Happy Mother +

2000

Happy Parenting

Love
M + D
Snesmid

EVERYDAY
BLESSINGS

ALSO BY JON KABAT-ZINN

Wherever You Go, There You Are:
Mindfulness Meditation
in Everyday Life

Full Catastrophe Living:
Using the Wisdom of Your Body and Mind
to Face Stress, Pain, and Illness

EVERYDAY BLESSINGS

The Inner Work
of Mindful Parenting

M Y L A A N D J O N
K A B A T - Z I N N

New York

Reprint permissions appear on p. 393

Library of Congress Cataloging-in-Publication Data

Kabat-Zinn, Myla.
Everyday blessings : the inner work of mindful parenting /
Myla and Jon Kabat-Zinn.
p.   cm.
ISBN 0-7868-6176-2
1. Parenting.   2. Parent and child.   3. Parents—Psychology.
4. Attention.   5. Meditation.   I. Kabat-Zinn, Jon.   II. Title.
HQ755.8.K317   1997
649'.1—dc21   96-44091
CIP

FIRST EDITION

2   4   6   8   10   9   7   5   3   1

For our children,
Will, Naushon, and Serena,
and for parents and children everywhere

Acknowledgments

In writing this book together, we wrote chapters by ourselves initially, then gave each other feedback on them through many iterations and changes. Side by side, we then went over it all, revising drafts and writing new material, and watched the book emerge. Every chapter became the product of our dual scrutiny in both the thinking and the writing. The final product is truly a collaborative effort of our hearts and our minds, and of course, of our lives together.

We want first and foremost to thank our children—for their irreverent humor, their honesty and insight, and their allowing us to share something of their lives with the world beyond our family. Ultimately, the stories from their childhoods that they have allowed us to share here reflect precious moments that are truly theirs alone. We honor and acknowledge their forbearance, and are blessed by their being and their love.

We also thank our parents, Sally and Elvin Kabat and Roslyn and Howard Zinn, for all that they have given to us.

At various stages of the writing, we asked for feedback from our friends. We wish to express our thanks and gratitude to them. Larry Rosenberg, Sarah Doering, Robbie Pfeufer Kahn, Becky Sarah, Norman Fisher, Jack Kornfield, and Trudy Goodman read the manuscript in its entirety and gave us invaluable perspectives and suggestions. We also thank Halé Baycu-Schatz, Kathryn Robb, Jenny Fleming, Mary Crowe, Sala Steinbach, Nancy Wainer Cohen, Sally Brucker, and Barbara Trafton Beall for their suggestions, which helped us greatly in our task.

A number of people contributed their own writing, and in that way, a part of their own hearts and souls to our effort, and we are deeply indebted to them for their generosity and their eloquence. We wish to thank Caitlin Miller for her poems in *Letters to a Young Girl Interested in Zen*, Susan Block for the material in *It's Never Too Late*, Ralph and Kathy Robinson for the poem written by their son, Ryan Jon Robinson, and for Ralph's account of Ryan's life and untimely death in *Impermanence*, Lani Donlon for the story in *Family Values*, Cherry Hamrick for her letter in *Mindfulness in the Classroom*, and Rebecca Clement, her student, for hers. Rose Thorne, Becky Sarah, Halé Baycu-Schatz, and Robbie Pfeufer Kahn also contributed material to the book, for which we are deeply grateful.

I (mkz) would like to thank Robbie Pfeufer Kahn in particular for our many conversations over the years regarding the needs of children. In addition, my daily walks and conversations with Halé Baycu-Schatz have been wonderfully supportive.

We also want to express our deep appreciation to all of the people who shared stories about their parenting experiences with us. Many of those stories are included anonymously at their request. Some, for reasons of space and content, we were unable to include in the book. Nonetheless, we are grateful to all those people who reached out to us with their poignant stories.

It was from Robert Bly that I (mkz) first heard the story of *Sir Gawain and the Loathely Lady*, told in his wonderfully soulful, heart-stirring way. Robert in turn credits Gioia Timpanelli, who has been telling the story for twenty some years. She in turn credits the medieval oral tradition, Chaucer's *Wife of Bath's Tale*, and the Goddess Mysteries of Great Britain. We have based our version primarily on Rosemary Sutcliff's in *The Sword and the Circle*, and have made ample use of her beautiful prose in our retelling.

Our editors, Leslie Wells and Bob Miller, were enormously helpful at key stages in the writing. Throughout the process, they accorded us the sovereignty we needed to give voice and shape to our views and to the book you have in your hands. Other members of the Hyperion family provided key elements of assistance at various stages. We are particularly indebted to Jennifer Lang for her help securing the permissions, and Claudyne Bedell for her work designing the interior of the book.

We also wish to thank Victor Weaver of Hyperion and Kate Canfield for designing the cover, Maria Muller for the painting of her water lily photograph, Beth Mallor for designing the interior graphic, and The British Museum, London, for allowing us to photograph the statue from which the lotus flower graphic was made.

Contents

Once the realization is accepted that even between the closest human beings infinite distances continue to exist, a wonderful living side by side can grow up, if they succeed in loving the distance between them which makes it possible for each to see the other whole against the sky.

RAINER MARIA RILKE, *Letters*

EVERYDAY

BLESSINGS

Prologue—jkz

First child off at college freshman year, arrives home 1:30 A.M. for Thanksgiving, driven by a friend. When he had called earlier to say he would not make it home for dinner as we had hoped, we were all disappointed, and for a few moments there had been more than a slight current of annoyance in me. We leave the door unlocked, as arranged, having told him to wake us when he arrives. No need. We hear him come in. The energy is young, vital, spilling over even in his attempts to be quiet. He comes upstairs. We call to him, whispering, so as not to wake his sisters. He comes into our darkened room. We hug. My side of the bed is closer to him than Myla's. He lies down across my chest, backwards kind of, extends himself, and embraces us both with his arms, but even more with his being. He is happy to be home. He lies here, draped over my body sideways, as if it were the most natural thing in the world. Any trace of annoyance at the lateness of the hour and disappointment about him not making it by dinnertime evaporate instantly.

I feel happiness radiating from him. There is nothing overexuberant or manic here. His energy is joyful, content, calm, playful. It feels like old friends reunited, and beyond that, familial celebration. He is at home now, here in our darkened room. He belongs. The bond is palpable among the three of us. A feeling of joy fills my chest and is joined by a series of images of my life with him, captured in the fullness of this moment. This huge nineteen-year-old, lying across me, who I held in my arms as much as possible until he could and would wriggle out and run in the world, now with his scruffy beard and powerful muscles, is my son. I am his father. Myla is his mother. We know this wordlessly, bathing in our different happinesses that unite as we lie here.

After a while he leaves us to watch a movie. He has too much energy to sleep. We try to go back to sleep, but we can't. We toss for hours in a daze of sleepless exhaustion. It crosses my mind to go into his room to spend more time with him, but I don't. There is nothing to chase after here, not him, not even needed sleep. The depths of our contentedness finally hold sway, and we sleep some. I am gone to work in the morning long before he wakes up. My whole day is suffused with knowing that I will see him when I get home.

*

Such moments, when they are not subverted by us, as I could easily have done in my initial annoyance, and when they are not passed over entirely unnoticed, as we do with so many of our moments, are part of the blessing and the bliss of parenting. Are they special? Is it just at the moment of arrival, the first time home from college, or at the birth of a child, or the first word or the first step, that we taste such deep connection and its blessing, or do such moments occur more frequently than we suspect? Might they not be abundant rather than rare, available to us virtually in any moment, even the more difficult ones, if we stay attuned both to our children and to *this* moment?

In my experience, such moments are abundant. But I find that they too easily go by unnoticed and unappreciated unless I make an effort to see them and capture them in awareness. I find I have to continually work at it because my mind is so easily veiled from the fullness of any moment by so many other things.

As I see it, all parents, regardless of the ages of our children at any point in time, are on an arduous journey, an odyssey of sorts, whether we know it or not, and whether we like it or not. The journey, of course, is nothing other than life itself, with all its twists and turns, its ups and its downs. How we see and hold the full range of our experience in our minds and in our hearts makes an enormous difference in the quality of this journey we are on, and what it means to us. It can influence where we go, what happens, what we learn, and how we feel along the way.

A fully lived adventure requires a particular kind of commitment and presence, an attention that to me feels exquisitely tenacious, yet also gentle, receptive. Often the journey itself teaches us to pay attention, wakes us up. Sometimes those teachings emerge in painful or terrifying ways that we would never have chosen. As I see it, the challenge of being a parent is to live our moments as fully as possible, charting our own course as best we can, above all, nourishing our children, and in the process, growing ourselves. Our children and the journey itself provide us with endless opportunities in this regard.

This is clearly a life's work, and it is for life that we undertake it. As we all know down to our very bones, there is no question about doing a perfect job, or always "getting it right." It seems more a quest than a question of anything. "Perfect" is simply not relevant, whatever that would mean in regard to parenting. What is important is that we be authentic, and that we honor our children and ourselves as best we can, and that our intention be to, at the very least, do no harm.

To me, it feels like the work is all in the attending, in the quality of the attention I bring to each moment, and in my commitment to live and to parent as consciously as possible. We know that unconsciousness in one or both parents, especially when it manifests in rigid and unwavering opinions, self-centeredness, and lack of presence and attention, invariably leads to sorrow in the children. These traits are often symptoms of underlying sorrow in the parents as well, although they may never be seen as such without a deep experience of awakening.

Maybe each one of us, in our own unique ways, might honor Rilke's insight that there are always infinite distances between even the closest human beings. If we truly understand and accept that, terrifying as it sometimes feels, perhaps we can choose to live in such a way that we can experience in its fullness the "wonderful living side by side" that can grow up if we use and love the distance that lets us see the other whole against the sky.

I see this as our work as parents. To do it, we need to nurture, protect, and guide our children and bring them along until they are ready to walk their own paths. We also have to be whole ourselves, each his or her own person, with a life of our own, so that when they look at us, they will be able to see our wholeness against the sky.

This is not always so easy. Mindful parenting is hard work. It means knowing ourselves inwardly, and working at the interface where our inner lives meet the lives of our children. It is particularly hard work in this era, when the culture is intruding more and more into our homes and into our children's lives in so many new ways.

One reason I practice meditation is to maintain my own balance and clarity of mind in the face of such huge challenges, and to be able to stay more or less on course through all the weather changes that, as a parent, I encounter day in and day out on this journey. Making time each day, usually early in the morning, for a period of quiet stillness, helps me to be calmer and more balanced, to see more clearly and more broadly, to be more consistently aware of what is really important, and over and over again to make the choice to live by that awareness.

For me, mindfulness—cultivated in periods of stillness and during the day in the various things I find myself doing—hones an attentive sensitivity to the present moment that helps me keep my heart at least a tiny bit more open and my mind at least a tiny bit clear, so that I have a chance to see my children for who they are, to remember to give them what it is they most need from me, and to make plenty of room for them to find their own ways to be in the world.

But the fact that I practice meditation doesn't mean that I am always calm or kind or gentle, or always present. There are many times when I am not. It doesn't mean that I always know what to do and never feel confused or at a loss. But being even a little more mindful helps me to see things I might not have seen and take small but important, sometimes critical steps I might not otherwise have taken.

Following a workshop in which I read the opening passage of this prologue (still in manuscript form) I received a letter from a man in his sixties, who wrote saying:

"I want to thank you for a special gift you gave me on that day. . . . It was when you read us the account of your son's homecoming for Thanksgiving. It touched me very deeply, particularly when you described how he enveloped you with his being, or words to that effect, when he lay down across your chest on the bed. Since then, I have experienced the first genuinely loving feelings towards my own son that I have felt for a long, long time. I don't know what has happened exactly, but it is as if up to now I needed another kind of son to love, and now I don't anymore."

It may be that the feeling of needing another kind of child to love visits all of us as parents from time to time, when things feel particularly bad or hopeless. Sometimes, that feeling can, if unexamined, turn from a short-lived impulse into a steady current of disappointment, and a yearning for something we think we don't have. But if we look again, as this father did, we may find that, after all, we can know and love well the children who are ours to love.

Prologue—mkz

The fiercely protective love I feel for my children has propelled me to do the inner work we call mindful parenting. This inner work has yielded unexpected gifts and pleasures. It has helped me to see my children more clearly, as they are, without the veils of my own fears, expectations, and needs, and to see what is truly called for in each moment. Parenting mindfully helps me to see myself as well, and gives me a way to work with the difficult moments and the automatic reactions that arise so easily in me at such times, reactions that are often limiting, harsh, or destructive to my children's well-being.

Although I have never had a formal meditation practice, I have always needed some time and space for non-doing, for being still, in silence. This was especially hard to find when my children were little. Moments of solitude and inner reflection would come as I lay in bed in the morning, awake but unwilling to move, aware of the images from my dreams, sometimes clear, sometimes elusive, receptive to whatever thoughts visited me in that place somewhere between wakefulness and sleep.

This was my inner, self-nourishing meditation. It brought some balance to my outer meditations—the ongoing, moment-to-moment awareness, tuning, responding, holding, and letting go that my children needed from me.

Meditative moments have come in many forms: sitting up in the middle of the night nursing my newborn, soaking in the peace and quiet, feeding her as I am being fed by the sweetness of her being; or walking with a crying baby, finding ways to soothe and comfort, chanting, singing, rocking, as I work with my own tiredness; or looking into the face of an unhappy, angry teenager, trying to discern the cause and intuit what is needed.

Mindfulness is about paying attention, and paying attention takes energy and concentration. Every moment brings something different and may require something different from me. Sometimes I am blessed with understanding. Other times, I am at a loss, confused, off balance, not really knowing, but trying to respond instinctively, creatively, to whatever is presented to me. There are deeply satisfying moments of pure bliss, when a child is thriving and glowing with a sense of well-being. There are plenty of difficult, frustrating, painful moments, when nothing I do is right, and sometimes very wrong. I've found it especially hard to see clearly with older children. The issues are much more complex and the answers rarely simple.

But what I have come to see is that each time I feel I have lost my way as a parent, when I find myself in a dark wood, the ground rough and uneven, the terrain unfamiliar, the air chilled, there is often something to be found in my pocket when I finally find my way back. I have to remember to stop, to breathe, to reach in, and look closely at what it is.

Each difficult moment has the potential to open my eyes and open my heart. Each time I come to understand something about one of my children, I also learn something about myself and the child that I once was, and that knowledge acts as a guide for me. When I am able to empathize and feel compassion for a child's pain, when I am accepting of the contrary, irritating, exasperating behaviors that my children can manifest, try on, experiment with—the healing power of unconditional love heals me as it nourishes them. As they grow, I grow. My transformations are inside.

Rather than being a disadvantage, my sensitivity has become an ally. Over the years, I have learned to use my intuition, my senses, my emotional antennae to try to see into the heart of whatever I am faced with. An essential part of this is attempting to see things from my child's point of view. I have found this inner work to be very powerful. Each time I choose to be kind instead of cruel, to understand rather than judge, to accept rather than reject, my children, no matter what their ages, are nourished and grow stronger.

This kind of parenting is trust-building. I work hard to maintain that trust and the underlying feelings of connectedness that have been built over many years of hard emotional and physical work. Moments of carelessness or the unconscious surfacing of old destructive patterns are betrayals of my children's trust, and I have had to consciously work to rebuild and strengthen our relationship after such moments.

For twenty-one years I have tried to bring some awareness to my moment-to-moment experiences as a parent: observing, questioning, looking at what I most value and what I think is most important for my children. Although there are myriad aspects of parenting that are not touched on in this book, it is my hope that in describing this inner process to you, we can evoke the richness of experience and potential for growth and change that reside in mindful parenting.

PART ONE

The Danger
and the Promise

The Challenge of Parenting

Parenting is one of the most challenging, demanding, and stressful jobs on the planet. It is also one of the most important, for how it is done influences in great measure the heart and soul and consciousness of the next generation, their experience of meaning and connection, their repertoire of life skills, and their deepest feelings about themselves and their possible place in a rapidly changing world. Yet those of us who become parents do so virtually without preparation or training, with little or no guidance or support, and in a world that values producing far more than nurturing, doing far more than being.

The best manuals on parenting can sometimes serve as useful references, giving us new ways of seeing situations, and reassuring us, especially in the early years of parenting, or when we are dealing with special problems, that there are various ways to handle things and that we are not alone.

But what these books often do not address is the inner experience of parenting. What do we do with our own mind, for instance? How do we avoid getting swallowed up and overwhelmed by our doubts, our insecurities, by the real problems we face in our lives, by the times when we feel inwardly in conflict, and the times when we are in conflict with others, including our children? Nor do they indicate how we might develop greater sensitivity and appreciation for our children's inner experience.

To parent consciously requires that we engage in an inner work on ourselves as well as in the outer work of nurturing and caring for our children. The "how-to" advice that we can draw upon from books to help us with the outer work has to be complemented by an inner authority that we can only cultivate within ourselves through our own experience. Such inner authority only develops when we realize that, in spite of all of the things that happen to us that are outside of our control, through our choices in response to such events and through what we initiate ourselves, we are still, in large measure, "authoring" our own lives. In the process, we find our own ways to be in this world, drawing on what is deepest and best and most creative in us. Realizing this, we may come to see the importance for our children and for ourselves of taking responsibility for the ways in which we live our lives and for the consequences of the choices we make.

Inner authority and authenticity can be developed to an extraordinary degree if we do that inner work. Our authenticity and our wisdom grow when we purposely bring awareness to our own experience as it unfolds. Over time, we can learn to see more deeply into who our children are and what they need, and take the initiative in finding appropriate ways to nourish them and further their growth and development. We can also learn to interpret their many different, sometimes puzzling signals and to trust our ability to find a way to respond appropriately. Continual attention, examination, and thoughtfulness are essential even to know what we are facing as parents, much less how we might act effectively to help our children to grow in healthy ways.

Parenting is above all uniquely personal. Ultimately, it has to come from deep inside ourselves. Someone else's way of doing things will never do. We each have to find a way that is our own, learning from all useful sources along the way. We have to learn to trust our own instincts and to nourish and refine them.

But in parenting, even what we thought and did yesterday that "worked out well" then, is not necessarily going to help today. We have to stay very much in the present moment to sense what might be required. And when our own inner resources are depleted, we have to have effective and healthy ways to replenish them, to restore ourselves, without it being at the expense of our children.

Becoming a parent may happen on purpose or by accident, but however it comes about, parenting itself is a calling. It calls us to recreate our world every day, to meet it freshly in every moment. Such a calling is in actuality nothing less than a rigorous spiritual discipline—a quest to realize our truest, deepest nature as a human being. The very fact that we are a parent is continually asking us to find and express what is most nourishing, most loving, most wise and caring in ourselves, to be, as much as we can, our best selves.

As with any spiritual discipline, the call to parent mindfully is filled with enormous promise and potential. At the same time, it also challenges us to do the inner work on ourselves to be fully adequate to the task, so that we can be fully engaged in this hero's journey, this quest of a lifetime that is a human life lived.

People who choose to become parents take on this hardest of jobs for no salary, often unexpectedly, at a relatively young and inexperienced age, and often under conditions of economic strain and insecurity. Typically, the journey of parenting is embarked upon without a clear strategy or overarching view of the terrain, in much the same intuitive and optimistic way we approach many other aspects of life. We learn on the job, as we go. There is, in fact, no other way.

But to begin with, we may have no sense of how much parenting augurs a totally new set of demands and changes in our lives, requiring us to give up so much that is familiar and to take on so much that is unfamiliar. Perhaps this is just as well, since ultimately each child is unique and each situation different. We have to rely on our hearts, our deepest human instincts, and the things we carry from our own childhood, both positive and negative, to encounter the unknown territory of having and raising children.

And just as in life itself, when faced with a range of family, social, and cultural pressures to conform to frequently unstated and unconscious norms, and with all the inherent stresses of caring for children, as parents we often find ourselves, in spite of all our best intentions and our deep love for our children, running more or less on automatic pilot. To the extent that we are chronically preoccupied and invariably pressed for time, we may be out of touch with the richness, what Thoreau called the "bloom," of the present moment. This moment may seem far too ordinary, routine, and fleeting to single out for attention. Living like this, it is easy to fall into a dreamy kind of automaticity as far as our parenting is concerned, believing that whatever we do will be okay as long as the basic love for our children and desire for their well-being is there. We can rationalize such a view by telling ourselves that children are resilient creatures and that the little things that happen to them are just that, little things that may have no effect on them at all. Children can take a lot, we tell ourselves.

But, as I (jkz) am reminded time and again when people recount their stories in the Stress Reduction Clinic and in mindfulness workshops and retreats around the country, for many people, childhood was a time of either frank or subtle betrayals, of one or both parents out of control to one degree or another, often raining down various combinations of unpredictable terror, violence, scorn, and meanness on their own children out of their own addictions, deep unhappiness, or ignorance. Sometimes, in the deepest of ironies, accompanying such terrible betrayals come protestations of parental love, making the situation even crazier and harder for the children to fathom. For others, there is the present pain of having been invisible, unknown, neglected, and unappreciated as children. And there is also the sense that, what with the rising stress on virtually all fronts in the society, and an accelerating sense of time urgency and insufficiency, things are strained to and often beyond the breaking point in families, and getting worse, not better, generation by generation.

A woman who attended a five-day mindfulness retreat said:

"I noticed this week as I was doing the meditation that I feel like I have pieces missing, that there are parts of me that I just can't find when I become still and look underneath the surface of my mind. I'm not sure what it means but it's kind of made me a little bit anxious. Maybe when I start to practice the meditation a little more regularly, maybe I'll find out what is stopping me from being whole. But I really feel holes in my body or in my soul that keep me pushing mountains in front of myself everywhere I go. My husband says: 'But why did you do that? There was a big opening here.' And I just say: 'I don't know, but if there is a way to block it up, I will.' I feel a little like a Swiss cheese. I have felt this from when I was small. I had some losses when I was small. I think parts of me were removed and taken from [me by] deaths and [by] other people; my sister died when I was young, and my parents went into a sort of depression, I think until they died. I think parts of me just got taken to feed them. I feel that. I was a very lively, young, go-getter when I was young, and I felt parts of me just being taken, and I can't seem to be able to regain those parts now. Why can't I be that way? What happened to me? Parts of me have gotten lost, and when I'm sitting here today, meditating, I realized that I'm looking for those parts and I don't know where they are. I don't know how to become whole until I find those parts that are gone. Now my whole family has died. They've taken all the parts and left, and I'm still here with the Swiss cheese."

A chilling image, that parts of this woman were taken to feed her parents. But this happens, and the consequences to the children reverberate throughout their lives.

To compound matters, in the name of love, parents often cause deep hurt and harm to their children, as when they beat them to teach them lessons, saying things like, "This is for your own good," "This hurts me more than it hurts you," or, "I'm only doing this because I love you," often the very words that were said to them as children when they were beaten by their parents, as was shown by the Swiss psychiatrist Alice Miller, in her seminal work. In the name of "love," frequently unbridled rage, contempt, hatred, intolerance, neglect, and abuse rain down on children from parents who are unaware of or have ceased to care about the full import of their actions, and who would never treat friends or strangers in such a way. This happens across all social classes in our society.

In our view, an automatic, unexamined, lowest-common-denominator approach to parenting, whether it manifests in overt violence or not, causes deep and frequently long-lasting harm to children and their developmental trajectories. Unconscious parenting also conspires to arrest our potential growth as parents as well. From such unconsciousness come, all too commonly, sadness, missed opportunities, hurt, resentment, blame, restricted and diminished views of self and the world, and ultimately, isolation and alienation on all sides.

If we can remain awake to the challenges and the calling of parenthood, this does not have to happen. On the contrary, we can use all the occasions that arise with our children to break down the barriers in our own minds, to see more clearly into ourselves, and to be more effectively present for them.

*

We live in a culture which does not place great value on parenting as valid and honored work. It is considered perfectly acceptable for people to give one hundred percent to their careers, or to their "relationships," or to "finding themselves," but not to their children. The implication is that giving a child such a high degree of consistent, devoted, highest priority attention will only "spoil" the child, that it cannot lead to good, and only stems from a parent's "neurotic" needs for control and attachment rather than from a respect for life and for the interconnectedness of all things, and from the unique joys of parent-child relationships.

Society at large and its institutions and values, which both create and reflect the microcosm of our individual minds and values, contribute in major ways to the undermining of parenting. Who are the highest-paid workers in our country? Certainly not day care workers, or teachers, whose work so much supports the work of parents. Where are the role models, the supportive networks, job sharing, and part-time jobs for mothers and fathers who want to stay home with their children for more than a few weeks after they are born? Where is the universal health coverage, the subsidies for young parents, support for parenting classes, adequate parental leave programs which would, by their prevalence, tell us that healthy parenting is of utmost importance and is valued highly by this society as a whole?

Certainly there are bright spots and reasons for hope. Countless parents across the country see parenting as a sacred trust, and manage to find heartful and creative ways to guide and nurture their children, often in the face of great obstacles and odds. There are imaginative efforts by people all across the country involved in programs that teach parenting skills, communication skills, violence prevention, stress reduction, and that offer counseling services to parents and families. There are also many groups engaged in community building and political lobbying on behalf of children. Mary Pipher's books, *Reviving Ophelia* and *The Shelter of Each Other*, Robert Bly's *The Sibling Society*, and Daniel Goleman's *Emotional Intelligence* give voice to the enormity of the problem, and point to our potential as a society to set it right if we are able to tap what is best in our country—in our families, and in ourselves. William and Martha Sears's *The Baby Book*, on "attachment parenting," provides a new framework for honoring the needs of infants and babies.

But the problems are staggering and all-pervasive, and are creating a society in which it is increasingly difficult for families to raise healthy children. In many households today, there is no adult at home when the children come home from school. The parents as well as the neighbors are out trying to make a living. Children are often left to their own devices. They may have more contact with the world of TV, and sometimes with the worlds of drugs and crime, than they do with caring adults. Teenage violence, the fastest growing sector of crime in this era, peaks between 3:00 P.M. and 8:00 P.M. each school day. Tangible and daily expressions of love, support, energy, and interest from living, breathing adults and respected elders are becoming more and more rare in our homes and in our neighborhoods.

While we are all subject to large social forces that shape our lives and the lives of our children, we also have the capacity as individuals to make conscious and intentional choices about how we are going to relate to our circumstances and to the era in which we find ourselves. We all have the potential to chart our own paths, to bring more attention and intentionality to our lives, and to attempt to see and honor the deep soul needs of our children as well as our own as best we can. Charting such a path for ourselves is made easier by having a larger framework within which to examine and come to understand what we are doing and what needs to be done—a framework that can help to keep us on course, even though things may be constantly changing and our next steps often unclear. Mindfulness can provide such a framework.

For example, new and important doors in our own minds can open just by entertaining the possibility that there are alternative ways of perceiving situations and that we may have more options open to us in any moment than we realize.

Relating to the whole of our lives mindfully—to both our inward and our outward experiences—is a profoundly positive and practical alternative to the driven, automatic pilot mode in which we operate so much of the time without even knowing it. This is particularly important for parents, as we try to juggle all the competing demands we carry from day to day while providing for our children and giving them what they need in an increasingly stressful and complex world.

What Is
Mindful Parenting?

Mindful parenting calls us to wake up to the possibilities, the benefits, and the challenges of parenting with a new awareness and intentionality, not only as if what we did mattered, but as if our conscious engagement in parenting were virtually the most important thing we could be doing, both for our children and for ourselves.

This book is a series of meditations on various aspects of parenting. It is about meeting our children's needs as fully and selflessly as possible by cultivating a certain kind of awareness. This awareness, known as *mindfulness,* can lead to deeper insight into and understanding of our children and ourselves. Mindfulness has the potential to penetrate past surface appearances and behaviors and allow us to see our children more clearly as they truly are, to look both inwardly and outwardly, and to act with some degree of wisdom and compassion on the basis of what we see. Parenting mindfully can be healing and transformative—for both children and parents.

As we shall see in Part 4, from the perspective of mindfulness, parenting can be viewed as a kind of extended and, at times, arduous meditation retreat spanning a large part of our lives. And our children, from infancy to adulthood and beyond, can be seen as perpetually challenging live-in teachers, who provide us with ceaseless opportunities to do the inner work of understanding who we are and who they are, so that we can best stay in touch with what is truly important and give them what they most need in order to grow and flourish. In the process, we may find that this ongoing moment-to-moment awareness can liberate us from some of our most confining habits of perception and relating, the straitjackets and prisons of the mind that have been passed down to us or that we have somehow constructed for ourselves. Through their very being, often without any words or discussion, our children can inspire us to do this inner work. The more we are able to keep in mind the intrinsic wholeness and beauty of our children, especially when it is difficult for us to see, the more our ability to be mindful deepens. In seeing more clearly, we can respond to them more effectively and with greater generosity of heart, and parent with greater wisdom.

As we devote ourselves to nourishing them and understanding who they are, these live-in teachers, especially in the first ten to twenty years of our "training," will provide endless moments of wonder and bliss, and opportunities for the deepest feelings of connectedness and love. They will also, in all likelihood, push all our buttons, evoke all our insecurities, test all our limits and boundaries, and touch all the places in us where we fear to tread and feel inadequate or worse. In the process, if we are willing to attend carefully to the full spectrum of what we are experiencing, they will remind us over and over again of what is most important in life, including its mystery, as we share in their lives, shelter and nourish and love them, and give them what guidance we can.

Being a parent is particularly intense and demanding in part because our children can ask things of us no one else could or would, in ways that no one else could or would. They see us up close as no one else does, and constantly hold mirrors up for us to look into. In doing so, they give us over and over again the chance to see ourselves in new ways, and to work at consciously asking what we can learn from any and every situation that comes up with them. We can then make choices out of this awareness that will nurture both our children's inner growth and our own at one and the same time. Our interconnectedness and our interdependence enable us to learn and grow together.

✲

To bring mindfulness into our parenting, it is helpful to know something about what mindfulness is. Mindfulness means moment-to-moment, non-judgmental awareness. It is cultivated by refining our capacity to pay attention, intentionally, in the present moment, and then sustaining that attention over time as best we can. In the process, we become more in touch with our life as it is unfolding.

Ordinarily, we live much of the time in an automatic pilot mode, paying attention only selectively and haphazardly, taking many important things completely for granted or not noticing them at all, and judging everything we do experience by forming rapid and often unexamined opinions based on what we like or dislike, what we want or don't want. Mindfulness brings to parenting a powerful method and framework for paying attention to whatever we are doing in each moment, and seeing past the veil of our automatic thoughts and feelings to a deeper actuality.

Mindfulness lies at the heart of Buddhist meditation, which itself is all about cultivating attention. The practice of mindfulness has been kept alive and developed within various meditative traditions across Asia for over twenty-five hundred years. Now it is making its way into the mainstream of Western society in many different contexts, including medicine, health care, education, and social programs.

Mindfulness is a meditative discipline. There are many different meditative disciplines. We might think of them all as various doors into the same room. Each doorway gives a unique and different view into the room; once inside, however, it is the same room, whichever door we come through. Meditation, whatever the method or tradition, is the tapping into the order and stillness embedded in and behind all activity, however chaotic it may appear, using our faculty of attention. It is not, as is so commonly thought, an inward manipulation—like throwing a switch or merely relaxing—into some "special state" in which everything feels different or better, or in which your mind goes "blank," or you suppress your thoughts. It is a systematic and sustained observing of the whole field of our experience, or of some specific element of it.

While it received its most elaborate articulation in the Buddhist tradition, mindfulness is an important part of all cultures and is truly universal, since it is simply about cultivating the capacity we all have as human beings for awareness, clarity, and compassion. There are many different ways to do this work of cultivation. There is no one right way, just as there is no one right way to parent.

Mindful parenting involves keeping in mind what is truly important as we go about the activities of daily living with our children. Much of the time, we may find we need to remind ourselves of what that is, or even admit that we may have no idea at the moment, for the thread of meaning and direction in our lives is easily lost. But even in our most trying, sometimes horrible moments as parents, we can deliberately step back and begin afresh, asking ourselves as if for the first time, and with fresh eyes, "What is truly important here?"

In fact, mindful parenting means seeing if we can *remember* to bring this kind of attention and openness and wisdom to all our moments with our children. It is a true *practice*, its own inner discipline, its own form of meditation. And it carries with it profound benefits for both children and parents, to be discovered in the practice itself.

For us to learn from our children requires that we pay attention, and learn to be still inwardly within ourselves. In stillness, we are better able to see past the endemic turmoil, cloudiness, and reactivity of our own minds, in which we are so frequently caught up, and in this way cultivate greater clarity, calmness, and insight, which we can bring directly to our parenting.

Like everybody else, parents have their own needs and desires and lives, just as children do. Yet, too often, in both big and little ways, the needs of the parent in any given moment may be very different from those of the child. These needs, all valid and important, are simply different, and are often in conflict. The clash of needs in any given moment may result in a struggle of wills over who is going to get "their way," especially if we, the parent, are feeling stressed, overburdened, and exhausted.

Rather than pitting our needs against those of our children, parenting mindfully involves cultivating an awareness, right in such moments, of how our needs are *interdependent*. Our lives are undeniably deeply connected. Our children's well-being affects ours, and ours affects theirs. If they are not doing well, we suffer, and if we are not doing well, they suffer.

This means that we have to continually work to be aware of our children's needs as well as our own, emotional as well as physical, and, depending on their ages, to work at negotiations and compromises, with them and within ourselves, so that everybody gets something of what they most need. Just bringing this kind of sensitivity to our parenting will enhance our sense of connectedness with our children. Through the quality of our presence, our commitment to them is felt, even in difficult times. And we may find that our choices in moments of conflicting and competing needs will come more out of this heartfelt connection, and as a result will have greater kindness and wisdom in them.

*

We see parenting as a sacred responsibility. Parents are nothing less than protectors, nourishers, comforters, teachers, guides, companions, models, and sources of unconditional love and acceptance. If we are able to keep this sense of parenting as a sacred responsibility in mind, and we bring a degree of mindfulness to the process as it unfolds moment to moment, our choices as parents are much more likely to come out of an awareness of what this moment, this child—at this stage of his or her life—is asking from us right now, through his very being and his behavior. In rising to this challenge, we may not only come to do what is best for our children; we may also uncover and come to know, perhaps for the first time, what is deepest and best in ourselves.

Mindful parenting calls us to acknowledge and name the challenges we face daily in trying to parent with awareness. For awareness has to be inclusive. It has to include recognizing our own frustrations, insecurities, and shortcomings, our limits and limitations, even our darkest and most destructive feelings, and the ways we may feel overwhelmed or pulled apart. It challenges us to "work with" these very energies consciously and systematically.

Taking on such a task is asking a great deal of ourselves. For in many ways, we ourselves are products, and sometimes, to one degree or another, prisoners of the events and circumstances of our own childhoods. Since childhood significantly shapes how we see ourselves and the world, our histories will inevitably shape our views of who our children are and "what they deserve," and of how they should be cared for, taught, and "socialized." As parents, we all tend to hold our views, whatever they are, very strongly and often unconsciously, as if in the grip of powerful spells. It is only when we become aware of this shaping that we can draw on what was helpful, positive, and nurturing from the way we were parented, and grow beyond those aspects that may have been destructive and limiting.

For those of us who had to shut down, to "not see," to suppress our feelings in order to survive our own childhoods, becoming more mindful can be especially painful and difficult. In those moments when we are ruled by old demons, when harmful beliefs, destructive patterns, and nightmares from our own childhood rise up and we are plagued by dark feelings and black or white thinking, it is particularly difficult to stop and see freshly.

By no means are we suggesting that, in parenting mindfully, there is some ideal standard we have to measure ourselves against or strive to achieve. Mindful parenting is a continual process of deepening and refining our awareness and our ability to be present and to act wisely. It is not an attempt to attain a fixed goal or outcome, however worthy. An important part of the process is seeing ourselves with some degree of kindness and compassion. This includes seeing and accepting our limitations, our blindnesses, our humanness and fallibility, and working with them mindfully as best we can. The one thing we know we can always do, even in moments of darkness and despair that show us we don't know anything, is to begin again, fresh, right in that moment. Every moment is a new beginning, another opportunity for tuning in, and perhaps coming—in that very moment—to see and feel and know ourselves and our children in a new and deeper way.

For our love for our children is expressed and experienced in the *quality* of the moment-to-moment relationships we have with them. It deepens in everyday moments when we hold those moments in awareness and dwell within them. Love is expressed in how we pass the bread, or how we say good morning, and not just in the big trip to Disney World. It is in the everyday kindnesses we show, the understanding we bring, and in the openness of our acceptance. Love is expressed by embodying love in our actions. Whether we are facing good times or hard times on any given day or in any moment, the quality of our attention and our presence is a deep measure of our caring and of our love for our children.

*

This book is for people who care about the quality of family life and the well-being of their children, born and unborn, young or grown. We hope it will support parents in their efforts to show their love through their being and their actions in their everyday lives. It is not likely that we can do this unless we can be authentic in our own lives and in touch with the full range of feelings we experience—in a word, awake.

Parenting is a mirror in which we get to see the best of ourselves, and the worst; the richest moments of living, and the most frightening. The challenge to write about it sensibly is daunting. There are times when we feel that things are basically sound in our family. Our children seem happy, strong, and balanced. The very next day, or moment, all hell can break loose. Our world fills with confusion, despair, anger, frustration. What we thought we understood is of no use. All the rules seem to have changed overnight, or in an instant. We can feel like we have no idea what is going on or why. We can feel like the biggest of failures, like we don't know or understand anything.

But even in those moments, we try to remind ourselves as best we can to hold on to the thread of some kind of awareness of what is happening, no matter how unpleasant or painful things are. Hard as it is, we try to acknowledge what is actually taking place, and even in those difficult moments, try to see what is really needed from us. The alternative is to get caught up in our own reactivity and automatic behaviors, and surrender what compassion and clarity we have to our fear or fury or denial. And even when this happens, as it inevitably does at times, we try to reexamine it later, with greater calmness, in the hope of learning something from it.

This book comes out of our own experience as parents. Our experience will undoubtedly differ in many ways from your experience as a person and as a parent. You may find some of the specific ways we chose to parent to be very different from how you were parented or how you have parented your children. You may find yourself reacting with strong feelings to some of the things we say or to some of the choices we have made. The whole topic of parenting can arouse deep emotions in all of us, because it is so intimately connected with how we think of ourselves and with how we have chosen to live our lives.

We are not suggesting that you should do everything as we have done it, or if you didn't, that you were lacking in any way. As we all know, there are few easy answers or consistently simple solutions in parenting. Nor are we saying that mindfulness is the answer to all life's problems, or to all questions regarding parenting. We are simply trying to point to a way of seeing and a way of being which can be integrated in many different ways into *your* way of parenting and into your life. Ultimately, we all have to make our own individual decisions about what is best for our children and for ourselves, drawing most of all on our creativity and our capacity to be awake and aware in our lives.

We share with you our experiences and this orientation called mindful parenting, in the hope that some of its transformative potential will resonate with your values and your intentions, and be of some use as you chart your own path in your parenting.

Ultimately, mindful parenting is about seeing our children clearly, and listening to and trusting our own hearts. It gives form and support to the daily work of parenting with awareness. It helps us find ways to be sources of unconditional love for our children, from moment to moment, and day by day.

How Can I
Do This?

No two families ever have exactly the same situations to deal with or resources to call upon. But no matter what the circumstances of people's lives, we believe that all families and individuals, by virtue of being human, have deep inner resources that can be called upon and cultivated—resources that can help enormously in making important choices as we struggle to bring balance into our lives and into our families.

At every level of economic and social well-being or lack of it, and no matter what enormous difficulties they are faced with, there are people who find ways to put their children first. Our view is unabashedly that the children deserve to be put first. Like a relay race with a long overlap in which the baton is passed—for at least eighteen years—our job as parents is to position our children to run their solo laps effectively. To do that, we need to give our all during our run alongside them. There are many ways to do this. No matter what our circumstances, if the will and the motivation are there, we can learn to draw on those resources of strength and wisdom, creativity and caring, that reside within us all. Each moment provides us with new occasions to do this.

Mindful parenting takes energy and commitment, as does any deep spiritual practice or consciousness discipline. We may find ourselves wondering from time to time whether we are capable of taking on such a task that is really the work of a lifetime, asking ourselves, "How can I do this on top of everything else I am already doing?" We may find it reassuring and inspiring to discover that, to a large degree, important elements of both the systematic discipline and the methods of mindful parenting are already familiar to all of us as parents. Mindful parenting as a practice and as an inner discipline is possible and practical because it arises naturally out of the experiences and challenges we already face every day as parents.

For instance, as parents, we are already constantly called upon to pay attention and we are already highly disciplined. We have to pay attention and be disciplined in waking up on time every morning, in getting the children up, fed, and ready for school, in getting ourselves ready for work and getting there if we work outside the home. We are disciplined and attentive in arranging our children's complex schedules, and our own, and in planning and then doing everything that needs to be done—all the shopping, cooking, cleaning, the countless repetitive tasks of daily life in a family.

We are also already highly accomplished. We deal every day with constant crises, juggle competing demands on our time and energy, and utilize the incredible sixth sense that parents develop early on which allows us to be continually aware of where our children are in each moment and of potential danger. We are also skilled at having conversations while doing other things, and dealing with constant interruptions while trying to keep a train of thought. People may sometimes feel hurt or put off when it seems as if we are not giving them our full attention. But as parents, we develop an ability to give our attention to many things at once: we can speak to other people at the same time that we are watching our child, or buttoning a jacket, or grabbing her before she gets into something harmful. Such skills and such disciplines go with the territory of parenting. The more we use and develop them, as we have to as parents, the better we get at them. They become a way of being.

We can make exceedingly good use of these skills and the discipline that is natural to us as parents in our efforts to parent more mindfully. The one is a natural extension of the other. Mindful parenting asks us to direct some of that energy and discipline and caring *inwardly*, toward our own minds and bodies and experiences, and toward attending more systematically to the inner as well as the outer lives of our children, to their soul needs as well as to their needs for clothing, food, and shelter.

We can bring mindfulness to any time, no matter how brief or how stressed, no matter how "off" we may be feeling. But to do so requires a strong commitment to cultivate mindfulness through everyday practice. Most of the thousands of people who have completed the mindfulness-based stress reduction programs offered in the Stress Reduction Clinic and in the Inner City Stress Reduction Clinic at the University of Massachusetts Medical Center are parents. Many come with serious, sometimes life-threatening medical problems, many with difficult social, economic, and personal problems as well. Some have horrifying family histories. Many already do remarkable things, day in and day out, to cope with extremely difficult situations in the present and from the past. In the eight-week program, they work at cultivating mindfulness in their lives, building on the foundation of what they are already doing to maintain their well-being and that of their families. In the process, their lives and their attitudes and the ways in which they see and relate to others, including their children, often change profoundly and enduringly. In spite of the inherent challenges in cultivating and sustaining the discipline of mindfulness in day-to-day situations, many people report that, in paying attention in new ways, they feel more relaxed, more hopeful, better able to cope with stress both at home and at work, and that they have a greater sense of peace of mind and self-confidence. They are able to see new openings in their lives through which to steer, using the practice of mindfulness itself. Some report feeling a greater sense of freedom, a greater sense of inner control and security, than they had thought possible before.

In the clinic's programs, the instructors introduce people to the various aspects of the meditation practice and make general suggestions for how it might be applied to daily life and to problem situations. But, for the most part, it is the participants themselves, while they are going through the program, who discover how to apply mindfulness in meaningful ways to the unique circumstances of their everyday lives. This is a creative and intuitive process that emerges naturally out of the practice itself.

It is the same with mindful parenting. We are not telling you what you should do, or what choices you need to make. Only you can determine that, because only you are living your life and could possibly know what your specific situation calls for in any moment. We are not even directing you in applying the practice, except in the most general terms. The detailed applications of mindfulness, and the specific choices you will be drawn to make, can only come out of your own motivation to practice, from your own commitment to honor each present moment by bringing your full awareness to it, and from the yearnings of your own heart. Mindful choices will then come out of the very situations you find yourself in with your children. They will come out of your own creativity, imagination, love, and genius, which, being human, are profound and virtually limitless.

Besides, with so many people now carrying all the parenting responsibilities alone as single parents; with the sharing of parenting in divorced families; with people having children later in life, when they may already have grown children; with people becoming parents through adopting children or being foster parents; with grandparents sometimes parenting their children's children and older couples having children for the first time; with same-sex couples, and couples who get along together and see more or less eye to eye about parenting, and couples who don't get along a good deal of the time or who see parenting very differently; with couples where the division of labor and parenting responsibilities is highly skewed; families where both parents work full time and more, and families with children with life-threatening diseases, or physical challenges, or developmental uniquenesses, families with closely spaced children, widely separated children, twins, triplets, families with vastly different numbers of children, same-sex combinations and different-sex combinations . . . with such a diversity of realities, there is no single way or knowledge that could possibly be relevant and useful in all circumstances.

But mindfulness, precisely because it is not formulaic, and because it has to do with the quality of our experience as human beings and the degree to which we can pay attention in our lives, is truly universal in scope, and therefore relevant in virtually all circumstances. Everybody has a mind; everybody has a body; everybody can pay attention intentionally; and everybody's life unfolds only in moments. Mindfulness doesn't tell us what to do, but it does give us a way to listen, a way to pay close attention to what we believe is important, and to expand our vision of what that might be in any situation, under any circumstances.

As parents and as people, no matter what we are facing in our lives, we are all capable of remarkable growth and transformation if we can learn to recognize and tap our deep inner resources and chart a path that is true to our values and to our own hearts. It does take work, but not much more than we are already doing. What it really involves is a rotation in consciousness, to where we can appreciate the deep seeing that comes out of present moment awareness, allowing what is best in us and in our children to emerge.

To enter now the world of mindful parenting and what it asks of us as well as what it has to offer, we begin by telling a story. For a time, we will be stepping outside of time, into the domain of the mythological, of the psyche, to return with perhaps a better sense of what it might mean to see in a deeper way, and to trust the mystery of our own hearts. It might be helpful to keep in mind that in this realm, all the characters in the story can be seen as different aspects of our own being, and that male and female, beauty and ugliness, kindness and hardheartedness reside to varying degrees in each of us.

PART TWO

Sir Gawain and the

Loathely Lady:

The Story Holds the Key

Sir Gawain and the
Loathely Lady

Long ago, in the days of King Arthur, for reasons we don't have to go into here, Arthur found himself on Christmas Day taking up a just cause that brought him face to face with his own impotence even though he was the King of the Land. His nemesis took the form of the Knight of Tarn Wathelan, "huge beyond the size of mortal man and armed from crest to toe in black armor, mounted on a giant red-eyed warhorse the color of midnight." As Arthur charged toward him to do battle on the plain before the knight's dark castle, the knight cast a spell upon Arthur which drained him and his horse of all power. "Like an icy shadow, a great fear fell upon him, the more terrible because it was not of the knight or of anything in this world; a black terror of the soul that came between him and the sky, and sucked the strength from him so that sword arm and shield arm sank to his sides and he was powerless to move."

"What—would you—of me?" gasped Arthur.

Rather than killing him or flinging him into his dungeons "to rot among other valiant knights who lie there, and take your realm for my own by means of the magic that is mine to wield," the Knight of Tarn Wathelan offers Arthur his life and freedom if he returns in seven days' time, on New Year's Day, with the answer to the question: "What is it that all women most desire?"

Filled with shame and rage, but helpless to do anything other than agree, Arthur made the bargain and rode off. That entire week he wandered the land, posing the question to every woman he met, whether a girl herding geese, an alewife, or a great lady, and dutifully writing down their answers, knowing all the while that none rang true.

And so, on the morning of New Year's Day, with a heavy heart, he turned his horse in the direction of the knight's castle, his one chance for life having eluded him, knowing now that he must submit and die at the knight's hand.

"The hills looked darker than they had done when last he rode that way, and the wind had a keener edge. And the way seemed much longer and rougher than it had done before, and yet it was all too quickly passed."

Not far from the knight's castle, as he rode chin on breast through a dark thicket, Arthur heard a woman's voice, sweet and soft, calling out to him, "Now God's greeting to you, my Lord King Arthur. God save and keep you."

He turned and saw a woman in a vivid scarlet gown the color of holly berries, sitting on a mound of earth beside the road between an oak tree and a holly tree. "At sight of her, shock ran through the King, for in the instant between hearing and seeing, he had expected the owner of the soft voice to be fair. And she was the most hideous creature he had ever seen, with a piteous nightmare face that he could scarcely bear to look upon, sprouting a long, wart-covered nose bent to one side and a long, hairy chin bent to the other. She had only one eye, and that set deep under her jutting brow. Her mouth was no more than a shapeless gash. Her hair hung in gray, twisted locks and her hands were like brown claws, though the jewels that sparkled on her fingers were fine enough for the Queen herself."

In his amazement, Arthur is struck dumb and has to be reminded by her of his code of chivalry and how a knight is to comport himself in the presence of a lady. She, mysteriously, knows on what errand he rides. She knows that he has asked many women what it is that all women most desire, and that all have given him answers, and not one the right answer. She then informs the astonished king that she and she alone knows the answer he is seeking, and that for her to tell him, he will have to swear a solemn oath that he will grant her whatever she asks of him in exchange. To this, he readily agrees. She beckons him to bend his ear to her lips, and whispers into it the answer he is looking for, so that "not even the trees may hear."

The moment he heard it, Arthur knew in his very soul that it was the true answer. He caught his breath in laughter, for it was such a simple answer, after all.

The answer that he was given to the question, "What is it that all women most desire?" was, *"Sovereignty."*

Arthur asked what she would have in return, but the lady refused to say until he had tested the answer on the Knight of Tarn Wathelan. So Arthur went off, and after some good sport at the expense of the huge knight, finally gave the true answer, and with it won his freedom. He then made his way back to the spot where the loathely lady was waiting for him.

Upon his return, the reward that Dame Ragnell, for that was the lady's name, asked of the King was that he bring to her from his court one of his own knights of the Round Table, brave and courteous, and good to look upon, to take her as his loving wife. Arthur, staggered and repulsed by this inconceivable request, has to be reminded that he owes his life to her and has made a knightly and kingly promise in exchange for her help.

Of course, for Arthur to assign the task to someone would be to disrespect the sovereignty of one of his own knights. The choice must be made freely. When Arthur returned to court and told the full story of his week's adventure to an astonished gathering of knights, his nephew Sir Gawain, out of loyalty to his uncle, the King, and out of his own goodness, offered to marry the lady himself. Arthur, ashamed and heavy-hearted, would not let Gawain make the vow without seeing her first.

So the knights rode out in company the next morning to the woods, and after some time, they caught a glimpse of scarlet through the trees. Sir Kay and the other knights were sickened by the sight of Lady Ragnell, and some were even insulting to her face. Others turned away in pity or busied themselves with their horses.

But Sir Gawain looked steadily at the lady; something in her pathetic pride and the way she lifted her hideous head caused him to think of a deer with the hounds about it. Something in the depth of her bleared gaze reached him like a cry for help.

He glared about him at his fellow knights. "Nay now, why these sideways looks and troubled faces and ill manners. The matter was never in doubt. Did I not last night tell the King that I would marry this lady? And marry her I will, if she will have me!" And so saying, he jumped down from his horse and knelt before her, saying, "My Lady Ragnell, will you take me for your husband?"

The lady looked at him for a moment out of her one eye, and then she said in that voice, so surprisingly sweet, "Not you, too, Sir Gawain. Surely you jest, like the others."

"I was never further from jesting in my life," he protested.

She tried then to dissuade him. "Think you before it is too late. Will you indeed wed one as misshapen and old as I? What sort of wife should I be for the King's own nephew? What will Queen Guenevere and her ladies say when you bring such a bride to court? And what will you secretly feel? You will be shamed, and all through me," said the lady, and she wept bitterly, and her face was wet and blubbered and even more hideous.

"Lady, if I can guard you, be very sure that I can also guard myself," Gawain said, glowering around at the other knights with his fighting face on him. "Now Lady, come with me back to the castle, for this very evening is our wedding to be celebrated."

To which Dame Ragnell replied, with tears falling from her one eye, "Truly, Sir Gawain, though it is a thing hard to believe, you shall not regret this wedding."

As she rose to move toward the horse they had brought for her, they saw that, beside all else, there was a hump between her shoulders and that she was lame in one leg. Gawain helped her into the saddle, mounted his own horse beside hers, and the whole group then wended their way back to the King's castle.

Word ran ahead of them from the city gates and the people came flocking out to see Sir Gawain and his bride go by. All were horrified beyond even their expectations.

That evening, the wedding took place in the chapel, with the Queen herself standing beside the bride, and the King serving as groomsman. Sir Lancelot was the first to come forward and kiss the bride on her withered cheek, followed by the other knights, but the words strangled in their throats when they would have wished her and Sir Gawain joy in their marriage, so that they could scarcely speak. "And the poor Lady Ragnell looked down upon bent head after bent head of the ladies who came forward to touch her fingertips as briefly as might be, but could not bear to look at her or kiss her cheek. Only Cabal, the dog, came and licked her hand with a warm, wet tongue and looked up into her face with amber eyes that took no account of her hideous aspect, for the eyes of a hound see differently from the eyes of men."

Dinner conversation was feverish and forced, a hollow pretense of gladness, through which Sir Gawain and his bride sat rigidly beside the King and Queen at the High Table. And when the tables were cleared away and it was time for dancing, many thought that now Sir Gawain might be free to leave her side and mingle with his friends. "But he said, 'Bride and groom must lead the first dance together,' and offered his hand to the Lady Ragnell. She took it with a hideous grimace that was the nearest she could come to a smile, and limped forward to open the dance with him. And throughout the festivities, with the King's eye upon the company and Sir Gawain's as well, no one in the hall dared look as though anything was amiss."

At last, the forced festivities came to a close and it was time for the newlyweds to go to the wedding chamber in the castle. There, "Gawain flung himself into a deeply cushioned chair beside the fire and sat, gazing into the flames, not looking to see where his bride might be. A sudden draught drove the candleflames sideways and the embroidered creatures on the walls stirred as though on the edge of life. And somewhere very far off, as though from the heart of the enchanted forest, he fancied he heard the faintest echo of a horn.

"There was a faint movement at the foot of the bed, and the silken rustle of a woman's skirt; and a low sweet voice said, 'Gawain, my lord and love, have you no word for me? Can you not even bear to look my way?'

"Gawain forced himself to turn his head and look and then sprang up in amazement, for there between the candle sconces stood the most beautiful woman he had ever seen.

" 'Lady,' he said at half-breath, not sure whether he was awake or dreaming. 'Who are you? Where is my wife, the Lady Ragnell?'

" 'I am your wife, the Lady Ragnell,' said she, 'whom you found between the oak and the holly tree, and wedded this night in settlement of your King's debt—and maybe a little, in kindness.'

" 'But—but I do not understand,' stammered Gawain. 'You are so changed.'

" 'Yes,' said the maiden. 'I am changed, am I not? I was under an enchantment, and as yet I am only partly freed from it. But now for a little while I may be with you in my true seeming. Is my lord content with his bride?' "

She came a little toward him, and he reached out and caught her into his arms. " 'Content? Oh, my most dear love, I am the happiest man in all the world; for I thought to save the honor of the King my uncle, and I have gained my heart's desire. And yet from the first moment I felt something of you reach out to me, and something of me reach back in answer. . . .'

"In a little, the lady brought her hands down and set them against his breast and gently held him off. 'Listen,' she said, 'for now a hard choice lies before you. I told you that as yet I am only partly free from the enchantment that binds me. Because you have taken me for your wife, it is half broken; but no more than half broken.' "

Dame Ragnell explained that she was now able to appear in her natural form for but half of each day, and Gawain must choose whether he wanted her to be fair by day and foul by night, or fair by night and foul by day.

"That is a hard choice indeed," said Gawain.

"Think," said the Lady Ragnell.

And Sir Gawain said in a rush, "Oh my dear love, be hideous by day, and fair for me alone!"

"Alas!" said the Lady Ragnell. "And that is your choice? Must I be hideous and misshapen among all the Queen's fair ladies, and abide their scorn and pity, when in truth I am as fair as any of them? Oh, Sir Gawain, is this your love?"

Then Sir Gawain bowed his head. "Nay, I was thinking only of myself. If it will make you happier, be fair by day and take your rightful place at court. And at night I shall hear your soft voice in the darkness, and that shall be my content."

"That was indeed a lover's answer," said the Lady Ragnell. "But I would be fair for you; not only for the court and the daytime world that means less to me than you do."

And Gawain said, "Whichever way it is, it is you who must endure the most suffering; and being a woman, I am thinking that you have more wisdom in such things than I. Make the choice yourself, dear love, and whichever way you choose, I shall be content."

Then the Lady Ragnell bent her head into the hollow of his neck and wept and laughed together. "Oh, Gawain, my dearest lord, now, by seeing that it is for me to decide, by giving me *my own way*, by according me the very sovereignty that was the answer to the original riddle, you have broken the spell completely, and I am free of it, to be my true self by night and day."

For seven years Gawain and Ragnell knew great happiness together, and during all that time Gawain was a gentler and a kinder and more steadfast man than ever he had been before. But, after seven years she left. No one knew where she went. And something of Gawain went with her.

PART THREE

The Foundations
of Mindful Parenting

Sovereignty

Let's look at the mysterious jewel lying at the heart of the Gawain story. It is the concept of *sovereignty*, offered up as the answer to the riddle— What do all women most desire?

As the "answer" to the riddle, the *knowledge* of sovereignty saved Arthur from certain death. But a deeper *feeling* for sovereignty, that came out of Gawain's empathy for Ragnell, solved (actually dissolved) a dilemma that no amount of thinking could have ever done. By giving the choice back to her, he accorded (opened his heart to) her sovereignty, and out of that came transformation.

This is the key to mindful parenting. In honoring our children's sovereignty, we make it possible for them to do two things: show themselves in their "true seeming," and find their own way. Both are necessary to come to full adulthood.

How many times do our children seem to be caught up in spells of their own, captivated by energies that carry them away, turned suddenly into demons, witches, trolls, ogres, and imps? Can we as parents in those moments, as Gawain did, see past the surface appearance, at which a part of us may recoil, to the true being behind the spell? Can we make room in ourselves to love them as they are without having them have to change to please us? And how many times do we as parents get caught up in spells of our own, show our children our "giant" side, the ogre within, or the witch? How much do we secretly yearn to be seen and accepted as we are by others, and to find our own way in our lives?

In *Reviving Ophelia*, Mary Pipher points out that the answer to Sigmund Freud's patronizing question, "What do women want?" is revealed over and over in her therapy sessions with women, and that, although they all want "something different and particular . . . each woman wants the same thing—to be who she truly is, to become who she can become," to be "the subject of her life and not [merely] the object of others' lives."

If sovereignty means being who one truly is and becoming who one can become, then could it not also be the answer to the larger question, "What does everyone at heart most desire?" And even, "What does everyone most deserve?"

In our view, sovereignty, understood in this way, is not an external seeking of power, although to be in touch with it is supremely powerful. It can be thought of as deeply connected to the Buddhist concept of *Buddha Nature*, which is another way of saying our true self. The figure of the Buddha represents the embodiment of a state of mind and heart, best described as in touch with itself, conscious, knowing, awake. The Buddhist view is that our individual mind and Buddha mind are fundamentally the same, and that our deepest work as human beings is to realize that essential unity. Buddha Nature underlies everything. Everything is perfectly and uniquely what it is, and yet nothing is separate and isolated from the whole. So, everybody's true nature is Buddha Nature, and in that we are all the same. Everybody's true nature is sovereign. We have only to recognize it, and honor it in other people—in all beings, in our children, and in ourselves.

Of course, having "only to recognize it" isn't so easy. It is the work of a lifetime, if not many lifetimes. We may not know or may have lost touch with what is most fundamental in ourselves, with our own nature, with what calls to us most deeply. When we don't recognize our true nature, and live far from it, we can create a lot of suffering for ourselves and for others.

The Buddha is sometimes called, "One who has Sovereignty over Himself or Herself." Events carry us away, and we lose ourselves. Walking meditation helps us regain our sovereignty, our liberty as a human being. We walk with grace and dignity, like an emperor, like a lion. Each step is life.

THICH NHAT HANH,
The Long Road Turns to Joy

Honoring what is deepest in people is symbolically reflected in the custom of greeting others by bowing to them. In many countries, instead of shaking hands in greeting, people put their palms together over their hearts and bend slightly toward each other. This means, "I bow to the divinity within you." It signifies a shared recognition of each other's intrinsic wholeness, of what is deepest and most fundamental, already and always present. You are bowing from your true nature to theirs, recalling that, at the deepest level, they are one and the same, even as we recognize that, on other levels, we are all different, unique expressions of this oneness. Sometimes, people bow to cats and dogs, sometimes to trees and flowers, sometimes to the wind and the rain. And sometimes the cats and dogs, the trees and the flowers, even the wind and the rain, bow back. For everything has its intrinsic nature, which makes it what it is and helps it take its place within the whole, and the relationship between them is always reciprocal. I (jkz) like to bow in this feeling way to babies, and to my children. Sometimes I do it when they are sleeping. Mostly, I bow inwardly.

*

At different ages, with different children, and in different circumstances, our choices as parents about how to go about according sovereignty will be very different. But what will not change, hopefully, is a deep commitment to recognize sovereignty and honor it as a fundamental attribute and birthright of each child. This calls for us as parents to remember and, ultimately, to trust the sovereignty, the intrinsic goodness and beauty in our children, even when we are least in touch with it or it is least in evidence.

As every parent knows or soon finds out, each child comes into this world with his or her own attributes, temperament, and genius. As parents, we are called to recognize who each one of them uniquely is, and to honor them by making room for them as they are, not by trying to change them, hard as that sometimes is for us. Since they are already always changing as part of their own nature, it may be that this kind of awareness on our part is precisely what is called for to make room for them to grow and change in those very ways that are best for them and that we cannot impose through our will.

Children are born with sovereignty, in that they are born perfectly who and what they are. We like to think that every child that is born really is an incarnation of what is most sacred in life, and that we as parents are guardians of the unfolding and flowering of their being and their beauty.

While sovereignty is fundamental to our very nature as human beings, our ability to feel it and draw upon it deepens through our life experience, beginning with how we are treated ourselves when we are young. And while it doesn't always happen, our knowledge of and feeling for our own sovereignty as a person, and that of others, can also wither through neglect or harming.

However, what we are calling sovereignty is so deep, so tenacious, so vital, so integral to our nature because it *is* our true nature, that many people manage to draw sustenance and strength from it even through extremely difficult childhood circumstances. At times, someone other than a parent may assume a key role in a child's life by seeing who he really is and offering kindness and encouragement, appreciation and acceptance. Many people credit one special person, who gave them soul recognition and encouragement to be who they were, as the source of their success in life. The mentoring of children and adolescents by people who themselves know in some way their own wholeness, and can thus give selflessly to bring out the beauty and wholeness in others, is the sacred responsibility of the adults in any healthy society.

*

The experience of sovereignty deepens as a child learns to encounter the world from a place of inward strength and confidence, secure in himself, knowing that he is loved and lovable, and accepted *as he is, for who he is.*

At first blush, the very notion of the intrinsic sovereignty of children might easily be misconstrued to suggest that we are advocating that children should be treated as kings and queens and therefore waited on hand and foot. We are not. In fact, nothing could be further from an understanding of sovereignty. According sovereignty to our children does not mean letting them run rampant over everyone, or promoting a sense of false "self-esteem" disconnected from their behavior and real experiences. It does not mean that they have license to do whatever they like, that whatever they do is fine, or that they should always get whatever they want because they have to have their own way and they have to always be happy.

Sovereignty, in the sense of one's true nature, is a universal quality of being, and life, above all, an occasion to understand what that true nature is and how it expresses itself for each of us. Children are sovereign within themselves, and so is everyone else, including their parents.

To nourish sovereignty in our children so that they will know their own way in the world, we have to ask, "How do we honor it in them and yet also respect our own sovereignty?" How do we help them to grow into all aspects of their being, to be in touch with their wholeness and learn from it how to be centered and confident? At the same time, how can we encourage them to see and respect the sovereignty of others?

Sovereignty is very different from unbridled entitlement. It does not mean that children should be given everything they want, or that others should do their work for them. It is our job to protect and nurture sovereignty in our children without fostering an attitude that whatever they do is fine, regardless of its effects, because only they are important, only their view or their desires count. Each person's sovereignty is interdependent and interconnected with everybody else's, because we are all part of a larger whole, and everything we do affects each other.

Another way of putting this is that actually, our children *are* entitled. They are entitled to a great deal. Adults are entitled as well, but there are important asymmetries in the relationship. The adults are responsible for the children. Children are *entitled* to be loved, cared for, and protected by their parents and by other adults. As adults and as parents, we cannot look to children to meet our emotional needs without betraying them. We have to look to ourselves and to other adults for that. But we do get to bask in the endless blessings that our children bestow on us unbidden, just by their being.

Indeed, as adults and as parents, we may very well need to explore, nourish, and develop a more abiding connection to our own underlying sovereignty, since it is so fundamental and, at the same time, so elusive. This is the work of awakening to our own true nature as human beings. Of course, most of the time, if we think about it at all, we might say that we are too busy to pay attention to such notions, for all the injunctions, such as Socrates', to "know thyself." But it may be that we can't afford *not* to pay attention to our own true nature and learn to live in accordance with it. For if we don't, in a very real way, we may sleepwalk through large parts of our lives; and at the end, we may not know who we are or were, and not know who our children are either, for all our thinking we did.

As we have seen, one vehicle for that inward journey of growth and discovery is mindfulness, cultivated in two complementary ways: as attentiveness brought to all aspects of daily life; and in the daily practice of a more formal meditative discipline, in which we stop for a period of time and observe in stillness and quiet the moment-to-moment activity of our own minds and bodies. Bringing mindfulness to our lives in one or both of these ways, and to the whole question of who we really are, can help us perceive our own sovereign nature as we accord sovereignty to our children.

*

What might a fundamental honoring of a child's own way mean for us as parents? After all, what does it mean to *have one's way*? What is one's true Way, with a capital W? What is the experience of sovereignty as an adult or as a child? How is it experienced at different ages and stages of life, and for children with vastly different temperaments?

For one, the honoring of a child's sovereignty means acknowledging to ourselves the reality of those very stages and temperaments. It might mean that the messages an infant gives us are responded to because we are the baby's major interface with the world. If the baby cries, we pick her up, we hold her, we move in with our presence, our listening. We attempt to provide comfort and a sense of well-being. By doing so, we honor her power to have the world respond to her, we accord her that respect and teach her that the world does respond, and that there is a place for her, that she belongs. And we do this as an intentional practice, whether we feel like it at any given moment or not.

According sovereignty might mean child-proofing our house so that our toddler is free to explore his environment safely. Yet, even in a relatively safe environment, toddlers need constant watching. Just keeping an eye out, moment by moment, accords the toddler sovereignty. It is an honoring, a statement that the child deserves that vigilant attention at arm's length that becomes, in parents of children that age, a sixth sense, like knowing when the glass is too close to the edge of the table and moving it just before the child grabs for it, even as we may be in mid-conversation with another person.

On the other hand, a steady diet of fearful warnings, such as, "Don't do that, you'll hurt yourself!" whenever the child is exploring something can undermine a child's confidence and instill our fears in her. An alternative might be quietly to position ourselves to assist or remove the child if necessary while allowing her to adventure without injecting our own fears into her bold explorations.

With adolescents, according sovereignty might mean being willing to see past the ways they choose to appear or assert themselves—ways that, as expressions of their inner power, often shock or repulse their elders—and relate to their underlying goodness. We accord them sovereignty by appreciating their unique views, insights, skills, their struggles, and strengths, and also by staying abreast of the myriad forces that may challenge and threaten them in these times. It might mean knowing when to be silent and leave them alone, and when to reach out, verbally and non-verbally, in ways that respect their growing autonomy. And sometimes it means setting definite and clear limits and sticking to them with kindness and firmness.

These are just a few passing examples of how we might accord sovereignty to children at different ages. As with Dame Ragnell, our true nature is not always so apparent. The clarity that enables us to see past the veil of appearances and act in the best interest of our children comes out of our moment-to-moment awareness. Sovereignty can neither be fully tapped in oneself nor fully accorded to another by one hopeful act, however important that act or moment might be. It emerges in both cases out of an ongoing, enthusiastic embrace of present moments with an open, discerning heart.

Not a day will go by when we do not feel challenged in one way or another, when we might question our own sovereignty or feel it is in conflict with our child's. This is another way of saying that parenting is exhausting at times, and always hard work in the same way that being mindful is hard work. As we have seen, it is a discipline, a constant calling upon ourselves to remember that it is possible to be present, to see and accept our children for who they are, and in doing so, to be and share with them our best self.

Part of this work means keeping in mind that we cannot solve all our problems or our children's problems through thinking alone. For there are other, equally important intelligences at work in our lives, and, as parents, we need to develop fluency in them ourselves in order to help them emerge in our children. One is the intelligence of *empathy.* Gawain *felt* something for Ragnell. In trusting his feelings, what we could call his intuition, his heart, he penetrated past appearances, and past the either-or veil of his own thinking. It is only when he lets go of his attachment to a certain outcome, and accepts both the dilemma *and* Ragnell's sovereignty, that an opening, and with it a seemingly impossible liberation, occur.

If each moment is truly an opportunity for growth, an occasion to be true to oneself, a potential branch point leading to one of an infinite number of possible next moments depending on how this one is seen and held, according sovereignty to a child in one moment makes room right then and there for his or her true nature to emerge, to be seen and silently celebrated. In this way, self-acceptance, self-esteem, self-confidence, and trust in one's own true nature and path take root, develop, and mature in the growing child.

The power of empathy and acceptance is immense, and deeply transformative both for the person receiving them and for the person according them. More than anything else, a careful nurturing of a child's sovereignty, and an honoring of it through empathy and acceptance, lie at the heart of mindful parenting.

*

Here is a striking example of a gift of sovereignty from a father to his son:

> "Daddy's going to be very angry about this," my mother said.
> It was August 1938, at a Catskill Mountains boarding house.
> One hot Friday afternoon three of us—9-year-old city boys—
> got to feeling listless. We'd done all the summer-country stuff,
> caught all the frogs, picked the blueberries and shivered in

enough icy river water. What we needed, on this unbearably boring afternoon, was some action.

To consider the options, Artie, Eli and I holed up in the cool of the "casino," the little building in which the guests enjoyed their nightly bingo games and the occasional traveling magic act.

Gradually, inspiration came: the casino was too new, the wood frame and white sheetrock walls too perfect. We would do it some quiet damage. Leave our anonymous mark on the place, for all time. With, of course, no thought as to consequences.

We began by picking up a long, wooden bench, running with it like a battering ram, and bashing it into a wall. It left a wonderful hole. But small. So we did it again. And again . . .

Afterward the three of us, breathing hard, sweating the sweat of heroes, surveyed our first really big-time damage. The process had been so satisfying we'd gotten carried away. There was hardly a good square of sheetrock left.

Suddenly, before even a tweak of remorse set in, the owner, Mr. Biolos, appeared in the doorway of the building. Furious. And craving justice: When they arrived from the city that night, he-would-tell-our-fathers!

Meantime, he told our mothers. My mother felt that what I had done was so monstrous she would leave my punishment to my father. "And," she said, "Daddy's going to be very angry about this."

By six o'clock Mr. Biolos was stationed out at the driveway, grimly waiting for the fathers to start showing up. Behind him, the front porch was jammed, like a sold-out bleacher section, with indignant guests. They'd seen the damage to their bingo palace, knew they'd have to endure it in that condition for the rest of the summer. They too craved justice.

As to Artie, Eli and me, we each found an inconspicuous spot on the porch, a careful distance from the other two but not too far from our respective mothers. And we waited.

Artie's father arrived first. When Mr. Biolos told him the news and showed him the blighted casino, he carefully took off his belt and—with practiced style—viciously whipped his screaming son. With the approbation, by the way, of an ugly crowd of once-gentle people.

Eli's father showed up next. He was told and shown and went raving mad, knocking his son off his feet with a slam to the head. As Eli lay crying on the grass, he kicked him on the legs, buttocks and back. When Eli tried to get up he kicked him again.

The crowd muttered: Listen, they should have thought of this before they did the damage. They'll live, don't worry, and I bet they never do that again.

I wondered: What will my father do? He'd never laid a hand on me in my life. I knew about other kids, had seen bruises on certain schoolmates and even heard screams in the evenings from certain houses on my street, but they were those kids, their families, and the why and how of their bruises were, to me, dark abstractions. Until now.

I looked over at my mother. She was upset. Earlier she'd made it clear to me that I had done some special kind of crime. Did it mean that beatings were now, suddenly, the new order of the day?

My own father suddenly pulled up in our Chevy, just in time to see Eli's father dragging Eli up the porch steps and into the building. He got out of the car believing, I was sure, that whatever it was all about, Eli must have deserved it. I went dizzy with fear. Mr. Biolos, on a roll, started talking. My father listened, his shirt soaked with perspiration, a damp handkerchief draped around his neck; he never did well in humid weather. I watched him follow Mr. Biolos into the casino. My dad—strong and principled, hot and bothered—what was he thinking about all this?

When they emerged, my father looked over at my mother. He mouthed a small "Hello," then his eyes found me and stared for a long moment, without expression. I tried to read his eyes, but they left me and went to the crowd, from face to expectant face.

Then, amazingly, he got into his car and drove away! Nobody, not even my mother, could imagine where he was going.

An hour later he came back. Tied onto the top of his car was a stack of huge sheetrock boards. He got out holding a paper sack with a hammer sticking out of it. Without a word he untied the sheetrock and one by one carried the boards into the casino.

And didn't come out again that night.

All through my mother's and my silent dinner and for the rest of that Friday evening and long after we had gone to bed, I could hear—everyone could hear—the steady bang bang bang bang of my dad's hammer. I pictured him sweating, missing his dinner, missing my mother, getting madder and madder at me. Would tomorrow be the last day of my life? It was 3 A.M. before I finally fell asleep.

The next morning, my father didn't say a single word about the night before. Nor did he show any trace of anger or reproach of any kind. We had a regular day, he, my mother, and I, and, in fact, our usual sweet family weekend.

Was he mad at me? You bet he was. But in a time when many of his generation saw corporal punishment of their children as a God-given right, he knew "spanking" as beating, and beating as criminal. And that when kids were beaten, they always remembered the pain but often forgot the reason.

I also realized years later that, to him, humiliating me was just as unthinkable. Unlike the fathers of my buddies, he couldn't play into a conspiracy of revenge and spectacle.

But my father had made his point. I never forgot that my vandalism on that August afternoon was outrageous.

And I'll never forget that it was also the day I first understood how deeply I could trust him.

MEL LAZARUS,

CREATOR OF THE COMIC STRIPS
"MOMMA" AND "MISS PEACH"
AND A NOVELIST

(from: "Angry Fathers," *Sunday New York Times*, About Men, May 28, 1995)

Empathy

Empathy played a key role in Sir Gawain's ability to free Dame Ragnell from the spell in which she was caught. He sensed her pain and he glimpsed, through her eyes, a beauty beyond appearance, hidden, but there nonetheless, ". . . something in her pathetic pride and the way she lifted her hideous head caused him to think of a deer with the hounds about it. Something in the depth of her bleared gaze reached him like a cry for help."

The dog of the castle symbolizes a soulful empathy that at times puts humans to shame. "Only Cabal, the dog, came and licked her hand with a warm, wet tongue and looked up into her face with amber eyes that took no account of her hideous aspect. . . ." Often, if we are paying attention, dogs and cats can teach us about sovereignty, empathy, and acceptance. Perhaps that is why we live with them and they with us. They provide the basic course. Raising children is advanced training. We enroll whether we are ready for it or not. And who is ever ready?

*

Reflecting on empathy in our own lives, perhaps it is useful to ask ourselves, "What did I most want from my parents when I was a child?"

We might take a minute or two to reflect, and see what words or images come to mind . . .

For many people, what is most deeply desired is to have been seen and accepted in the family for who they were, a desire to have been treated with kindness, compassion, understanding, and respect; to have been accorded freedom, safety, and privacy, and a sense of belonging. All of these depend on a parent's ability to empathize.

Empathy is not limited to immediate emotional responses. It is easy to empathize with a child when he is hurting. It is much harder to do when he is kicking and throwing things and screaming. It is also hard to do when his interests or views seem to conflict with ours. Our ability to empathize in a broader range of situations takes intentional cultivation.

When we cultivate empathy, we try to see things from our child's point of view. We try to understand what he or she may be feeling or experiencing. We attempt to bring a sympathetic awareness to what is happening in each moment. This includes an awareness of our own feelings as well.

What might it be like to empathize with a newborn baby, to imagine how she might feel arriving in this world after nine months of being in a very different one?

We might start by imagining what it was like in the uterus, in a place that is warm, wet, and protected, with constant, rhythmic sounds, a feeling of being contained, held, rocked . . . a world of undifferentiated wholeness, where there is nothing wanting, nothing missing.

In a letter written by a young man of nineteen to his mother on Mother's Day, we are given a heartfelt glimpse into this world:

"Much peace and strength from my heart to you. For the nine months of sweetest meditation. In which water I could breathe like fish. When food was so pure not the mouth nor throat were used . . . Blessings."

When we are born, we leave this harmonious world and emerge into a new and totally different one. There might be harsh light and cold air. We may hear loud, unpredictable noises and feel roughness or hardness against our skin. We feel hunger for the first time. All of this occurring as raw, pure experience, with no filters of knowing anything. Imagine being thrust into this foreign environment, where you depend entirely on the inhabitants' ability to understand your language and to be sensitive and responsive to your whole being, and to what you may need in any given moment.

What quality of experience would *you* choose: a cold, neoprene nipple or a warm, soft, sweet-smelling breast? To be held tenderly in loving arms or to lie in a crib or plastic babyseat? To be left to cry until you fell asleep, or to feel a sympathetic responsiveness? To experience that when you cry, you will be picked up, or put to the breast, or made warm and dry with a diaper change, or rocked and held or sung to?

Why is it so hard for us to see our infants as fully feeling, fully experiencing beings? Why is it okay to let infants "cry it out" when we would never ignore the cries of a friend or lover or even a stranger? What might we be resisting, or protecting ourselves from, when we distance ourselves from a baby's distress?

One thing we may be protecting ourselves from, of course, is more work. It's much more labor-intensive in the short run to parent moment by moment in responsive ways. Tuning in to a child's body language, trying different things, being sensitive not to underrespond or overrespond, holding, comforting, crooning, all take time and energy. More often than not, they can also interrupt our sleep—literally and metaphorically. It is certainly easier to empathize with our children when it also meets our own needs. The real test for us comes when it feels as if their needs are in conflict with ours.

A lack of empathy in such situations may also be a way of protecting ourselves from the pain we may have experienced when our own physical or emotional needs were not responded to when we were little. Empathizing with a child's vulnerability can be a painful reminder of our own.

One way to avoid having to acknowledge, as adults, our suffering as children, is to revert to a coping mechanism we may have relied on when we were babies ourselves. In the face of an unresponsive environment, many babies close off emotionally, withdraw, and tune out. If that is the way we learned to deal with pain and frustration when we were children, we may continue to do this as adults, in ways that may be entirely automatic and below our level of awareness. Rather than tuning in to our baby's feelings and our own feelings in response, we might instead ignore them or minimize them with rationalizations such as, "Kids are tough, she'll adjust," "Crying won't hurt her," "We don't want to spoil her." Then we might reach for food, alcohol, drugs, TV, or the newspaper to calm ourselves and tune out the pain.

We may not realize that we have powerful inner resources that extend far beyond such vehicles of escape. Tuning in and connecting empathically in such moments is a far healthier alternative, and far more satisfying for both parent and child. Even if we did not learn this in childhood, our babies and children can call up this primordial capacity from our deepest souls, if we are prepared to give ourselves over to such deep callings.

In studies where researchers asked mothers to deliberately over- or underrespond to their infants, rather than matching their feelings in an attuned, empathic way, the infants responded with immediate dismay and distress. Reporting on these studies, Daniel Goleman, in *Emotional Intelligence*, writes that

> Prolonged absence of attunement between parent and child takes a tremendous toll on the child. When a parent consistently fails to show any empathy with a particular range of emotion in the child—joys, tears, needing to cuddle—the child begins to avoid expressing, and perhaps even feeling, those same emotions. In this way, presumably, entire ranges of emotion can begin to be obliterated from the [child's] repertoire for intimate relations, especially if through childhood, those feelings continue to be covertly or overtly discouraged.

The implications of such studies are profound. According to the researcher and psychiatrist Daniel Stern, cited by Goleman, the small, repeated exchanges that take place between parent and child form the basis for the most fundamental lessons of emotional life. If this is so, the importance of parents engaging wholeheartedly in this dance of interconnectedness with their children is vital to their children's ongoing unfolding as whole, emotionally competent, sovereign beings.

From this point of view, the "good" baby who stops crying after ten minutes and goes to sleep may be a baby who has learned to give up. But is giving up what we really want to teach our children? Is adapting to *not* getting their needs met the way we want our children to develop "independence"? Is shutting down emotionally and losing some of their aliveness and openness what we want for our children? Or do we want to teach them that their feelings count, that we will respond to them, that there are people who they can trust and rely on to be sensitive to them, and that it is safe to be open, expressive, to ask for what they need, to be *interdependent*?

＊

As babies become toddlers and start to explore the world, they have a natural curiosity and pleasure in everything around them. At the same time, the world offers many frustrations as they try to do things they cannot yet do and are limited by skills they do not yet have. So while they are continually venturing out, they still need a loving, emotionally available person to come back to. Toddlers depend on their parents' sensitivity and understanding to create an environment (or in the case of child care, to choose an environment) that feeds their curiosity, gives them the freedom to safely explore and discover, and at the same time provides the warmth and security they need, in the form of a welcoming lap or being held or carried.

As our children get older, empathy takes a less physical form, although there are times when what is most needed is a silent hug, or holding hands. The cues we get from them can be confusing and difficult to understand. One day or one minute they may be friendly and communicative; the next they might be angry and rejecting.

Our ability to communicate, or even its possibility, will depend a great deal on the sense of an enduring and strong commitment on our part to our child, even when he or she may be questioning their relationship with us, or rejecting our overtures or inquiries.

Being empathic in the face of rejection requires us to not let our own hurt feelings get in the way of seeing the pain our child may be feeling. In some sense, our children have to feel us holding on to them, no matter what repugnant (to our mind) spells come over them, no matter what dark disguises they try on. This mindful holding on comes not out of a desire to control them, or to hold them back, or to cling to them out of our own neediness, but out of a commitment to be appropriately present for them no matter what, to let them know that they are not alone, that we have not lost sight of who they are and what they mean to us.

And isn't it true for all of us that when we are feeling lost, sad, and often quite toadlike, it helps enormously to feel that the people closest to us are still our allies, are still able to see and love our essential self? *So, as parents, it is our job to continually rebuild and restore our relationships with our children.* This takes time, attention, and commitment. If we are perpetually absent—or present in our bodies but absent in our attention and in our hearts—there is no way our child will feel the trust, the closeness needed to let us know what problems she or he is facing.

Children have a wonderful ability to cut to the heart of an issue. A friend told us the following story. One night when her daughter was eight years old, she sat with her as she tried to go to sleep. Her child was overwhelmed by an acute fear of robbers and kidnappers, something that had surfaced at nighttime for a number of years. The mother sat on the bed, listening, struggling inwardly with her desire to reassure her child, to convince her that there was nothing to fear, and knowing the futility of trying to use reason in the face of her daughter's deep and persistent dread.

Taking a different tack, she told her daughter that when she was her age, she also was very fearful at night. The young girl looked at her mother solemnly and said, "You were?" She responded with a nod. Her daughter was thoughtful for a moment and then asked with great seriousness, "Could you tell your mommy?" The mother paused, thinking back to when she was a child, and replied, "No, I couldn't."

At eight years old, her daughter knew from her own direct experience how important it is to be able to tell someone close to you how you feel. She knew what it was like to feel an openness and acceptance, an empathic presence from a parent. Her fears weren't dismissed, joked about, or belittled. In the grip of this very real terror, she unquestion-ingly felt safe enough to tell her mother. She didn't have to feel alone in her fear.

As parents, we can learn a great deal about ourselves by bringing mindfulness to the thoughts and feelings that come up when a child is sharing something difficult with us. If we can observe our own discom-fort brought on by certain feelings, and note any impulse that might arise to smooth over, dismiss, or belittle particular concerns or fears, the pos-sibility exists of changing our own automatic behavior and becoming a more empathic and supportive parent.

Sometimes, in moments when we are called upon to listen, to em-pathize, to respond in a caring manner, we may instead find ourselves overwhelming a child with our own strong feelings and reactions. She may end up feeling that she has to take care of us, rather than the other way around.

If we can bring mindfulness to those moments in which we find ourselves moving down a tributary we didn't mean to pursue, we may be able to see what is happening and stop, perhaps even reverse course and chart another. This kind of moment-to-moment sensitivity keeps us knowing where the energy is going. It reminds us that we need to be se-lective, to decide in a conscious way when it is helpful to share our own feelings and when it is unnecessary, even destructive. We need to learn, through an *inner* listening, when to reach out and when to let things be, when to speak and when to keep silent, and how to be present in silence so that this is felt by another as empathic presence, rather than as rejec-tion and withdrawal. No one can teach us these things. We have to learn from our own experience, from attending to the clues and cues we are given, and to our own mind states as they come and go.

Children who grow up without empathy from parents, other adults, and from peers, can feel as though they are living in an emotional desert, surrounded by people who do not really know them or care to know them, however well-intentioned some of them may be. Children who grow up with parents who are empathic, who feel a parental acceptance of a wide range of their behaviors and feelings, who can depend on their parents emotionally as well as physically, have a certain open, lively expression on their faces. They are free to express anger and sometimes fury, as well as exuberance and affection. They can be caring and concerned when someone is hurt or distressed. At the same time, their strong sense of self enables them to set healthy boundaries with others.

The continual weaving and restoring of empathic connections to our children is a foundation of mindful parenting. Seeing things from a child's point of view can guide us in the choices we make, and helps us to bring a sympathetic presence to whatever comes up in each moment.

Acceptance

Along with sovereignty and empathy comes the crucial need for acceptance as a fundamental element of mindful parenting. The three are intimately interwoven and complement each other. Acceptance is an inner orientation which acknowledges that things are as they are, whether they are the way we want them to be or not, no matter how terrible they may be or seem to be at certain moments.

Gawain accepted Lady Ragnell as she was. Mel Lazarus's father accepted that what the boys had done was already done. In doing so, he saw that the next moment called for something new, something to further healing, completion, and respect. Acceptance of what *is* underlies our ability to choose *how* to be in relationship to whatever is actually happening. Acceptance is not passive. It has nothing to do with resignation or defeat. Just as sovereignty does not mean unbridled entitlement, so acceptance does not mean that everything our children do is okay with us. But even as we are totally clear with them that certain behaviors are not acceptable, our children can still feel from us that we accept them completely. Acceptance is a door that, if we choose to open it, leads to seeing in new ways and finding new possibilities.

*

I (mkz) am in a shoestore with my daughters. One is four and the other is an infant. The four-year-old wants shoes, and there are none that are quite right. As we are leaving, she starts to yell and scream and grabs a shoe on display, refusing to let go. With a baby to hold, I grab her hand and get to the door, where I ask an employee to take the shoe from her. A tugging match ensues. I'm feeling angry and helpless and out of control. I finally manage to get us outside. She is still screaming and crying, her face bright red. She is wild, furious that she cannot have new shoes. It is a struggle to get her into her car seat. In the process, her foot kicks the half-open car door and breaks the plastic side panel.

How I respond to this whole episode is determined by how I see or don't see my child in that moment. At the time, feeling completely overwhelmed by the intensity of her reaction, I felt angry and not very sympathetic. I wasn't feeling particularly empathic, but I didn't lash out at her, either. It took all my attention and effort just to get us home and keep her from hurting anyone. It was only later that I was able to look at what had gone on and feel sympathy for her as I started putting together clues in an attempt to understand what had happened.

The possible causes were as disparate as her being overtired, being hungry and having low blood sugar, reacting to the fumes from the leather products in the store, and her frustration over not getting what she wanted, made worse by having to share me with her baby sister. In all likelihood, it was some combination of these factors.

In looking back on what happened, I could see that she wasn't kicking and crying and destroying the car out of maliciousness or to drive me crazy or to control me. Her anger over not getting shoes set off a huge reaction that she couldn't control. She was in the grip of something, as if under a spell.

*

There are so many different ways to view what we often call "difficult" or "negative" behaviors in our children. What might be completely unacceptable to someone else might be normal behavior to me, and vice versa. Very often we're locked into seeing things in only one way, conditioned by views and feelings that are frequently unexamined, and that often put social decorum—what other people might think, or how embarrassed we are feeling—above the emotional well-being of our children.

In such moments, it is easy to feel controlled and manipulated by our children, to feel completely helpless, and then of course to feel tremendously angry. We might easily find ourselves lashing out at them in an attempt to assert our authority and regain control of the situation.

Since such occasions abound in parenting, especially with young children, we are given plenty of opportunities to decondition ourselves from these reactive patterns, and to develop, out of our awareness and discernment, a much more appropriate and nourishing repertoire of emotional responses.

This is where mindfulness of our emotional reactions can combine with formal meditation to help us see more clearly, as we will describe in Part 4. Formal meditation is like a laboratory that allows us to develop a high degree of familiarity with our mind states and feeling states and how they affect us. It gives us a lot of practice in watching our thoughts and feelings arise from moment to moment and coming to see them as occurrences that do not have to be reacted to. An awareness of our emotions simply means consciously acknowledging their presence. We accept that they are our feelings in the moment, whether we like them or not, without judging them.

As we learn to observe and accept our own wide range of feelings, including very turbulent ones, as part of our effort to be mindful, we naturally become more aware of other people's feelings, especially our children's. We come to know something of the landscape of feelings and their changing nature, and are more likely to be sympathetic and less likely, at the same time, to take them personally. We are better able to accept their experience and their feelings, even if we may not like how they are behaving. In doing so, we are able to step out of the limited realm in which we as parents can often find ourselves, where we are so carried away by our own feelings and our attachment to our view of things that we cut ourselves off from our children and in some deep way, without realizing or intending to, abandon them.

Again, our children will give us countless opportunities to practice seeing and accepting things as they are through the veils of our own emotional reactivity, and then acting as best we can, based on our understanding of the larger picture.

*

How we see things will completely affect what we choose to do. When a baby is crying, do we see it as a willful attempt to control us or as a cry for help? When children begin crawling and exploring the world around them, do we view their unstoppable curiosity as a sign of intelligence, strength, and spirit, or as a threat to our control, as an act of disobedience? How do we view it when a son is wildly teasing his sisters, or when a teenage daughter is moody and distant, critical and demanding, or when a child is so angry that she threatens to run away from home?

The situations we struggle with that are the most difficult for us are also the ones in which we need mindfulness the most. It can help us remember, right in those most horrible moments, to accept our children as they are, and attempt to act out of that awareness, with compassion.

Accepting our children as they are. It sounds so simple. But how often do we find ourselves wanting our children to act, look, or be different from the way they actually are in *that* moment? How often do we want them to be, or look, or relate the way they were in a different moment, at a different time, and not accepting—despite all the evidence—that right here, right now, things are not the way we want them to be but are undeniably the way they are?

We tend to label as "negative behavior" any kind of acting out on the part of a child that we perceive as an attack on our authority. When things feel out of control, the impulse is to reach for whatever methods we have at our disposal to "discipline" the offender and restore order.

This cycle of "bad behavior," followed by some kind of discipline imposed by us, frequently does not include any attempt to empathize with what the child is experiencing. Rather than a difficult moment leading to greater understanding and a deeper connection between parent and child, distance and alienation are created instead.

The alternative to this is a process which is much less clearcut. There is no set formula for it. But we can say that it begins with an attempt to be open, to see our child freshly in that very moment and remember his or her sovereignty, or true nature. When we try to do this, we often find that our view is colored by our own needs, by our fears and our expectations, and by the extent or lack of our resources in that moment. These can combine, either to filter our vision so that everything is colored in one particular way, or to cloud our vision completely. In either case, we are no longer seeing the whole picture. Only certain colors and certain details come through. Our own partial seeing often leads to habitual negative labeling and judging of our child's behavior, and to sustained anger and emotional distancing.

If we bring mindfulness into those very moments when we sense ourselves losing perspective or clarity, allowing ourselves to be fully present, perhaps using our breath to ground us in our bodies, and if we try looking carefully at what is really happening with our child, we often find that there is much more going on than what we are reacting to on the surface. If we assume that there is some underlying reason for a child's "difficult" behavior, even if we don't see it immediately and don't understand what is going on, we are able to be more sympathetic and accepting.

How we view what is happening, whether it is with judgment and disapproval or with an openness to trying to see beneath the surface, strongly affects our relationships with our children. Viewing our children's difficult behavior in a more non-judging, compassionate, and open manner allows us to remain their ally and keep a heartfelt connection with them even when we don't like how they are acting.

When we are able to put aside our habitual, often critical ways of seeing disruptive or difficult behavior, we may begin to see that wild, loud, angry behavior is not necessarily "negative" at all. Sometimes, children are acting out as a way of regaining equilibrium. They may have felt constrained by school or by the demands of certain kinds of work, and need outlets for their energy, their vitality, their power.

Over the years, when our children have been particularly wild, silly, goofy, or generally provoking, it has helped me (mkz) to view it as discharging or releasing, an important way for them to let things out rather than hold them in. Our bodies do this all the time in the form of sweating and skin eruptions. Even vomiting and diarrhea can be seen in a positive light, the body's way of getting rid of toxins and cleansing. We can view emotional discharging in a similarly accepting and positive way.

Sometimes, children are bursting with uncontrolled energy. At other times, they may be expressing deep, subterranean emotion. Even when they are falling apart, yelling, screaming, kicking and banging, seeing such behavior as an expression of their aliveness makes me more tolerant. Viewing it as a healthy and normal release helps me to get some perspective on it and not take it so personally. I can choose to be more sanguine. It also gives them the freedom to try out different behaviors instead of being locked by parental authority into a narrowly defined framework of what is acceptable in the domain of being.

Every time that we have resisted, fought with, attempted to control, or commented negatively about this energy, we only made it worse. In such moments, we need to find ways to move *with* our children rather than only to offer resistance; to work with them, rather than against them.

Sometimes it involves engaging their energy. If a toddler or even a school-age child is getting wild and a bit out of control, he might like to wrestle with you, or play some other very physical game that allows him to let out his energy, but in a more focused, grounded way. Once you have connected with him, you can more easily help him to make the transition to whatever it is he needs in that moment.

There are times when we might find it helpful to view an outburst the way we view suddenly inclement weather. Sometimes we just have to sit out such an eruption, the way we might a thunderstorm. Do we think of thunderstorms as "manipulative," a word that often comes up when children are not acting the way we want them to? Sometimes the only way children have to start fresh is to erupt first. When disequilibrium builds up, for whatever reason, discharging it may be the only way to achieve the peace that follows in its wake, the sigh, the letting go. Children sometimes have to push us away and find a new space within themselves before there can be a reconciliation, a reconnecting, and a new beginning.

If we are observant, over time we can begin to identify the early warning signs that a storm is brewing. We can also work with our children in peaceful moments, when they are more receptive, and encourage them to pay attention to how they feel in those pre-storm moments. They can begin to ask themselves, "Am I hungry?" "Am I tired?" "Am I mad, or sad?" Slowly, our children can learn to ask for what they need, whether it's a quiet time in their room alone, a hug, a warm bath, a snack, or a rough-and-tumble game. In this way they begin to experience self-awareness and self-acceptance.

Parents may find it just as hard as their children to learn to direct their focus inwardly and pay attention to their own feelings and to the cues they are getting from their bodies, especially in times of emotional turbulence. Finding appropriate and satisfying ways to meet our own true needs, as well as those of our children, takes energy, attention, and on-going practice.

*

Being open, accepting, and sympathetic doesn't mean that we are naive or passive. There are many times every day that we have to step in and take decisive action. Of course, what we do will depend very much on a child's age and the particular circumstances. At times, our children are simply doing too much, moving too fast, flying too high. They may not be able to self-regulate yet, or they may have tried, but the pressures around them were too powerful. So they need us to rein them in, give them some boundaries, provide something to hit up against to slow them down, to bring them down to earth.

There are also times when our child may be waving a red flag at us, sending a serious distress signal, saying: "Pay attention! Something is not right!" These red flags can take many different forms, such as a pattern of angry outbursts, fearfulness, being withdrawn, physical symptoms, or not wanting to go to school. At such times, if we automatically attribute the worst motives to their behavior and react with punitive harshness or cynicism, or if we ignore them, we diminish our children as well as our-selves. When we label their behavior "negative" or "disrespectful" or "manipulative," and react with disapproval and discipline, we essentially cut ourselves off from them in those moments, just when they might need us the most. Our judging throws up a barrier. It becomes a dead end. We miss an opportunity to support our children's inner growth and transformation, and to build trust and a sense of connectedness with them. We also miss an opportunity to deal with what may be very real problems and empathize with the underlying pain that accompanies them.

At such times we have to look beneath the surface to see what is going on. It can be hard to track down the source of these red flags. But rather than a negative, fearful, judging perspective, we might try cultivating a more open and caring perspective: "What do these signs mean?" "What can we work with here?" If we are sensitive and attentive to the cues and clues our children give us, and combine them with what we know about them, we can usually begin to see what the underlying issues are and what it is that we may need to do.

Of course, when a toddler is kicking and screaming, or a school-age child is yelling and slamming doors, these are not the best times to wonder what is really going on. We need to get through the immediate crisis first. Whatever the cause, when children are upset, they are not in a thinking mode. They are usually immersed in strong feelings, and don't want us to reason with them. They need us to stay with them through the storm, and to not lose our own center just because they have lost theirs. We might imagine that we are a large sheltering oak tree in this storm, a solid, overarching friend, not necessarily understanding or having answers, but a sympathetic presence.

Once the storm has passed, that is the time to ask ourselves what is going on here? We become detectives. We consider the possible source of their unhappiness or disequilibrium. Is it something at school or something at home? Is it physical, emotional, or both? Is it something relatively simple, like being overtired, hungry, or overstimulated, or did something troubling happen? Is there a pattern of things happening? What are the stresses in their lives? What inner and outer resources do they have or need? Are their emotional and soul needs being met?

Being accepting of who our children are and what they are going through means asking these kinds of questions and looking deeply into what we may find.

*

My ten-year-old daughter, in bed, lights out, says to me:

> "Mommy, I feel so confused."
> I reply: "What are you confused about?"
> She says: "I don't know, I just feel confused."
> I struggle with my urge to make it better . . . "It's okay to feel
>   confused."
> She says: "It is?"
> I say: "Yes, it is."
> She is silent and drifts off to sleep.

She didn't need a discussion or a solution in that moment. Feeling held by me, she could accept uncertainty, confusion. My acceptance led her to an acceptance in herself.

*

It is not always easy to be accepting of our older children, especially when everything they say seems to be a direct criticism of us. This usually happens at the end of a long day, when everybody is feeling tired and depleted. Along with what sometimes feels like a steady stream of negative comments and putdowns are requests for us to do things for them, and complaints about how tired they are and how much they have to do. The more alienated we feel from them, the angrier and more critical and demanding they become. In turn, their behavior can trigger anger in us, and can make us feel even more unaccepting and rejecting of them.

My (mkz) teenage daughter comes into the kitchen, shivering, dressed in a T-shirt, and we have the following exchange:

"It's cold in here."
"Put something else on."
(Annoyed): "I don't need to put something more on, it's cold in here."
"It's not very cold in here, why don't you go and put something warmer on?"
(Getting angry): "I shouldn't have to put something on, it's cold in here."

Each interaction pushes us further apart. I am annoyed by her behavior and not feeling sympathetic because of all the times recently when I have felt relentlessly picked on. Later, things dissolve into a hugely upsetting scene, after which she goes to her room and refuses to talk to me. This has the effect of throwing cold water on me, and I finally see past my own anger and wake up to the difficult time she is going through. I see that the more distant we have grown in the past few weeks, the angrier she has become; and the more she has snapped at me, the angrier and more alienated from her I have become. A horribly vicious cycle, culminating in this present impasse. How does it end?

Clearly, *I* have to end it. I see that she can't get all of what she needs from me. She wants something, but she doesn't want it from me . . . she does and she doesn't. In that lies a conundrum.

When she complained of being cold and refused to put something on, I could have hugged her, which she may or may not have wanted. Or I could have been sympathetic and just turned up the heat, which would have given her warmth in a way she might have accepted. There were all sorts of options; but, instead, I let my own anger from the previous days make me intolerant. I closed myself off from her, and made her the problem.

During this time, she needed me to be particularly loving and accepting, not to take her criticisms of the past few weeks personally, but to see them as a sign of her own internal struggles. I couldn't change things in the rest of her life, but I could have been more sympathetic, and interpreted her behavior as asking for love in a difficult time.

*

It may be much harder for us to show teenagers the warmth and affection that may have come to us so easily when they were little. We need to continually find ways to remind them that we are on their side, that they are as precious to us as they were when they were adorable, red-cheeked cherubs.

*

Some of the ways in which our children behave may be much more difficult for us than others. The times they need our acceptance and our love the most are, inevitably, those times when it is hardest for us to give.

No matter what their age, some things they do can trigger volcanic feelings and destructive behaviors in us. These reactive patterns might have been part of the landscape of our own childhood, and we may have adopted them ourselves without even knowing it. They surface in particular situations when similar conditions arise. Our reactions can take the form of unconscious posturing, tension, self-righteousness, contempt, intolerance, cruelty, and catastrophic thinking. To cultivate acceptance, we need to be exquisitely aware of our own feelings as our children act out. Every time we are able to see a little more clearly what our own issues are and where they come from, we have the possibility of choosing not to react in automatic and often destructive ways, and creating new and healthier possibilities instead.

Any behavior can be seen in its worst light, or it can be seen in a more accepting and benign way. When we have been raised in an environment of mistrust, when we have been hurt by suspicion and judgment, when we have been belittled or ridiculed, it is easy to fall into these familiar patterns and repeat them with our own children. To break out of them takes ongoing, moment-to-moment awareness. We need to be aware of *what* we are saying, *how* we are saying it, and *what effect* we are having on our children.

Too many children live with the feeling that they are not accepted for who they are, that, somehow, they are "disappointing" their parents or not meeting their expectations, that they don't "measure up." How many parents spend their time focusing on the ways in which their child is "too this" or "too that," or "not enough of this or that"? A great deal of unnecessary pain and grief is caused by this withholding, judging behavior on the part of parents. When has parental disapproval, in the form of shaming, humiliating, or withholding, ever been a positive influence on a child's behavior? It might result in obedience; but at what cost to the child, and to the adult that child becomes?

Parents don't have to like or agree with everything their children do, or the ways in which they choose to live when they are older. There are always going to be differences. Ultimately, each child has to find his or her own way. When a child, no matter how old, feels our acceptance, when he feels our love, not just for his easy-to-live-with, lovable, attractive self, but also for his difficult, repulsive, exasperating self, it feeds him and frees him to become more balanced and whole. Children can face all sorts of difficulties and challenges if they can come back to the well of our unconditional love. For it is in our honoring of their whole selves that inner growth and healing take place.

PART FOUR

Mindfulness:

A Way of Seeing

Parenting Is
the Full Catastrophe

When we become parents, whether intentionally or by happenstance, our whole life is immediately different, although it may take some time to realize just how much. Being a parent compounds stress by orders of magnitude. It makes us vulnerable in ways we weren't before. It calls us to be responsible in ways we weren't before. It challenges us as never before, and takes our time and attention away from other things, including ourselves, as never before. It creates chaos and disorder, feelings of inadequacy, occasions for arguments, struggles, irritation, noise, seemingly never-ending obligations and errands, and plenty of opportunities for getting stuck, angry, resentful, hurt, and for feeling overwhelmed, old, and unimportant. And this can go on not only when the children are little, but even when they are full grown and on their own. Having children is asking for trouble.

So why do it? Maybe Pete Seeger said it best: "We do it for the high wages . . . kisses." Children give us the opportunity to share in the vibrancy of life itself in ways we would not touch were they not part of our lives. Especially when children are young, our job as a parent is to be there for them and, as best we can, nurture them and protect them so that they are free to experience the innocence and genius of childhood, gently providing what guidance we can out of our own hearts and our own wisdom as they learn to find and define their own paths.

Children embody what is best in life. They live in the present moment. They are part of its exquisite bloom. They are pure potentiality, embodying vitality, emergence, renewal, and hope. They are purely what they are. And they share that vital nature with us and call it out of us as well, if we can listen carefully to the calling.

Once we have children, we are in touch with the rest of the universe in an entirely different way. Our consciousness changes, rotates from one way of seeing to another. We may find ourselves feeling connected to the hopefulness and the pain in others in ways that we might not have felt before. Our sphere of compassion tends to broaden. Concern for our children and their well-being may give us a different perspective on poverty, the environment, war, and the future.

As for trouble, Zorba, the crusty old character in Kazantzakis's novel *Zorba the Greek*, who, when asked whether he had ever been married, replied, "Am I not a man? Of course I've been married. Wife, house, kids, the full catastrophe," also said: "Trouble? Life is trouble. Only death is no trouble."

Ultimately, we make our own choices, mindfully or not, and we live with their consequences. Even so, we never know what is coming next. Immanent uncertainty is a big part of the full catastrophe. The question is, can we learn to use all of life's circumstances, even the most trying and stressful ones, to grow in strength and wisdom and openheartedness, much as a sailor makes skillful use of all kinds of wind conditions to propel a sailboat toward a particular destination? For our own ongoing growth is an absolute necessity if we are to serve as effective parents of our children over the long haul, so that they may be sheltered and grow well in their own ways and in their own time.

Live-in
Zen Masters

We were married in a Zen ceremony in which our wedding vows were to help each other "attain 'big mind' for the sake of all beings." The Zen tradition has had a deep appeal to me (jkz) from my first contacts with it some thirty years ago. Zen training is arduous and demanding, intense and unpredictable, wild and crazy, and very loving and funny. It's also very simple, and not so simple. It's all about mindfulness and non-attachment, knowing who we are at the deepest of levels, and knowing what we are doing, which paradoxically includes both not knowing and non-doing.

For me, the wild ride of Zen training seemed like it had a lot in common with parenting. They both appeared to be about waking up to life itself, with no holds barred. So it was not such a big jump to think that I could see our babies, who, like all babies, really do look like little Buddhas, with their round bellies, big heads, and mysterious smiles, as live-in Zen Masters. Zen Masters don't explain themselves. They just embody presence. They don't get hung up in thinking, or lost in theoretical musings about this or that. They are not attached to things being a certain way. They are not always consistent. One day does not necessarily have to be like the next. Their presence and their teachings can help us break through to a direct experiencing of our own true nature, and encourage us to find our own way, now, in this moment. They do this, not by telling us how, but by giving us endless challenges that cannot be resolved through thinking, by mirroring life back to us in its fullness, by pointing to wholeness. More than anything, Zen Masters embody wakefulness and call it out of us.

Children are similar in many ways, especially when they are babies. The older they get, the harder it may be for us to see it. But their true nature is always present, and always mirroring our own, if we are willing to look, and to see.

Children have what might be called "original mind"—open, pure, unencumbered. They are undeniably and totally present. They are constantly learning, developing, changing, and requiring new responses from us. As they grow, they seem to challenge every place that we might be holding an expectation, a fixed opinion, a cherished belief, a desire for things to be a certain way. As babies, they so fill our lives and require so much attention to their physical and emotional needs that they continually challenge us to be present totally, to be sensitive, to inquire into what is actually happening, to risk trying something, and to learn from their responses to our attempts. They teach us how to be attuned to them, and to find joy and harmony in our connectedness with them. There is little time for theory, and it doesn't seem to help much anyway unless it is connected to practice.

Of course, children are not really Zen Masters. Children are children and Zen Masters are Zen Masters. But if we are able to look at our children with openness and receptivity, and see the purity of life expressing itself through them, at any age, it can wake us up at any moment to their true nature and to our own.

Nothing anyone ever tells us prepares us for what it is actually like to be a parent. We learn on the job, in the doing, charting our own paths, relying on our inner resources, including the ones we never knew we had, taking our cues from our children and from every new situation that presents itself. We have to live inside of parenthood to know what it is. It is a deep and abiding inner work, a spiritual training all its own, if we choose to let it speak to us in that way, literally moment to moment.

We can ignore entirely, or resist as inconvenient or unimportant, or too messy or difficult, the continual stream of teachings from our children and from the circumstances we find ourselves in; or we can look deeply into them, letting them serve as indicators of where we need to pay attention and discern what is happening and what needs doing in any moment. It is entirely our choice. If we resist, we may occasion a great deal of unnecessary struggle and pain, for to ignore or struggle against the life force of children exploring and learning and growing, to not recognize and honor their sovereignty, denies a reality that is fundamental and will make itself known and felt one way or another.

For example, to forget momentarily that a two-year-old is a child and to rigidly and unfeelingly impose our own expectations about how she should be behaving, is to forget that what she is doing is what two-year-olds do. If we want it to be different from what is happening in that moment, and we resist or contract in our mind and try to force what we want on the situation, we will be creating a lot of trouble all around. We have all undoubtedly experienced the consequences of such a situation at one point or another as parents.

On the other hand, if we can let go of our idea in such a moment of how things "should be," and embrace how they actually are with this child; in other words, if we can remember that we are the adult and that we can look inside ourselves at that very moment and find a way to act with some degree of wisdom and compassion, and in the best interest of our child—then our emotional state and our choices of what to do will be very different, as will be the unfolding and resolution of that moment into the next. If we choose this path, she will have taught us something very important. She will have shown us how attached we can be to having things happen a certain way, that our mind wavers when we are challenged, and that we have various choices available to us. One of those choices would be to allow ourselves to be carried away by our own reactivity and ignorance, forgetting that two-year-olds do two-year-old kinds of things; another might be to affirm that we are capable of seeing our own reactivity and choose to go a different route, one in which we work both with our reaction and with what is actually happening with our child. We may have "known" all this, theoretically speaking, the moment before, or in another circumstance, but perhaps not in a way that prevented us from reacting automatically, from *embodying* our understanding. So our two-year-old showed us, through her being, Zen Master-like, that we can easily lose ourselves in emotional reacting, and that we don't have to. An important teaching, applicable in many different areas of our life. After all, our mind goes everywhere we do, and it usually reacts in a similar way when it doesn't feel in control or like what is happening.

If we can bring attention and intentionality to our own growing edges—in parenting and elsewhere in our lives—painful and frightening as that can be, that very orientation, that tenacious willingness to be present and to look at *anything*, can bring us into greater harmony with the way things actually are. But for that to happen, we must learn to listen carefully to what the world offers us, to look deeply into our experience as it is unfolding.

The funny thing is that if we bring awareness to what is in front of us in every moment, without insisting on it being a certain way, then the discipline of doing just that gives rise to a stability of mind and an openness and clarity of heart that are unattainable by struggling to achieve them through forcing a particular resolution or outcome. For such harmony underlies everything. It is here now, in us, and in our children, if we can but make room, over and over again, for it to emerge.

*

First we braid grasses and play tug of war,
then we take turns singing and keeping a kick-ball in the air.
I kick the ball and they sing, they kick and I sing.
Time is forgotten, the hours fly.
People passing by point at me and laugh:
"Why are you acting like such a fool?"
I nod my head and don't answer.
I could say something, but why?
Do you want to know what's in my heart?
From the beginning of time: just this! just this!

RYOKAN,

EIGHTEENTH-CENTURY

JAPANESE ZEN MASTER, HERMIT,

CALLIGRAPHER, POET

An Eighteen-Year
Retreat

Just as it might be useful to look at our children as little Buddhas or Zen Masters in order to help us to parent them better and to continue to grow ourselves, I (jkz) have often felt that parenting could be looked at as an extended meditation retreat—an opportunity to do a certain kind of deep and concentrated inner work of potentially profound and continuing benefit to children and parents alike within a family.

Usually, meditation retreats last for days, weeks, or months; but in this case, the "parenting retreat" would last on the order of at least eighteen years per child. Of course, the demands of parenting from day to day are very different from those of a secluded and intensive meditation retreat, but seeing them as related ways of doing sustained inner work has energized and sustained me at times in bringing a tenacious and overarching perspective to the inner calling of parenting, and to the years of constant and ultimately selfless attention, caring, and wisdom that it asks of us.

What, then, is a meditation retreat? What is its purpose? And how might seeing parenting as a kind of retreat help us understand and deepen what is being asked of us when we engage in mindful parenting, even for those of us who don't meditate regularly or who have no personal experience of such retreats? And how might looking at parenting in this way contribute to our own growth and development?

A meditation retreat is an opportunity to do a certain kind of inner work on ourselves that is extremely difficult to do outside of the retreat setting because of all the competing obligations, distractions, and enticements of everyday life. On retreat, because we are off in a special place for an extended period of time, away from the demands of family and work, we have a rare and precious chance to simplify our lives and give enormous care and attention to the domain of being.

Meditation retreats are often guided by one or more skilled teachers, who serve to encourage, inspire, guide, instruct, and listen to the experiences of the retreatants. The basic practice consists mostly of periods of sitting and walking, all in silence, typically from early morning to late at night. Just sitting. Just walking. Usually there is a period of work as well, also silent, so that the same mind that we cultivate in sitting and walking can be brought to cleaning the bathroom, or washing pots, or weeding the garden. What the task is is not so important . . . the mind that we bring to it is exquisitely important.

Attention is directed primarily inwardly, toward a few basic aspects of life experience that are ordinarily taken completely for granted, such as the breath flowing in and out, and what there is to be perceived moment by moment in your own body and in your own mind. Other than that, you eat, also in silence, and you sleep. Usually there is no reading, no writing, and no telephone calls, so you are really on your own, except for occasional interviews with the teacher. Such retreats can be extremely arduous and challenging—and deeply healing.

Over time, the mind gradually settles into the retreat. It can become deeply concentrated and one-pointed, remaining focused and relatively balanced and still over extended periods of time. Through the disciplined cultivation of attention, coupled with recognition and acceptance of what you are observing, you can come to know the landscape of your own mind and your own heart in radically new ways. A highly penetrative awareness develops, which can provide a deep look into the very nature of your being, underneath surface appearances, attachments, and personal history. Intensive and sustained attention of this kind can sometimes catalyze profound insights—awakenings that are truly enlightening—and can reveal you to yourself in ways you never knew or thought possible.

Intensive meditation practice is both a mirror and purification process. We may come to a larger and more accurate way of seeing, which can give rise to deep learning about ourselves, and an equally deep letting go, perhaps most importantly, a letting go of whatever we find we identify with in absolute and rigid ways . . . our attachments to things, ways of seeing, ideas.

In paying sustained attention to your own mind, you can discover that the mind actually behaves in fairly structured ways, in patterns that are recognizable, if sometimes excruciatingly repetitive and unrelenting. You might come to see, just by sitting and walking in silence, how ceaselessly the stream of thinking flows, how chaotic the thought process is (order within it is sometimes difficult to discern), and how unreliable and inaccurate most of our thoughts are. You might come to see how reactive the mind is, and how powerful its emotional storms.

You might see that the mind spends enormous amounts of time in the past, reminiscing, resenting, or blaming, and in the future, worrying, planning, hoping, dreaming. You might see that the mind tends constantly to judge itself and everything else, depending on whether an experience is felt to be pleasant, unpleasant, or neutral at any particular moment. You might see how strong the mind's attachments are, its incessant identification with things and opinions, and how so much of the time it is driven by wishful thinking and the desire to be somewhere else, to have things and relationships be different from how they actually are.

You might see how hard it is for the mind to settle into the present moment as it is, but also that, over time, the mind can actually calm down enough to see much of this ceaseless activity that it is engaged in, and come to an inner stillness and calmness and balance that is less easily disturbed by its own activity.

If you are motivated enough to stick with the practice through the hard times, if you can stay with the pain in your body that may come from long periods of sitting still, if you can stay with the yearning in the mind for talk, or for entertainment and distraction and novelty, if you can stay with the boredom, resistance, the grief, terror, and confusion that can and do arise on occasion, and if, all the while, you ruthlessly and with utter kindness and gentleness, without expectations, persist in simply observing whatever comes up in the field of your awareness, moment by moment, you may come to encounter, at certain points in your practice, great oceanlike depths of silence, well-being, and wisdom within your own mind.

For, in many ways, the mind does resemble a body of water, a veritable ocean. On the surface, depending on the season, the weather, and the winds, the surface can be anything from completely calm and flat to hugely tumultuous and turbulent, with forty-foot waves or higher. But even at its most stormy, if one goes down deep enough, the water will be very still.

Persisting in the practice, we might come to see on such a retreat that our own mind is much the same—that calmness and deep stillness are intrinsic to its nature, that they are always present, and that even when we are caught up in huge storms of emotional turmoil, for whatever reasons, the calmness and the stillness and the capacity to be aware are still here, underneath, embedded in and an integral part of our being. They can be called upon, and used, not to extinguish the surface turbulence of the mind (just as we don't try to flatten the waves on the ocean), but to understand it and to provide a larger container for it, a context in which the very turbulence itself can be held, seen, and even used to deepen our understanding.

We may come to see that our thoughts and emotions do not have to carry us away or blind us in one way or another, as so frequently happens in life. Nor do we have to make any effort to suppress them to be free from much of the suffering they contain or engender.

Working in this way with the activity of our own mind, we might also come to see that it is a fiction that we are isolated, separate, and alone. We might see that "I," "me," and "mine" are themselves thoughts, powerful, deeply rooted and tenacious habits of mind, but thoughts all the same. Beneath the sense of ourselves as being separate and preoccupied so much of the time with concerns about our individual self and our own personal gains and losses, we might see that we are part of a flowing movement of wholeness that is larger than we are and to which we belong.

We might see that there is a deep mystery in our individual life emerging from the union of our parents and, before them, from their parents, and so on back into time; that we are an intermediary between our parents and our children, between all those who have come before, whom we will never know, and all those who will come after our children's children's children, whom we will also never know.

We may come to see that the deepest nature of the universe is that it is one, a seamless whole, and that everything that is is an aspect of everything else. We may come to see that everything is embedded in and reflected in everything else, that everything and every being is whole *and* part of a larger wholeness, and that interconnectedness and interdependence are the root relationships out of which meaning and the particulars of our fleeting and constantly changing individual lives arise.

And you may come to see with fresh eyes and a new understanding and appreciation that, together with the ways in which the unfolding of life is impersonal, it is all the same very personal. You may realize directly, as the veils of thinking and strong attachment thin, that right now and right here, you are who you are; that the being that is you is unique, with your own face and character and desires, with a particular history that is the legacy of having the parents that you had and growing up the way you did, and with your own unique and mysterious path or calling that can infuse your life with vision and passion. You work where you work, you live where you live, your responsibilities are your responsibilities, your children are your children, your hopes are your hopes, your fears your fears.

We might come to see that "separate" and "not separate" are themselves just thoughts, attempts to describe a deeper reality that is us. We might see the possibility of living more gracefully, knowing that the things that happen to us are happening to us, yet also knowing that it is not wise to take them entirely personally, because everything is also impersonal, and it is problematic—Buddhists would say, impossible—to point to a solid, permanent "you" who is here to take them personally. You are certainly who you are, and you are responsible for many things; but you are certainly not who you think you are because thinking itself is limited, and your true nature is limitless.

On retreat, we might also come to know that we are not our body, not our thoughts, not our emotions, not our ideas and opinions, not our fears and our insecurities and our woundedness, even though they are an intimate part of our experience and can influence our lives enormously, much as the weather influences the surface of the ocean. Their influence is particularly strong if we form strong and unconscious attachments to them, to which we cling for dear life, and through which we see everything as through dark, or light, or colored, or kaleidoscopic glasses.

We are not our ideas and opinions. If we could live our lives knowing this, and take off the glasses through which we filter our experience, what a difference it might make in the way we see, in our choices, and in the way we conduct our lives from day to day. This insight alone might cause us to see ourselves very differently, to see our parenting very differently, and indeed, to live differently.

We may also see that, like everybody else, we are only here very briefly, but that brief moment we call a lifetime is also infinitely long if we can bring awareness to our moments, since there are infinite moments in any lifetime. In living in the present, we step out of clock time into a timeless present. Such experiences may show us that we are not by nature entirely bound by time.

We might, thus, also begin to taste impermanence in a new way, since nothing we focus our attention on endures for long. Each breath comes and goes, sensations in the body come and go, thoughts come and go, emotions come and go, ideas and opinions come and go, moments come and go, days and nights come and go. We may see that, similarly, seasons and years come and go, youth comes and goes, jobs and people come and go. Even mountains and rivers and species come and go. Nothing is fixed. Nothing is permanent, although things may appear that way to us. Everything is always moving, changing, becoming, dissolving, emerging, evolving, in a complex dance, the outer dance of the world not so different from the inner dance of our own mind. We might see that our children are also part of this dance. . . . that, like us, they too are only brief visitors to this beautiful and strange world, and our time with them even briefer, its duration unknown.

Might not this realization strike us deeply and teach us something of great value? Might it not suggest how precious the time we do share together with our children is, and how to hold our essentially fleeting moments with them in awareness? Might it not influence how we hug and kiss our children, and say good-night to them, and watch them sleep, and wake them in the morning? Might such understanding not influence how hard a time we give them when, in seeking to find their own ways, they scrape up against our ideas and opinions, the limits of our patience, and our ego investments in being right and all-knowing, forgetting in those moments what we actually know that is far larger and more life-affirming?

Perhaps taking on parenting as a kind of meditation retreat, and doing the inner work of mindful parenting day by day and moment by moment in the same spirit of concentrated and sustained effort of attention and presence as on a retreat, might help us to realize the enormous power in seeing and remembering the larger context of wholeness, so that we are not lost in the surface waves of our own minds and our sometimes narrowly conceived and clung to lives. Perhaps we would hold our moments differently. Perhaps they would not slip by so unnoticed, so unused, so filled up by us with busyness or diversions. Perhaps we would appreciate more what is given to us, from our own body and life, to our relationships, to our children and our parents, and our children's children, to the world in which we get to live and which we pass on to those who will follow.

Perhaps we would care more, and care differently, and attend more, and attend differently, if we held in our own minds and hearts what we already deeply know, but usually forget, or haven't developed to the point where it can serve us as a way of being, a way of seeing, a way of truly living wakefully. Perhaps we would know how to stand in our own life, on our own feet, and feel the earth beneath us and the wind in our face and around our body, and know the place as here, and the time as now, and honor the mysterious wisdom that resides within all beings and within our children.

These glimpses are some of what one might see and realize through intensive practice on an extended mindfulness meditation retreat. Retreats are of great and abiding value when we can arrange our lives to go off from time to time to practice in this way. But there are also many times when it may be neither possible nor advisable to go off someplace else for an extended period, especially when juggling the responsibilities of parenting, family life, and work.

This is where the metaphor of seeing the whole experience of parenting as an extended meditation retreat may be useful. It is not that parenting is a retreat from the world, although to some extent a healthy family can buffer the stress of the outer world and create feelings of inner security and peace. It is, rather, that we are using the very circumstances of the world and of parenting, as best we can, and usually under difficult conditions, to help us cultivate mindfulness, look deeply into our lives, and let our doing come out of our being—not just from time to time, but concertedly, as a way of life.

The daily schedule of family life, of course, is much more complex and chaotic than on retreat, dictated as it frequently is to a large extent by the head teachers, who are our children. It will change as they change and grow, sometimes from day to day, sometimes moment by moment. But the practice is always the same: To be fully present, looking deeply, as best we can, and without judging or condemning events or our experience of them. Just presence, and appropriate action, moment by moment. It can be anchored by a daily period of formal practice at a convenient time, but the major commitment will of necessity be the cultivation of mindfulness in everyday life, responding to the call of parenting, allowing each day and each moment to provide the arena for a deepening of awareness.

In this way, waking up in the morning is waking-up meditation. Brushing your teeth is brushing-your-teeth meditation. Not getting to brush your teeth because the baby is crying is not-getting-to-brush-your-teeth-and-taking-care-of-the-baby-first meditation. And so on. Getting the children dressed, getting food on the table, getting them off to school, going to work, diapering, shopping, making arrangements, cleaning up, cooking, everything becomes part of our practice of mindfulness. Everything.

The Importance of Practice

To affect the quality of the day, that is the highest of arts.

THOREAU, *Walden*

There is no doubt that just hearing about the importance of being more present, more aware, more empathic, and more accepting in one's life and, particularly, in one's parenting can be suggestive enough to some people to put them on a different track, to awaken them to their own capacity to, as Thoreau put it, "affect the quality of the day" intentionally, to inspire them to new openness and sensitivity in their lives and in their parenting.

But we also know that the human mind has its own particular way of operating, which makes it difficult to "just wake up" all of a sudden. To get in touch with the present moment usually requires effort and consistency. Seeing clearly is not something that easily sustains itself. For instance, we may catch only occasional glimpses or vague intimations of our own sovereignty and our capacity to embody it in everyday life. Insight and transformation do not, as a rule, come easily to us.

We have to *practice* learning to live in the present. We have to *practice* seeing with eyes of wholeness. Why? Because, perhaps due to the nature of the human mind, especially if it was not embraced with kindness and fully nurtured in childhood, we spend much of our lives practicing the exact opposite of mindfulness. We *practice* not living in the present moment. We practice being carried away from our center, from our sovereignty, from our interconnectedness, by our thoughts and feelings, our likes and dislikes. We practice anxiety. We practice getting angry. And the more we practice, through repeating these patterns in our lives, the "better" we get at them, and the harder they are to break out of. We practice being firmly attached to views and models of reality that are only partially accurate or don't pertain at all, feeding the automatic pilot mode in ourselves, generating consequences with our less-than-sovereign, less-than-empathic, less-than-accepting actions, which then come back to compound our problems, our confusion, and our lack of clarity regarding our own lives.

This is why mindful parenting is best seen as a *practice*, a discipline, and not simply as a philosophy or a good idea. As a practice, it helps us liberate ourselves from the deep patterns in our minds and in our lives that keep us apart from ourselves and from the only moments we have in which to live and grow and affirm our connectedness.

We are using the word "practice" somewhat differently from the way it is ordinarily thought of. "Practice" here means *embodying wholeness right now*. It is not like practicing the piano, or a dance step. It is not an exercise or a rehearsal. It is not to get better at something by repeating it over and over again, although a deepening does happen the more you practice being mindful.

Every time you pick up your baby, if you do it with awareness, it is practice. It is a matter of being fully there. And what does "being fully there" mean? It means knowing that you are picking up your baby while you are picking up your baby. It means being in touch with feeling, smelling, touching, holding, breathing, with whatever is happening, and holding it all in your awareness as you do whatever it is that your intuition, and your baby, and the moment tell you is what needs doing—whether it is feeding, diapering, dressing, singing, or something else. This something else can include nothing at all. It may be that *nothing* is called for other than just being as present as you can be in that moment.

You do not have to be "good" at this, and certainly judging yourself is not part of the spirit of being mindful. You just have to be there for that particular moment. Why? Because you already are. Why not be there completely? Then you might be able to taste wholeness in that very moment, because it is always here, now, to be seen, felt, and embraced.

So practice simply means intentionally remembering to be fully present with whatever comes up so that you are not always on automatic pilot or acting mechanically. When you are picking up the baby, you are there with picking up the baby. When you are hugging your child, you are there with hugging your child. Your mind is not off someplace else, or if it is, you are aware of that too, and so can bring it back. It is simple, but it is not so easy, because our minds are so readily carried off elsewhere.

There are many, many ways to practice. There is no aspect of life or of parenting that cannot become practice simply by bringing it intentionally into awareness and holding it in awareness as it unfolds. The more we are willing to pay attention, the more firmly grounded we become in mindfulness and in mindful parenting. We each have all the equipment we need to do this inner and outer work. Every moment is our teacher. Each child, each circumstance, each breath is our teacher. It is all here, waiting to be embraced right now, in this moment. If we approach life in this way, then, as Thoreau was suggesting, affecting the quality of the day truly becomes an art form. It is the art of conscious living, an endless refining of how we live and are in the world, an endless allowing ourselves to be refined by what the day provides. We become full participants in this process, bringing it forth in ourselves and for our children.

Breathing

How then do we get started with mindful parenting in a way that feels comfortable and authentic? Do we wait for "the right moment," or do we take our moments as they come, such as they are? Do we have to begin in pregnancy or with the birth of our first child in order for this to "work," or can we begin any time, wherever we are in our lives?

Habits of mind being what they are, we will probably be breaking healthy new ground for ourselves if we decide not to wait for a largely fictitious "opportune time" to begin, but rather seize the moments that we have, ragged and ratty and messy as they may be.

Resolving to begin where we are, and now, with the resources at hand, already puts us in the spirit of mindfulness practice. We can explore for ourselves the value of being fully present no matter what is happening and precisely where we are right now, whether we are just starting out as a parent, have grown children, or are grandparents.

One way to get started on the practice of mindful parenting is to cultivate a certain intimacy with your own breathing, in quiet moments and right through the day. Your breath is flowing constantly. It is always present. It is deeply connected to your life, to your body, and to your emotional states. Becoming aware of the breath brings mind and body into the present moment with wakefulness and clarity of perception.

You might try touching base with your breath right now, and see if you can keep it in the forefront of your awareness for a few minutes. The basic idea is to *feel* the breath as it moves in and out, knowing that the breath is coming in as it's coming in, and that the breath is going out as it's going out. You can ride the waves of your breathing with your attention, feeling their rising and falling much as you would feel the movement if you were in a rubber raft, floating on gentle waves. Later, you can try bringing awareness of your breathing to whatever it is that you find yourself doing, and as you deal with whatever it is you are facing.

You may quickly discover as you do this that your mind, like all our minds, has a life of its own. It may not want to remember the breath and stay in touch with it. It isn't used to sustaining awareness. You will find that, like all our minds, it goes here and there constantly, to the past, to the future, and, invariably, from one thought to another and one feeling to another. It is even more this way when we are feeling pressed for time, or dealing with problems, or conflicted in one way or another. Anybody who sits down to follow their breathing in stillness for the first time for even a few minutes discovers this state of affairs right away. It applies even when the outer conditions are peaceful.

Through ongoing practice, it is possible to develop an intimacy with the breath that extends your awareness into whatever else is happening in your world at that moment. Cultivating awareness in this way allows the deep potential in each moment to become available to you.

The value of cultivating an awareness of your own breathing will grow on you as you work at it. It lights up the present moment and helps you hold it with greater calmness and clarity. But extending an awareness of the breath into any activity in any moment takes energy and commitment. It is a looking out for and a looking into, so it is a looking *and* a seeing, what might be called *discernment*, or wise attention. You can bring this awareness to any aspect of your life: the breath *and* diapering, the breath *and* shopping, the breath *and* eye contact, the breath *and* playing with your children, or reading to them, or putting them to bed, or talking with an older child, the breath *and* cooking dinner, the breath *and* juggling ten things at once and feeling like you are about to lose it, the breath *and* having lost it and now having to somehow pick up the pieces and move on. This takes no extra time. Only remembering.

Diapering, cleaning up messes, breaking up fights, rushing here and there, sitting around worrying and feeling anxious, working or playing, "on" time or "off" time are all appropriate occasions for using the breath to be more present.

Practice
As Cultivation

You can cultivate mindfulness in your life and in your family just as you can cultivate tomatoes or corn in a garden, and this cultivating is what we mean when we speak of *practice.* The key role in any cultivation is tending that which has been planted, whether we are talking about our intention to be more mindful, or about tending to the growth of our children. Tending means attending, which comes from attention. These words all carry in them the quality of being present, wakeful, stretched toward, in readiness, conscious. The feeling extends to being tender, an *extending* of oneself through care and caring.

This tending or attending is the heart of mindfulness practice. Just as young plants require protection as part of their tending, so it is with children, and so it is, as well, with a nascent mindfulness practice. If you wish to undertake mindful parenting, the very intention, as well as your efforts to practice, need to be protected or they will be easily trampled by the chaotic circumstances and constant demands of our lives, and soon abandoned. Our efforts and intentions are best protected by creating commonsensical boundaries to circumscribe and support our work of cultivating mindfulness, just as we put up fences and poles to protect and support young plants.

These boundaries take the form of specific formal and informal exercises and disciplines, which all together make up the practice of mindfulness. The formal practices take some time. Whether you want to practice, and how much, is always up to you. As we have seen, the informal practices, such as being in touch with your breathing throughout the day, don't take any time. They just take attention, and remembering.

Although we are all mindful from time to time in a conventional sense, to sustain meditative, non-judgmental, non-reactive awareness, we have to generate and regenerate the *intention* to be mindful. Part of it is learning how to get out of our own way, to not be so ruled by our thoughts and emotions. Usually, we have to learn that lesson over and over again. It is done by observing our thoughts and feelings and practicing not getting carried away by them.

As with cultivating corn or tomatoes, discipline is critical here, too. Not the outwardly imposed discipline of punishment, but the inner self-discipline of mindfulness, of being one's best self as much as possible. As we have seen, it is a spiritual discipline, a means for staying in touch, or touching base periodically, with what T. S. Eliot called "the still point of the turning world."

Because mindfulness practice and raising children really demand the same basic grounding in attention, it is not that big a stretch to attempt to cultivate them together. In doing so, the one feeds, deepens, and supports the other.

In the Zen tradition of meditation, people are fond of saying that the practice is nothing special. The practice is nothing special in the same way that being a mother or giving birth is nothing special, that being a father is nothing special, that being a farmer and bringing things forth from the land is nothing special, even that being alive is nothing special.

That is all true in a way, but try telling that to a mother or a father or a farmer. "Nothing special" also means "very special." The utterly ordinary is utterly extraordinary. It all depends on how you see things, and whether you are willing to look deeply, and live by what you see and feel and know.

Free Within
Our Thinking

When we ask people who have completed mindfulness training in the Stress Reduction Clinic what were the most important things they got out of the program, they invariably say two things. The first is, "The breathing." The second is, "Knowing that I am not my thoughts."

Of course, everybody was breathing before they came to the program, so what they mean by "The breathing" is a new awareness of their breathing and the discovery of how powerful mindfulness of the breath can be when cultivated in periods of quiet, and when brought to the activities of daily living.

The second statement points to the fact that most of us are at best only vaguely aware that we are thinking all the time. We may not experience this in a forceful way until we start systematically paying attention to our breathing and we begin observing, non-judgmentally, what is on our minds, and how difficult it is to stabilize our attention, to keep our focus on anything—even on such a simple thing as the breath.

When we start paying attention to the breath *and* to what is on our minds that carries us away from the breath, we come to see almost immediately that thinking is going on virtually all the time. We see that much of our thinking is preoccupied with judging and evaluating our perceptions, and generating ideas and opinions about things. We also see that our thinking is complex, chaotic, unpredictable, and frequently in-accurate, inconsistent, and contradictory.

This ceaseless stream of thinking goes on, largely unexamined and unknown by us. Our thoughts really do seem to have a life of their own. They are like clouds coming and going, momentary events in the field of our consciousness. Yet from them, we are constantly creating models of reality in our minds in the form of ideas and opinions about our-selves and others and the world, and then believing them to be true, and frequently denying evidence to the contrary.

Not knowing that thoughts are just thoughts can get us into trou-ble in virtually every aspect of our lives. Knowing it can help us stay out of the traps our own mind sets for us. This is especially true in parent-ing. For instance, if you have the thought, "Tom is lazy," you will easily believe that this is true about Tom, rather than just your opinion. Then, every time you see Tom, you will tend to see him as lazy, and not see all the other aspects of who he is that are blocked or filtered out by your strong opinion, for which you may or may not have much evidence. As a consequence, you may only relate to him in a limited way, and his re-sponse to how you treat him may only confirm and reinforce your view.

In reality, you have made Tom lazy in your mind, and are not able to see Tom as Tom, for who he is as a whole being. Instead, you see just the one attribute that you are preoccupied with, which may only be true to a degree, if at all, or may change. And this may make it impossible for you to connect with him in any meaningful way because everything you say or do will be "loaded" in a way that he might feel and feel uncomfortable about, and that you might not even recognize as coming from you.

Teachers sometimes do this. Parents do, too. For, in truth, we are all doing this, not just with children and other people but with ourselves. We tell ourselves that we are "too" this or "not enough" that. We label ourselves. We judge ourselves. Then we believe it. In believing it, we narrow our view of what is real and what is true, and our view takes on aspects of a self-fulfilling prophecy. This limits and confines us and our children. And it blinds us to the possibilities for transformation in ourselves and in others because we carry around a rigid view of things that tends to be fixed and does not see things in terms of multiple dimensions, complexity, wholeness, and constant change.

So when practicing mindfulness, it is important to see your thoughts, as thoughts, and not simply as "the truth." Feeling states can also be looked at in this way.

When we look at our thoughts and feelings in this way, we can sometimes experience a loosening of the domineering and tenacious grip of personal pronouns over the mind. In such moments, it may no longer be "my" thought, but just "a" thought, not "my" feeling, but simply "a" feeling. This can free us from a strong attachment to "our" thoughts and opinions and feeling states, and give us more perspective and latitude. Whether it is a feeling of annoyance or embarrassment, impatience or anger, recognizing its presence in mindfulness and knowing what it is opens up new choices for us, so that we won't necessarily get lost or stuck in it or react mindlessly. This doesn't at all mean that we won't take our feelings or our thoughts very seriously, or that we won't act on them. But an awareness of thoughts as thoughts and feelings as feelings can help us to act more appropriately, and to be more in touch with ourselves and with the needs of the situation.

*

Be empty of worrying.
Think of who created thought!

Why do you stay in prison
When the door is so wide open?

Move outside the tangle of fear-thinking.
Live in silence.

Flow down and down in always
widening rings of being.

RUMI

Discernment
Versus Judging

Mindfulness is defined as moment-to-moment, non-judgmental aware-ness. The non-judgmental part is crucial. If we spend any time noticing what is going on in our own minds, we will soon notice that we have something of an inner "censor" at work almost all the time, judging not only everything around us but ourselves and our experience as well. Without knowing it, we can be virtual prisoners of all this judging. It takes up a great deal of our energy, and frequently prevents us from seeing clearly.

As we saw in the previous chapter, we often form opinions quickly and hold to them with utter conviction as if they were the truth, when actually, they are just thoughts, and the *content* of those particular thoughts are the conclusions that our minds have arrived at about things or peo-ple or ourselves. And just as with other thoughts in the mind, we can lock in to these conclusions, whether they be positive or negative, and lose the ability and freedom to see beyond them to anything else. To the extent that we get attached to our ideas and opinions, we become di-minished and constricted. Our possibilities for growth narrow.

If we live in this way a great deal, we may look back years later, and see, with deep regret, that our opinions at a particular time in our lives were just that, opinions. We may come to see that they kept us from pursuing, even seeing, other options and possibilities, and led us down paths that were not quite true to our innermost being. Our opinions can obscure our sovereignty, as clouds block the light of the sun. They also block our ability to see the sovereignty of others, including our own children.

What is called for in the cultivation of mindfulness, and in mindful parenting, rather than judging, is *discernment,* the ability to look deeply into something and perceive distinctions keenly and with clarity. Discernment is the ability to see this *and* that, as opposed to this *or* that, to see the whole picture, and its fine details, to see gradations. Being discerning is an inward sign of respect for reality because we are taking note of subtleties as well as the gross outline of things, aware of complexity and mystery. There is a fairness in it, a rightness in it, because it is truer to the whole of reality. In the story of the Loathely Lady, Sir Kay and the other knights judged Dame Ragnell narrowly, on the basis of her appearance, and in doing so, betrayed their own code of chivalry and decency. Sir Gawain discerned something deeper, and did not judge her, in spite of her appearance.

So when we speak of mindfulness being a non-judgmental awareness, that does not mean that we don't see what is going on because we are refusing to perceive necessary and important distinctions. In fact, it is only through being non-judgmental that it might be possible to see and feel what is actually happening, past surface appearances and the filters of our own limited opinions, our likes and dislikes, beliefs, fears, our unexamined and sometimes unconscious prejudices, and our deep longing for things to be a certain way.

Being non-judgmental means that we are aware of those aspects of our own mind that are judging all the time, and that we intentionally suspend judgment and bring the mind back to observing the distinctions from moment to moment. This orientation is not only important to the inner work of meditation and of parenting; it is also essential to scientific endeavors, which seek to discern an underlying order behind appearances, at the boundary between the known and the unknown. The scientific method recognizes the critical importance for scientists to be acutely aware of their own biases and prejudices, and of the tendency of the mind to jump prematurely to conclusions or become too comfortable with what it thinks it knows.

A discerning awareness can hold even our own judging in mind and know it for what it is. We can observe this ingrained habit of mind with some degree of compassion, and not judge ourselves for being so judgmental. In seeing the significance of what we are seeing, discernment gives rise to wisdom. It frees us to act more wisely with our children, without getting so caught up in our own likes and dislikes that we can no longer see clearly. It is in the nature of the mind to judge. But without discernment, our judgments will tend to be inaccurate, unwise, and unconscious.

If a mother is continually seeing danger in every situation with her five-year-old boy and hovers over him constantly, naming all the terrible things she is afraid are going to happen if her son does this or that, she is locked into a very narrow way of seeing that does not include an awareness of her own thinking and behavior or the effects that she may be having on her child. In this way, she may only add to the child's fears, or put barriers in his way and constrict him unnecessarily.

If she were able to look into and discern her own behavior and the mind-set which is giving rise to it, she might modulate some of her fear-based impulses, and be freer and less constricted herself. She might perceive that she has a wider range of choices than she saw the moment before, and perhaps might find a better balance between her fear, which has important elements of concern for her child's safety, and the child's need for autonomy and to give rein to his curiosity and desire to explore.

Fathers, of course, can fall into the same fear-driven behavior, and it can be directed as much toward daughters as toward sons.

It is helpful to bring a degree of generosity to our deeply ingrained habit of seeing things in terms of only this or that, good or bad, dangerous or safe, okay or not okay. For example, if you have done a number of things that you regret as a parent, it is also important to be able to see those things that you have done well, and vice versa. A rigid, black and white, either/or view is invariably inaccurate; it serves only to perpetuate illusions and delusion, and conflict between spouses and with children.

When we bring mindfulness and discernment to our parenting, we come to see how much we tend to judge our own children as well as ourselves as parents. We have opinions about them and who they are and how they should be, and hold them up against some standard that we have created in our minds. When we judge our children in this way, we cut ourselves off from them and them from us. We also cut ourselves off from ourselves by contracting and becoming rigid. By intentionally suspending judgment and cultivating discernment, we create the potential to reconnect with them.

Discernment includes seeing that even as we attempt to see our children for who they are, we also cannot fully know who they are or where their lives will take them. We can only love them, and accept them, and honor the mystery of their being.

Formal Practice

Even if you choose not to practice formally, or only do so occasionally, it is helpful to become familiar with the instructions for formal meditation practice because they provide a clear map of how to cultivate mindfulness, and a useful tool for bringing it into all aspects of daily life. When you attend to your experience in this way, as we have seen, your whole life becomes your meditation practice. All your moments are occasions to cultivate awareness and to wake up.

For those of us who are drawn to developing a formal meditation practice, either for parenting or for stress reduction, or to nourish ourselves in a deep way, we might make use of whatever quiet moments we have—even if they are rare, or even if they have to be arranged by, say, getting up earlier than usual or shutting off the telephone at certain times.

Solitude, time by oneself, alone, is an important form of deep sustenance for human beings. It is rapidly becoming lost as the pace of life accelerates. For parents, finding time for formal practice when we are not exhausted may feel virtually impossible at certain stages. We each need to make our own choices about whether, how, and when we might make some time in our lives for stillness.

A quiet period of stopping does not have to be long . . . it could be for one or two minutes if that is all the time you can find. It could be stretched out on the couch in the middle of the day, or in bed before you go to sleep, or five minutes during your lunch break, or in a parked car while the baby is sleeping. If the motivation were there, most of us could probably find or free up a few minutes, or even fifteen minutes or so, somewhere in the twenty-four hours of a day. But there does have to be a strong intention to make it happen, especially if we find meditation difficult or boring at first. Otherwise, we will quickly fill up any "free" moments we might have with the newspaper or television, or the radio, or some form of doing or "passing the time."

Quiet moments of wakefulness feed body and soul. Parents of young children may need it more than anyone else. Time for ourselves—time alone—is what many parents have least and desire most. Yet often we don't know what to do with it when we do have it, especially if it is only a few minutes here and there, not long enough to do anything special with, or coming at the wrong time.

Formal mindfulness practice does unavoidably take some time. But it is a time worth taking, if you are drawn to it, and it does not have to be long to be of profound value. This is in part because when you are in the present moment and truly let go of the past and the future, and step out of the stream of thinking, the experience is of timelessness. Even a few minutes by clock time can be restorative because timeless "moments" are liberating moments. There is no place to go, nothing to do. You are momentarily released from the press of time and obligations and can enter into the experience of being whole and complete and at the same time part of a larger wholeness and interconnectedness.

If you want to try to integrate formal meditation practice into your life, this is one way to get started: Find or make a few moments of quiet time by yourself. Then lie down, or sit in a dignified posture. Put your mind in your belly for a few moments and feel it moving with the breath; or put your attention at the nostrils and feel the flow of the air there. In either case, try not to push or pull the breath or the belly, but just allow your breathing to flow, and your belly to move however it does.

Paying attention to the breath and to your body doesn't mean interfering with it. It simply means attending to the feelings in your body and the sensations associated with the breath as it moves in and out. Those sensations might be of the abdomen rising, expanding with each in-breath and falling, deflating with each out-breath, or of the feeling of the air passing back and forth at the nostrils. After experimenting for a while, it would be good to choose one of these to focus on and keep your attention there.

As we have discussed, you will soon discover that the mind is often turbulent, like the surface of the ocean, or a flag being blown first in this direction, then in that. The mind tends to be preoccupied. It gets carried away by thoughts and feelings. Your attention may wander off the breath or be pulled from it time and time again, often without any moments of seeming peace or continuity, even for one breath's-worth of time. It may also seem anything but relaxing to try to stay with the feeling of the breath. You may experience mostly anxiety, or ceaseless distraction.

That is all fine. It's not supposed to feel relaxing, although it often can. There is no way in particular you are supposed to feel. Rather, you are just to be aware of how things actually are with you from moment to moment. So if you are feeling tense, you note that you are feeling tense; if angry, then angry; if dull or sleepy, then dull or sleepy. That's all. You just watch your own mind and your own body. No judgment is necessary. In fact, we are attempting to cultivate a non-striving, non-reactive, non-judgmental orientation toward our experience of *any* moment, just perceiving and feeling what is here, and if possible, letting go of any tendency to attach personal pronouns to the feeling states.

The other crucial instruction to keep in mind when you are starting out with formal mindfulness practice is simply this: Whenever you notice that your attention is no longer on your breathing or in your body, note where it is. In other words, you notice what is on your mind. This noting is very important, because it brings thoughts and feelings and images into awareness, and deepens our familiarity and intimacy with our own mind states. Once you have allowed whatever is on your mind in this moment to be held in awareness, you purposefully let go of it and come back to the breath itself, either at the belly or at the nostrils, and just pick up with the sensations and direct experience of this in-breath, this out-breath. If the mind wanders away from the breath a thousand times, you just bring it back in this way a thousand times, after first bringing mindfulness to the particulars of what is on your mind, no matter what it is. You neither pursue the content of your thoughts nor do you attempt to suppress any of the activity of your mind. You simply observe it, let it be, and let it go, returning to the breath. With time, you can expand your practice to include other objects of attention within and beyond the breath.

Formal and informal practice go hand in hand. The one strengthens the other. Ultimately, meditation is no different from life itself. You are not going to parent while sitting still, so every moment has to count. We have only to let our children, and everything else in our lives, become our teachers, and to keep our intention to be present as strong and as vibrant as possible.

There are many other ways in which to practice mindfulness meditation formally if you make the time for it. In the Stress Reduction Clinic, people practice using a number of different methods, including a body scan, sitting meditation, and mindful hatha yoga. More details about what these are and how to practice them, as well as other methods, are given in *Full Catastrophe Living* and *Wherever You Go, There You Are*. Guided meditation tapes of varying lengths to help with developing and deepening formal meditation practice also are available and are listed at the back of this book.

Letters to a Young Girl
Interested in Zen

One day, I (jkz) received a letter from Caitlin, the daughter of a friend. She had chosen to do a project for school on Zen Buddhism, and wanted to go beyond what she could learn from the written sources that were available to her. Her father had suggested she write to me. Her letter was so beautifully composed, her tone so self-possessed, her questions so filled with genuine interest, that I sat down on the spot and tried, as best I could, to convey to her a sense of the beauty and the depth of the Zen perspective on meditation practice. I realized later that my response touched on elements of meditation practice in ways that might be helpful to adults, and so include it here.

In general, we believe that we have to be very careful in offering meditation to children. It is wonderful, of course, when they see us meditating. Sometimes, when our children were little, they would come and sit on my lap as I was sitting, and I would wrap them up in my blanket and arms, continuing to sit silently. When they were ready to go, I would open the blanket and they would emerge. But, in the spirit of bringing mindfulness to all aspects of parenting, it is important to be sensitive to what is coming from our children, and what we may be forcing on them from our desire to have them value what we value.

In Caitlin's case, the impulse to learn about meditation came from her. You might say that my response was an attempt to provide her with some tools for cultivating her own garden. What I found out was that she was quite a gardener already. With her permission, I share parts of my letters to her and some of the poems she sent me.

*

February 11, 1996

Dear Caitlin:

Thank you for your wonderful letter of January 31. I was happy to hear that you are excited about Zen and Buddhism, and I think it is great that you are taking your interest out beyond the usual sources from which we gather information when we have a project such as yours. Books can be very helpful, and I have enclosed a few of my favorites here, which I hope you will keep your whole life and dip into every five years or so, as what they say to you will change over time. But especially in Zen, you have to go beyond what the books say, to *EXPERIENCE* what they are pointing to, to really understand what it is about.

What Zen and Buddhism are really about is *KNOWING WHO YOU ARE*. You might say, "Well, that is silly. Of course I know who I am!" Then you might say, "I am Caitlin and I am 11 years old." But "Caitlin" is just a sound (we call it a name, and a very beautiful one) that your parents gave to you when you were born. And 11 years old is just the number of times the Earth has circled the Sun since you were born. Weren't you "you" before you got the name Caitlin? Also, are you the same "you" that you were when you were five, or when you were two? Of course you are; and also you're not, because you are always growing, and changing. What you thought then, or wanted then, or felt then may not be what you think or want or how you feel now. But the deep something that is "you" is still you and will always be you.

But can you see that this is also a little mysterious, the question of who you are? So Zen is about knowing yourself, understanding yourself, and knowing what that means. Part of what it means is knowing that some kinds of knowing and understanding are beyond words, and beyond thinking, and beyond anybody being able to tell you about. This knowing is very personal and intuitive. That is why much of Zen is in the form of poetry and impossible riddles. They cut through the thinking mind, and point to something beyond it, which is freer, and more fundamental. That doesn't mean that thinking is "bad." Thinking is great, and very important, and it is necessary to learn how to think well. But it is not all there is, and thinking, if you're not careful, can dominate your life and make you forget the deeper, more feeling, more intuitive, more artistic aspects of your being, of your true self (as the Buddhists call it . . . who you "really" are . . . beyond your name, your age, your opinions, your likes and dislikes). Sound confusing? That is only because I have to use words to talk about what is beyond words. It is really very simple, and that is one of the beauties of Zen . . . its utter simplicity. But that also makes it seem mysterious on the surface when it's really not. You just have to understand what it is pointing toward.

So here are some traditional Zen pointers. A friend of mine recently wrote a tiny book full of them, which she illustrated (*When Singing, Just Sing—Life as Meditation*, by Narayan Liebenson Grady).

When sitting, just sit.

When eating, just eat.

When walking, just walk.

When talking, just talk.

When listening, just listen.

When looking, just look.

When touching, just touch.

When thinking, just think.

When playing, just play,

And enjoy the feeling of each moment and each day.

You ask me if there are any Zen riddles (they are traditionally called *koans* in Japanese) that are meaningful to me and that really stay with me throughout the day. Yes, there are, and I have found them to be quite wonderful and helpful over the years. The key, as you suggest, is to be open to letting them visit you and revisit you throughout the day.

Here are a few:

Does a dog have Buddha nature?

What was your face before your parents were born?

Where are you coming from?

Who are you?

Have you finished your breakfast? Then go wash your
    bowl!

Remember, you cannot answer these adequately or understand them by thinking about them and speaking in the usual way. One of my teachers, a Korean Zen Master, used to say, "Open your mouth and you're wrong." (This is sometimes the way Zen Masters speak.) They have a saying, "Don't mistake the finger pointing at the moon for the moon." So think about Zen riddles and stories as fingers pointing to something. The pointing is not the something. (You wouldn't climb on top of a sign with an arrow saying "New York City" and think you had gotten to New York City, would you?) In the case of Zen koans, the "something" that is being pointed to is not even a "thing." So it's best to just keep the riddle or the question or the story in mind, to hold it, to cradle it in your mind and in your heart, whatever that means to you, and not try to answer it, or even understand it in the usual thinking way. This is what meditation is really about. It is keeping in the front of your mind the mystery and the beauty of living, of "having" a body, of being alive, of being connected to your family and friends and to nature, and to the planet, of not having all the answers, or even knowing where you are going all the time. It is all OK. What is important is to be *AWAKE*, to be present in this moment, with the whole of your experience, with your feelings, your intuition and imagination, your body and everything it feels and does, and with your thinking. It is all part of who you are, but you are more than all of it, being whole, and always growing as well, being and becoming, knowing and not knowing. Not only is it OK, it is absolutely wonderful. That means, *you* are absolutely wonderful already, and so you don't have to become wonderful, or better, you just have to let yourself be yourself, and learn not to get in your own way all the time (this is a problem you may not have, but a lot of people do, unfortunately, and that is why meditation can be so helpful to them). This was the Buddha's original discovery. It's both very special, and not so special, since everyone's mind is potentially the same as the Buddha's. It's just a matter of being awake and paying attention. (That's why my friend Joko Beck's book, which I have enclosed, is called *Nothing Special*. By the way, she is a 78-year-old American grandmother Zen Master, and if you met her, you would think she was just a regular person, because she is. Just like you and me and your mom and dad. Nothing special, only very special.)

So, this brings us to techniques, which is your third question. Yes, there are techniques to help cultivate this understanding of who you are, and of a full appreciation of being alive and sharing in life with all living things. But it is important, before I tell you a few of them, for me to say that you will have to remember that the techniques are also just fingers pointing at the moon. They are not the goal, they are merely signs pointing to your own experience, and helpful aids, like training wheels on a bike, to use formally until you get the "feeling" of what it is really about to be present from moment to moment (remember, "when walking, just walk. . . ."), for that, in a nutshell, is what it means to have "Zen Mind."

It turns out that "just walking" or "just sitting," in fact, *just* doing anything, isn't so easy. Take walking for instance. If you try to "just walk," you may find that, in addition to walking, you are also thinking about where you are going, or worried about being late, or what will happen when you get there, so that you are not fully aware of your body, say your feet, or your hands, or your spine, or your breathing. So just walking is not so easy. You have to work at it, and this working at it is called "practice" or "meditation practice." That's right. Meditation is simply working at being aware of each moment, no matter what you are doing, and not being carried away by your thoughts or feelings, whatever they are, whether they are in-teresting, happy, unhappy, or blah. It is not about trying to change anything. The point is just to be aware of this moment as you are experiencing it.

If you learn this when you are young and it becomes a way of life with you, it can have an incredible effect on your life for years and years and years, because it develops your deep inner capacity for being a wise and a loving, caring, happy, and playful person. We all have it, especially when we are young, but age and life can sometimes weigh on people to such an ex-tent that they forget that they are miraculous beings, and that they have tremendous capacities for wisdom and compassion and creativity. Meditation practice is a way to keep yourself from ever forgetting this, and a way to develop WHO YOU ARE, fully, across the entire lifespan. Then, it turns out, things will change in marvelous ways sometimes, and difficult ways other times, and you will be able to participate in those changes and contribute to them, and give direction to your life out of your own wisdom and awareness. Then your life choices will be very healthy, and you will be better able to handle all man-ner of things, even very difficult times, and lots of stress.

So, if you want to practice, there are many different tech-niques. Paying attention to your breathing is probably the best one to start with, because you can't leave home without it. You are not always walking, or talking, or sitting, or eating, but you are always breathing. So you can pay attention to your breath-ing, and become friends with it at any moment. If you do, it will calm you down when you are upset, but more importantly, it will help keep you in touch with the present moment. This moment is it. You will never have it again. So Zen says, don't miss it. "Don't let an opportunity like this go by" (the great Indian/Sufi poet, Kabir, said that).

One more thing. Just as the techniques are not what it is really about, but just a systematic way to get more intimate with your own life, so the practice of meditation is not limited to just sitting or lying down and tuning into your breathing for a period of time each day. It is really about being present, awake, and aware in your life, moment by moment, and day by day, in everything you do. And since your breathing goes with you, wherever you are, you can always use it to bring you into your body and back into the present moment so that:

> when you are walking, you are just walking,
>
> when you are eating, you are just eating,
>
> when you are helping your little brother, you are just helping your little brother,
>
> (when you are teasing your little brother, you are just teasing him)
>
> when you are talking on the phone, you are just talking on the phone,
>
> when you are studying, you are just studying. . . .

I think you get the idea.

One more thing: the idea is to practice moment-to-moment awareness of your breathing or anything else without judging, and without a lot of emotional reacting. It's not that these won't happen. Of course they will. But the idea is to be aware of your constantly judging mind, and try to suspend judgment and just let things be as they are, at least while you are practicing. If you are always judging everything and everybody, and have opinions about everything, your mind and your heart will already be filled up with thinking and judging, liking and disliking, and your opinions will cloud your ability to see clearly.

Here is a favorite Zen story: A university professor came to see a Zen Master to ask him what Zen was really all about. He had done a lot of reading, and was now following up to get the real story.

The Zen Master invited the professor to sit down across the table from him and proceeded to serve him tea. He poured the tea into his guest's cup, and when the cup was full, he just kept pouring and pouring, and the tea ran out of the cup and over the saucer and all over the table and floor.

The astonished professor yelled, "What are you doing? Can't you see the cup is already full?"

"Yes, I see," said the Zen Master. "Similarly with your mind. How can you expect me to put anything in it when it is already so full of ideas and opinions?"

So remember, try not to judge everything all the time and have a strong opinion about everything. I know this is difficult, because school and the whole of society is constantly trying to get us to have opinions. But you are not your opinions, and it's good to know that. In fact, you are not any of your thoughts. You might say, you are the thinker, the feeler, the seer. But, coming back to page one of this letter, who is that? That is the question to keep in mind. Trust awareness and wakefulness above all else. Trust your true self, your own heart, your own intuition. Another way to say this is that is it fine to have opinions, but if you are not aware of them, you will get so attached to them and closed-minded that you will not be able to learn anything new.

You asked me why I chose to start practicing these techniques and teachings. Because I knew in my heart that there had to be more to life than what I was experiencing when I was a graduate student studying molecular biology, and I didn't want to miss my own life as it went by. So I got into yoga and meditation and the martial arts because I found that they fed something deep in me that nothing else was feeding. And as a result, I became a lot less angry, and a happier person. Meditation helps me to be calmer and clearer and more loving and accepting, and to take more effective action in my life than I think I would have been able to do if I had not started practicing it, now some thirty years ago. And I still keep at it every day . . . not to get anywhere or even to feel good. I do it because it is one good way to love life and to be in touch with what is important. I love listening to silence.

You ask how Buddhism and Zen affect the world? I think they are pointing to something universal in life and in people that is important for our survival as a species, and for our happiness in society and as individuals. As the world gets more and more complicated, and as it goes faster and faster, and we feel more and more time pressure and stress, we will need to learn how to take better care of ourselves, how to nourish our hearts and our souls and who we are, as well as putting energy into what we do. Otherwise, we might easily become nervous wrecks, and also live sad lives, with no stillness or real understanding. Buddhist wisdom can help us out a lot here. There is such a thing as "Buddhist economics." Perhaps you have heard of the phrase, "small is beautiful." That is part of it. Not causing harm to living creatures is another part of it that the world could learn from. I think that we need more awareness and more selflessness in politics and in business, and in the world in general. Nowadays, millions of Americans are practicing meditation. This is very different from even twenty years ago. This is a very positive change.

Finally, you ask about unusual beliefs or practices that I find interesting and insightful. I guess you might say that all of the above is somewhat unusual. I suppose that we should just come full circle here, to say that watching your own mind is what it is about. Beliefs are fine, but it's important not to get so attached to them that they blind us to other aspects of reality. In the end, it is just a matter of being yourself, and feeling comfortable in your own skin. The practices are all to help us to do that, and to remind us that we are already OK, and very precious. And unique.

There is a saying that goes, "I asked him what time it was, and he told me how a watch works." Maybe it's the same here, I don't know. All I know is that I loved your letter and the enthusiasm behind it, and so I find that I have written many pages in response. I hope you don't feel overwhelmed by this letter. Perhaps I have said too much, or made it too complicated. If that is the case, just take the parts that make the most sense to you and throw away the rest.

Feel free to write if you like. And good luck on your project.

With warm best wishes,

Jon

*

February 22, 1996

Dear Caitlin:

Thank you for your letter, and for your poems. I am awestruck by each and every one of them. Just writing a poem, any poem, is hard enough, but to write Zen poems . . . and good ones, that capture moments, and images that drop down into the truth of your immediate experience, inward and outward, where does this come from? Surely you have a remarkable gift: the ability to see, to listen, and to write faithfully, with subtly and tremendous power. Never, never stop writing.

What a wonderful project you have chosen (or did it choose you?). William Stafford, one of our great contemporary poets, who died recently, wrote a poem every morning, before he did anything else, for thirty years. Quite a meditation practice!

Clearly, you have discovered a territory for yourself that many adults never touch or are touched by their whole lives. And while you are right to think that your understanding of Zen and Buddhism will grow over the years, I can see from your letters and from your poetry that you have "soaked up a lot," as you put it. This idea of being "awake" is absolutely fundamental to living the life that is yours to live, and to developing what is deepest and most beautiful in yourself so that you can share the flower that is you with the world. The world needs all of its human beings to flower. We can help each other to do that, but only if we can cultivate the garden of our own heart and mind, soul and body. You obviously already know this. The trick, and what Zen and meditation are really about, is keeping this knowing alive, so that you don't forget it or take things that are precious for granted. Writing is a very wonderful meditation practice in itself. Did you know that?

Thank you for the pleasure of getting to know you in this way. Whatever you are doing, and wherever it is coming from, mysterious as I am sure it is (it should be mysterious), keep at it and let it, and all of life, teach you.

Good luck with your project. Feel free to write any time.

With warm best wishes,

Jon

*

CAITLIN'S POEMS

Branches
Thin, intertwining
A silhouette no artist could cut
But nature.

*

I was awake in the night and I saw
Millions of sunrises that were sunrises.
I woke up in the morning
and saw a sunrise that was life.
It had every color in it.

It was like the eight-spoke Buddhist wheel,
Or the paths of life.
If you just look at red,
You can't appreciate orange.
If you stand back and are filled with awareness
You can see all the colors of life,
then plunge into one
The one which catches your eye
and your soul
and your heart
and your mind.

*

I was walking in shadow on a dark pebble path
Walking, Walking, Running
An unfeelable mist just STIRRED MY WRATH
Walking, Running, Running
I wasn't walking but staying right here
Walking, Running, Running
For my mind was on homework, schedules, and fears,
Running
The smoke of a factory of unappreciation
Running
Was filling my soul with a conveyor belt sensation
Walking
STOP Two maple trees blocked my mist
Their trunks of faith and loyalty erased my lists
I climbed while gripping their amber wood

Then jumped ahead and felt where I stood
Those alarm clock trees to make me aware
Had disappeared in the clear crisp air.

✻

stress
feelings like hot spaghetti
boiling over
put a lid on it
forget it, cover it up
calms down to the eye

bursts finally

release

run under cold water
calms down to soul
and heart and mind

empty finally

✻

Vacuum while washing while reading a book
Is looking at the snow fall
And being blinded by the white
You'll never see a single flake

It's like the pictures of Seurat,
You'll never notice each separate dot.

*

A single drop of water
Is like a still tulip
It is not a pose or picture
but a part
of an ongoing circle
Tulips wilt
and reseed
Drops fall
and join a stream
A single pebble
is one
But also a whole
rock garden

*

Mara takes the many shapes
Of gold and jewels and satin drapes
Of diamond rings and plastic hearts
Of false I-love-you from Hallmark cards
It chases, tempts, and hooks you on
And entraps you with its phony song
To search for the Truths as Buddha told
You must listen to riches from days of old

The trees, the air, and NATURE's song
Have been the *real* pleasures all along.

[Mara tempted the Buddha with worldly delights just prior to his enlightenment]

*

Zen
Still, distinct
Appreciating, being, watching
A single flower in the starlight
Awareness

The Stillness
Between Two Waves

Mindfulness and the clarity that can come from it are very simple. It is truly nothing special, except that it is also very special. T. S. Eliot, in *Little Gidding*, the last of his *Four Quartets*, referred to this "nothing special" as

> A condition of complete simplicity,
> (Costing not less than everything)

All children are unique, each a fathomless universe of possibilities and feelings. Can we learn to listen carefully enough to hear the texture and resonances of their voices, their songs, their lives? Can we hear, as Eliot put it, "the hidden laughter of children in the foliage"? For there is only right now in which to do this work.

> Quick now, here, now, always—
> A condition of complete simplicity
> (Costing not less than everything)

Quick now, only in *this* moment is anything, whether it is our children or the fluctuations of our own mind, to be seen or felt or heard. But that can only happen if we are willing to pay exquisite attention and be present and completely available, to look, and listen and remain open. Otherwise, countless opportunities for seeing and for relating to our children can remain opaque to us.

> Not known, because not looked for

But if we do look, perhaps we will catch a glimmer. If we listen inwardly, perhaps we may hear our own life, our true self calling to us:

> But heard, half-heard, in the stillness
> Between two waves of the sea.

That is, when our own awareness can hold the space between thoughts, in the stillness, we can hear

> The voice of the hidden waterfall
> And the children in the apple tree

Over and over again, the poet's deep insight reminds us of the calling, the yearning, the potential latent in each present moment—that space, that stillness between two waves of the sea that reveals our essence and our possibilities.

Rainer Maria Rilke, the great German poet of the early twentieth century, describes the same interval, invoking explicitly musical imagery:

> I am the rest between two notes
> Which are somehow always in discord,
> Because death's note wants to climb over—

But in the dark interval, reconciled,

They stay here trembling.

    And the song goes on, beautiful.

Inner stillness delivers to us, over and over again, with every breath, in every moment, the opportunity—and it is only an *opportunity*—to be present, to *hear* the children in the apple tree, the hidden laughter of children in the foliage. Quick now, here, now always . . .

And such a practice—and it is a *practice*, as Eliot well knew, and Rilke too, and Thoreau as well, and countless others—does, parenthetically, take everything we've got. This simplicity costs everything. It requires everything for us to have *this* here, *this* now. And in truly choosing to have this now, we also have "always," a lingering, a stretching out into the future, because this moment is the last moment's future, and the next moment's past. The one colors the other, to the point where it becomes mysterious.

Go, said the bird, for the leaves were full of children,

Hidden excitedly, containing laughter.

Go, go, go, said the bird: human kind

Cannot bear very much reality.

Time past and time future

What might have been and what has been

Point to one end, which is always present . . .

T. S. ELIOT,

"BURNT NORTON," *Four Quartets*

This work of being a human being and of being awake to the fullness of life, the work of mindfulness, is hard, and mindful parenting even harder. Or is it easier, given that we have such marvelous occasions to catch hold of and simply be here for?

Anyone who stops and sits down to meditate for even the shortest of times, feels and knows directly that our "notes" are somehow always in discord, the discord of pain and anguish, uncertainty, impatience, nostalgia, loss and grief, as well as death, and the incessant torrent of thinking in the mind. Learning how to let all those varied "notes" be reconciled in Rilke's dark interval, in Eliot's stillness between two waves of the sea, is the heart of the practice of seeing, and of letting go and letting be. The dynamic tension of our moments trembling, pregnant with more moments and possibilities yet to unfold which we get to participate in shaping one way or another, itself invites the music of life to sound and resonate, and to go on.

Perhaps we might affirm through our own practice, in our own lives, with our own children that when we do embrace the stillness and the fullness of the present moment, the song does go on, and that that song is beautiful. Eliot ends the final great poem of his life with an ancient medieval affirmation, raised to new heights of imagery and music to the point that it almost becomes an incantation:

> And all shall be well and
> All manner of thing shall be well
> When the tongues of flame are in-folded
> Into the crowned knot of fire
> And the fire and the rose are one.

Here now, the closing stanza of the fourth quartet (*Little Gidding*) in its exquisite fullness, giving voice, as does the entire poem, to a knowing that directly touches the transcendent within the ordinary for all who are committed to listening, and to seeing:

We shall not cease from exploration
And the end of all our exploring
Will be to arrive where we started
And know the place for the first time.
Through the unknown, remembered gate
When the last of earth left to discover
Is that which was the beginning;
At the source of the longest river
The voice of the hidden waterfall
And the children in the apple-tree
Not known, because not looked for
But heard, half-heard, in the stillness
Between two waves of the sea.
Quick now, here, now, always—
A condition of complete simplicity
(Costing not less than everything)
And all shall be well and
All manner of thing shall be well
When the tongues of flame are in-folded
Into the crowned knot of fire
And the fire and the rose are one.

This unceasing exploration is the great work of awareness. We can bring it to anything. But what better place to cultivate such a way of seeing, such a way of being, than in parenting?

PART FIVE

A Way of Being

Pregnancy

Pregnancy is a natural time to begin or deepen the practice of mindfulness. The increasingly dramatic changes that occur in our bodies and in our very perceptions, thoughts, and emotions invite new degrees of wakefulness, wonder, and appreciation. For some of us, being pregnant may be the first time we experience being fully in our body.

The changes in our body are of interest not only to ourselves but often to people around us. We are constantly reminded of our special state of being by the reactions we get from other people, ranging from warm inquiries to unasked-for advice to sudden pats on the belly.

The myriad physical and emotional changes we experience give us unique opportunities throughout pregnancy to work intimately with many aspects of mindfulness practice—paying attention to our experience, being fully present, being aware of our expectations, cultivating acceptance, kindness, and compassion, particularly toward ourself and our baby, experiencing feelings of deep interconnectedness.

These opportunities are also available to fathers and partners. Pregnancy is a time when they can become more mindful of their own feelings about our changing bodies and the changes that the birth will inevitably bring to their lives. They have their own outer and inner work to do, participating in all the planning and in the choices that need to be made, and developing greater empathy and selflessness in honoring our special state and the miracle and the mystery of the whole process of two becoming three, and sometimes more. At the same time, they can use this challenging period to deepen their own self-awareness, which will be so essential to their parenting.

*

Prior to getting pregnant, we may have been living our lives in a state of constant doing, in a sort of hyperdrive: fast, relatively unconscious, focused on doing more and more. Then all of a sudden we may find ourselves in a slower, more receptive, "being" mode. The extreme fatigue we feel at times may force us to slow down, as our body works hard to create, grow, and nourish our baby via the newly formed, amazing placenta, and our greatly increased blood supply. If we ignore these changes as we push on with life as usual, we can miss out on a rich and quickly passing opportunity to experience the world in a different, slower, more conscious and sensitive way. Even as the impending birth continually pulls our thoughts and imaginings toward the future, our ever-changing state also draws us more and more into the miracle of what is happening now.

The naturally inward focus of pregnancy gives us a chance to tune in to ourselves, using the breath to ground ourselves and deepen our connection to the present moment. We become more aware of our thoughts, our feelings, of our body and our baby. Allowing the breath to become slow and deep, acknowledging where we feel tension, we can begin to let the tension in our bodies flow out with each out-breath. The energy that we may have used in the past to cover up or ignore anger, fear, or anxiety will be freed up as we begin to observe our feelings with receptivity, watching them change from moment to moment.

Pregnancy can be a time of highly charged and rapidly changing emotions. No matter how much we have wanted to be pregnant, along with our happiness we may also experience moments of fear, ambivalence, regret, and uncertainty. How will our lives change? Are we ready to be parents? During pregnancy, women often feel more emotionally vulnerable, and more sensitive to sights, sounds, and smells.

Every pregnancy is different, every woman is different, and every day is different. The range of experience is enormous, from feeling healthier than we have ever felt before, radiant, with a sense of total well-being, to feeling incredibly sick, miserable, and immobilized. We may find ourselves disappointed or angry or frustrated because what we are experiencing doesn't coincide at all with the expectations we had about what our pregnancy would be like and how we would be feeling.

Being mindful while pregnant doesn't mean that we are "supposed" to feel a certain way, or that there is some ideal state that we have to achieve that will be best for our baby or for ourself. It means acknowledging and accepting the full range of how we are feeling and what we are experiencing and working with it as best we can. This orientation, grounded in awareness and acceptance, can often lead, paradoxically, to greater calmness and relaxation and feelings of well-being.

We all carry with us, to varying degrees, painful experiences, difficult family relationships, and old wounds that may or may not have healed. It is especially important, as we prepare to become a parent, that we begin to heal the wounds created by the judgments, criticisms, and conditional love that may have been our steady diet as children. We can begin by bringing awareness to the moments in the day when we catch ourselves judging or belittling ourselves or others. We can remind ourselves that these thoughts are just that—thoughts—and intentionally bring our attention to our breath and back into the present moment.

Another way we can begin to heal is by making some time in the day to focus inwardly and bathe ourselves in a compassionate, non-judgmental energy. For some, it may feel natural and easy to direct loving kindness and acceptance to their innermost being and their baby. For others, generating this kind of energy and directing it toward themselves may be very difficult or feel stilted or awkward. It might help to think of a person or an animal for whom we have felt love and acceptance, and then, as we get in touch with the feelings of loving kindness and acceptance we have for them, allow those feelings to begin to flow around ourselves as well.

As we focus inwardly, aware of the many changes we are experiencing, we can also direct our awareness to any deep-seated and emotionally laden beliefs that we may be carrying about pregnancy, labor, birth, and parenting. We all have such beliefs, conscious as well as unconscious, stemming from our own experiences and from stories we have heard from family, friends, and acquaintances. These deep-seated, frequently unexamined beliefs can color our hopes and our fears for the coming birth.

It is important for us to keep in mind that our beliefs about birthing, whatever they are, are not necessarily "true." They are just beliefs, or, as one of our children at the age of four put it, "believements." Becoming more intentionally aware of them as thoughts, examining them on purpose, trying to understand their origins and the context that originally fed them, is the beginning of defusing any negative influence they may exert on our psyche.

Toxic seeds, in the form of negative beliefs or attitudes toward pregnancy, birth, and parenting, can be planted unwittingly by what seem like casual comments made by friends and family. These comments can have even more of an effect on us when they come from those we consider powerful and knowledgeable authorities, whether they be our own parents, health care providers, or friends.

A common one that came up when I (mkz) was teaching childbirth classes was, "My doctor says my pelvis is small." The "inadequate pelvis" remark could set in motion all sorts of doubts and fears that could have a negative effect on the course of labor. Many a cesarean was done because the woman's pelvis was supposedly too small. In her next pregnancy, that same woman may have then gone on to have a bigger baby vaginally, with the assistance of a caregiver with the experience, positive beliefs, and skill to guide and support her in giving birth without unnecessary medical intervention.

One way to become more aware of our own beliefs about giving birth is by talking with our mothers and our grandmothers about their experiences and other family birthing stories, trying to elicit as much detail as possible. We might then seek out practitioners who have been present at many births that occurred without unnecessary medical intervention and ask them to interpret frightening birth stories we may have heard, from their base of knowledge, experience, and their own beliefs.

For instance, a birth story, recounted by someone who gave birth twenty or thirty years ago, that ended in a traumatic forceps delivery and a depressed baby might be seen in the larger context of a drugged mother, laboring on her back (a poor position in which to labor and birth a baby), and with no support. A more recent birth story, with a difficult vacuum-assisted delivery and a depressed baby, might be seen in the larger context of a woman laboring under epidural anesthesia, unable to squat and use gravity to assist her, and not being able to feel enough to push effectively. Understanding the medicalized context in which many births take place, and hearing stories of women birthing without unnecessary interventions, we can begin to see and trust the power and wisdom that our bodies naturally have to give birth.

Through educating ourselves about normal birthing, we may come to see and understand that, while we cannot control everything, there is much we can do to create a positive birthing environment with minimal or no medical intervention, which is healthier for the baby and for ourselves as well.

An important part of this process will be choosing who to have assist us in our preparations and at the birth itself. Childbirth educators, birth attendants, and practitioners are formed by their training and their own unique experiences, just like everybody else. As we have said, they too have their own belief systems. Those who believe in the body's ability to give birth without unnecessary intervention and who have been present at many such births are more likely to be wise in the ways of being supportive of pregnant women, ways that empower them and acknowledge their sovereignty. Meeting with practitioners in preparation for the birth is a time to see with clarity, to put aside our naïveté and any elements of blind faith we may have in "authorities."

It is not enough that the practitioner seems like a "nice" person. We need to pay close attention to how we feel in their presence. Are they able to listen, to hear our concerns, and what is important to us? By interviewing several prospective caregivers, by asking them specific questions, such as where they practice, who covers for them, what their cesarean-section rate is, how frequently they do episiotomies and what their criteria are for performing them, we can acquire important information about their attitudes toward birthing and how they practice. Speaking with other women who have used these caregivers and hearing the details of their experiences can also be helpful.

Listening closely to the language practitioners use, questioning the kinds of experiences they have had, and the parameters within which they feel comfortable working, we can begin to see their different points of view and decide which ones, if any, are compatible with our own. As we gather information through reading, and by speaking with people and paying attention to our own feelings and reactions, we can become increasingly aware of and honor what *we* feel comfortable with, and more familiar with what is important to us.

After we have prepared ourselves in this way, the ultimate question will be where and with whom will we feel most safe and most comfortable? Some people start out thinking they would feel safest in the hospital, only to find further down the road that they want to have a home birth. Others may think they want a home birth at first, only to find themselves feeling more comfortable with the idea of giving birth in a hospital or a birthing center.

Working both inwardly and outwardly, using a combination of information-gathering, self-awareness, and intuition, can help us make informed decisions and chart a course that will best meet our needs and the needs of our baby.

Birth

The power and intensity of labor pull us right into each moment. Each labor is unique. Like life, you never know how things will unfold. Every labor has its own rhythms, its own tempo. Sometimes labor and birth have a quiet, holy feeling. Each person does his or her part, and the labor steadily progresses and builds until the baby is born. But birth can also feel like a wild comedy, with things happening so quickly that people are rushing about in a frenzied and chaotic atmosphere.

Birth requires the people present to put aside their expectations and judgments and be open to whatever comes up in each moment and work *with* it with their whole being. We may have had positive images of being massaged and stroked during our labor, only to find that when we are actually in labor, we don't want to be touched. We may have made plans to have beautiful music playing and many friends in the room, only to find that we want quiet and just a few people with us. We may have had an image of a serene madonna laboring quietly, only to find ourselves angry, or frustrated, at times cursing or complaining, and making all sorts of outrageous sounds.

Labor is an opportunity to take off the quiet, kind, thoughtful, neat, taking-care-of-others, "good girl" mantle so often adopted by women in our society, and allow ourselves the freedom to be whoever and however we find ourselves, completely free to be inwardly focused and fully engaged in the work at hand. If those around us can accord us our own way, our own sovereignty, in this miraculous process in which we play the central and critical role, birthing can be a powerful affirmation and a powerful healing of our own psyche, an initiation into a new domain of being.

If you have been using the breath to cultivate mindfulness during your pregnancy, by the time labor begins, you will have some familiarity with its use in helping you to be present, relaxed, and focused. As labor becomes more and more intense, you can use the breath to enter fully into the pain and the demanding, moment-to-moment work of birthing. Regardless of how your labor actually unfolds, and as intense and painful as it can sometimes be, a ferocious, moment-to-moment awareness, conjured up as we face the huge and unknown process as consciously as possible, can help bring the experience into the realm of full awareness, acceptance, and ownership. The result is not only a new baby to welcome and nurture, but a powerful experience we will carry with us our whole lives.

To cultivate mindfulness during labor, we can remind ourselves to keep the breath slow and deep as we feel the intensity of the contraction building, using the in-breath to stay with the intense sensations, and using each out-breath to release any tension or holding back that we feel in the body. The end of each contraction always brings a rest, no matter how short, giving us an opportunity to change position, have a drink, a hug, a laugh. Being aware, being present, we are better able to see or sense what we need in each moment.

Using the breath to be fully present during labor, to breathe into any pain or discomfort, takes less energy than either trying to distract ourselves from it or fighting against it. The body has its own inner wisdom. Resisting and tightening up only make it harder for our bodies to do the work of opening and birthing. Breathing slowly and deeply, working with what we are feeling by changing our position, having a support person apply pressure or hot compresses, expressing our feelings, our frustrations, holding on to our partner or friend—all can help us to be more fully present as we labor.

Women often find that their fear of the pain of childbirth is worse than the pain itself; that if they intentionally experience each contraction without thinking or worrying about how long it is going to last, or about the next one, that they have more positive energy to give to the work at hand in *this* moment. Being fully present from one moment to the next in this way during labor and birth requires courage, concentration, and the love and support of the people around you.

We are used to associating pain with pathology. The pain of labor and birth is the healthy pain of an intensely physical process, as the uterus contracts to first open the cervix and then push our baby out. Women can bring positive "believements" to labor by associating the power, the intensity, and even the pain they are feeling with images intentionally evoked in the mind, such as the cervix opening like a flower, or the baby slipping and sliding lower and lower down with each contraction. Making open *ohhh* and *ahhh* sounds with each contraction, which allows the throat to open, and associating in our mind's eye the opening of the throat with the opening of the cervix and vagina, gives us another way of working intentionally "inside" the very intensity of our labor.

Birthing is a process in which, like parenting, each situation, and veritably, each moment brings a different challenge. At times we meet it fully. At other times we may retreat, close down, go on automatic pilot. There may be times when we completely lose it, or find ourselves complaining and cursing and rejecting what feels like a miserable experience.

When we find ourselves retreating and shutting down, we can simply bring our attention back to the breath. This will help bring our focus back into each moment and to work with it as it is. Each moment truly is a new beginning, and new beginnings are exactly what is called for after each contraction, especially if one is feeling spent, anxious, or discouraged. Our willingness to embody new beginnings mirrors the biggest new beginning of all. After all the preparation and hard work, the child is born, and with it, the mother.

*

Sometimes in birthing, as in life, what occurs is unexpected. We cannot anticipate or control everything that may happen. At those times, our expectations for the "perfect" birth, or the "perfect" baby, can get in the way of experiencing what is actually happening to us and with us in each moment. Being mindful in the face of the unexpected involves a combination of seeing clearly and working with what is. There is nothing passive about it. Even in very difficult circumstances, it is possible and very important to trust our feelings and our intuition and try to make informed, wise, spur-of-the-moment decisions. Ultimately, we do the best we can, with our eyes as open as we can manage to keep them, in the moments that we get to work with.

Working as best we can with whatever arises, and letting go of our strong expectations for things to be a certain way, is not easy to do. It involves giving ourselves permission and time to fully experience all our feelings—frustration, anger, disappointment, fear, grief. Feeling compassion for ourselves, for our difficulties, for our efforts, for our limits, for our humanness, is an essential part of healing and restoring ourselves.

We spend most of our energy while we are pregnant focusing on the birth of our baby, and it is not until our baby is born that we truly understand that the birth is just the beginning. But the inner work we do during pregnancy and birthing is good training for mindful parenting. As we give birth, the power and immediacy with which we are pulled into the present moment and are forced to let go of our preconceptions puts us in touch with the essence of mindfulness practice. In giving birth to our babies, we may find that we give birth to new possibilities within ourselves.

Well-being

When we start to bring mindfulness into our lives and to our parenting, our new awareness may lead us to reexamine and question many basic assumptions that we usually take for granted.

For instance, new parents are often asked: "Is the baby sleeping through the night yet?" We may notice, as we listen carefully to the intent behind this question, that it has more to do with how much sleep the parents are or aren't getting than it does with concern for the baby. It is predicated on the supposition that babies are supposed to sleep all night long. The unspoken assumption is that the parents' needs should take priority.

This assumption often surfaces in the form of unsolicited advice to new parents, such as, "Make sure you have time alone together. Give attention to your relationship. Leave the baby with a sitter and have a date." If we look closely at this, we may see that, once again, the focus is predominantly on the parents' well-being rather than on the child's. Babies are seen as tough and resilient, while the parents are seen as vulnerable and in need of protection. Of course new parents do need to take care of themselves, and do need the loving care and support of others during this intense period of adjustment, when all sorts of new demands are being placed upon them. But it is important that in the process, the baby's needs are not minimized or lost sight of. If we can act with some degree of awareness, our choices in taking care of ourselves will not be at the expense of our baby's well-being.

In deciding how we are going to parent, and what our priorities are, we need to be aware of the paramount importance of building and maintaining trust and feelings of connectedness with our baby, both for his long-term well-being, and for the long-term well-being of the family as a whole. As we noted in the chapter on empathy, scientists who study infants have found evidence that the most basic lessons of emotional life are laid down in the small, repeated exchanges that take place early on between parent and baby. Of all such intimate moments and exchanges, the most critical seem to be those that "let the child know her emotions are being met with empathy, accepted and reciprocated." This process is called *attunement*. Knowing that attunement in infancy forms the basis of a child's later emotional competencies might motivate us to pay much greater attention, moment by moment, to how we actually interact with our children, especially when they are little, and to the choices that we make about their care.

Let's say a baby isn't sleeping through the night. The parents, tired and frustrated, decide to let the baby "cry it out" until she "gets the idea" and falls asleep. But consider for a moment what the baby might be learning from this. In all likelihood, the lessons she is learning from this lack of response are that she can't rely on others and that shutting down emotionally is the best way to survive.

Instead of seeing the baby's well-being as in some way competing with our own, mindful parenting focuses on the mutual interrelatedness of our needs. According to William and Martha Sears, authors of *The Baby Book*, "There is a biological angle to mutual giving. . . . When a mother breastfeeds her baby, she gives nourishment and comfort. The baby's sucking, in turn, stimulates the release of hormones that further enhance mothering behavior. . . . The reason that you can breastfeed your baby to sleep is that your milk contains a sleep-inducing substance. . . . Meanwhile, as you suckle your baby, you produce more of the hormone prolactin, which has a tranquilizing effect on you. It's as if the mommy puts the baby to sleep, and the baby puts the mommy to sleep." Having a greater awareness of the many ways in which we are so highly interconnected, we might look very differently on many aspects of parenting—including nursing, and having our baby in bed with us.

To parent mindfully does not mean that we won't at times have strong feelings of frustration, or wish that a certain situation wasn't happening when we feel as if our needs are in direct conflict with our baby's. For example, there will be nights when our baby wants to play or wants to be held or walked with at three in the morning. Our first impulse might be to resist the situation. Intentionally bringing mindfulness and discernment to such moments, we can acknowledge our feelings of anger, resentment, and frustration, *and* also our feelings of empathy and understanding. In the spirit of seeing everything we face as part of the practice of mindful parenting, we can choose to see our resistance to meeting our child's need in that moment, drop down below our either/or thinking, no matter how rational and reasonable it seems, and respond with greater wisdom from our hearts. This way of holding the present moment in a difficult time allows us to find truly creative solutions that do not come at the expense of our child's well-being. In this way, our own well-being is nourished as well, as we grow against the envelope of our limitations.

Babies are not babies for very long. This formative stage in which they are completely dependent on us is relatively brief and very precious.

During this time, their sense of well-being is intimately related to how attuned we are to what they are feeling and needing in each moment, and the quality and constancy of our responses. So in parenting mindfully, we try as best we can to cultivate the kind of responsiveness that honors the sovereignty of our children.

Nourishment

Taking nourishment is a fundamental human function to which we usually bring remarkably little moment-to-moment awareness, although it occupies enormous amounts of time, energy, and thought. A similar lack of awareness clouds our ability to see and appreciate some of the most important aspects of providing nourishment for our babies, although it is an activity that parents engage in many times throughout the day and night. If we go into parenting with the understanding that human connection and interaction are of paramount importance, the seemingly ordinary but formative choices we make around feeding, and, more importantly, the quality of the attention that we bring to it as we engage in it, will be more in tune with the full range of our infant's needs, and likely to feed more aspects of our child's being than just his belly.

There is a kind of immersion, a soaking in bliss, that happens in those moments after a baby has been fed. At times, a mutual gazing arises, a wonderfully peaceful feeling and sense of palpable connectedness and devotion, captured in many Renaissance paintings in which the Madonna is gazing at her child.

The Ojibwa word for mirror, *wabimujichagwan,* means "looking at your soul," a concept that captures some of the mystery of image and substance. If it is true that we are mirrors to our infants and that looking forms the boundaries of a self, then perhaps we are also helping to form a spiritual soul self during those concentrated love gazes during which time stops, the air dims, the earth cools, and a sense of deep rightness takes hold of our being.

LOUISE ERDRICH, *The Blue Jay's Dance*

Whether we choose to bottlefeed or breastfeed, we can feed our children in a way that is responsive to the cues they give us, feeding them when they want to be fed, holding them with sensitivity, close to the warmth and comfort of our bodies, making sure that there are plenty of times when we put down our book or newspaper, shut off the TV, give them our full attention, and cultivate the art of gazing. It is a meditation in itself.

When a baby is fed on a schedule rather than in response to her cues, the food comes at an adult-determined "time for feeding," whether she is hungry or not. Instead of getting to experience hunger and then feeling the hunger satisfied as we respond to the myriad ways she subtly or not-so-subtly communicates with us, the experience can easily become one of disconnection from herself and the person feeding her. She is denied the ability to self-regulate and is placed in a passive role. There is no control, no empowering, no experience of exercising her will and getting an appropriate response. Being fed can become a dissociative experience, rather than an enlivening one in which feelings of trust and connectedness between parent and child are continually nourished and strengthened.

Whether babies are breastfed or bottlefed, feeding them in response to *their* cues reinforces and builds a sense of their own power. They experience their ability to get what they need and to elicit an appropriate response from the world around them. This inner quality of confidence, built upon repeated experiences of successfully achieving a desired effect, is known as *self-efficacy*. Many studies show self-efficacy to be the single strongest factor predicting health and healing, an ability to handle stress, and the ability to make healthy lifestyle changes in adults and in children. The foundation for a robust and wide-ranging self-confidence begins in childhood with these kinds of intimate and mutually responsive interactions.

If you choose to breastfeed, it helps enormously to have support from experienced individuals or groups. The initial period can be frustrating and difficult, depending on the particular needs of both your baby and your own body. It is easy to feel overwhelmed as difficulties arise, but there are often very simple solutions to sometimes seemingly impossible or frustrating problems. With knowledgeable support and a willingness to work with the problems that come up, you can make it through the first few weeks and come through feeling a strong sense of confidence in yourself and your body, and what it is beautifully designed to do. At a certain point nursing can become effortless, the foundation of a child-centered way to parent that nourishes baby and mother at the deepest level.

Although there is some public awareness of the health benefits of breastfeeding, there has not been much talk or research into other equally important dimensions of breastfeeding, such as emotional comfort, physical and psychological tuning of biological rhythms (how the bodies and minds of the mother and the baby interact), maternal-infant bonding, and its long-term neurological and developmental effects.

Observing our children when they were babies and toddlers, I (mkz) could see the deep states of relaxation that they would immediately move into as they nursed. No matter what was going on in the moment, no matter what upset had just occurred, I could usually count on nursing to rejuvenate them. It provided a momentary withdrawal from the stimulation of the world into a quiet, peaceful place of comfort, nurturance, and renewal. As toddlers, they would move from playing and exploring at a distance, back to me for refueling. By that time, they were eating lots of different foods. They weren't really nursing for food. They were nursing to renew their inner resources, their psyche, their spirit.

Another important aspect of breastfeeding is the concentrated effort required of the infant to suck milk from the breast. With nursing, the milk doesn't come pouring down into their mouths; they have to work for it. The initial sucking may give them very little milk, and then at a certain point, if you watch closely, you can see them switching to the long, slow sucks that show you that your milk has let down and is flowing. The child relaxes into a satisfying rhythm—focused, working, but relaxed. When the breast is emptied, they often continue to suck to meet their needs for comfort, calming, relaxation, and centering.

Some years ago, I attended a conference sponsored by La Leche League, an organization devoted to informing women about breastfeeding and providing support. It was in a large auditorium full of women listening to a presentation as they held infants and toddlers in their laps, some nursing, some snuggling. It was remarkable to feel the babies *centering on their mothers*. The importance of this embodied relationship is discussed in sociologist Robbie Pfeufer Kahn's insightful book, *Bearing Meaning: The Language of Birth.*

Breastfed babies and toddlers see their mothers as the "source." Venturing out is balanced by a return to the source of their contentment, their fulfillment, their security. It is as if they are always held. This "holding" has nothing to do with controlling or holding back. They stay within the maternal sphere because they are strongly connected. They are able to come and go, grounded in their relationship to her and to her body.

In that auditorium full of small children, I was struck by the sustained quiet in the room, the feeling of contentment with being held or nursed, embraced by the aura of the mother.

Soul Food

When our children were little, people would frequently comment on how rosy their cheeks were. I (mkz) would smile to myself, knowing where those rosy cheeks came from. They came from nursing.

Once I had made it through the sometimes painful and frustrating first few weeks of nursing, in which my body was trying to find the right balance between too little and an overabundance of milk, I found that nursing relaxed me and slowed me down. As I felt my milk let down, a wonderful haziness descended on me, and everything else became less important. I let go of the things I had planned to do, and instead let myself be pulled into the present moment, into being totally with my baby. It was a deeply meditative time for both of us.

Nursing was a huge cornerstone of my mothering. It gave me great confidence to know that I had what I needed to feed and comfort my babies anytime, anywhere. They often had a look of delight as I positioned them at the breast. First they would nurse for milk. Then, as the breast emptied, they would go on to suck for comfort, and from there, would move into a completely relaxed state of being. If they were at all tired, they would usually fall asleep. Getting them to sleep without a big fuss when they needed a nap was as easy as nursing them as they snuggled up to me. If they woke up at night, they would either already be sleeping next to me, or I would go and get them and bring them into our bed and nurse them, both of us never fully waking up, drifting back to sleep together.

As they got to be toddlers and were eating all sorts of foods, nursing remained a deep source of comfort. If their day had been wearing, overwhelming or overstimulating, I could count on nursing to rejuvenate them. No matter where we were, a quiet space could be created just by climbing onto my lap, nestling into my arms. Tensions were released by the quiet concentration of sucking, the warmth of my body, the rhythm of my breath. This ongoing connection to me through nursing gave them a deep security and self-confidence. I could feel it in every aspect of their being. Their experience of the world was grounded in the body—in their relationship to me and my body, and in their experience of their own body, nursing, being held. They knew the source of their satisfaction and renewal. It was visible, tangible, dependable. That grounding helped them to meet the world with curiosity and self-possession. Nursing allowed them to be snuggled, nurtured, to be treated like a "baby" for brief periods throughout the day and the night. Perhaps because they had an acceptable way to still be little, they felt secure enough to give up wearing diapers at a relatively early age.

When they started speaking, the nursing brought out an impish, playful, humorful side to them. When my son was one and a half, he made his first joke. He gave me a mischievous look, blew on my breast as if to cool it, and then said, "Hot!" laughing with delight. When he was about two and a half, we were nursing one morning and I said, "Let's go down and have breakfast." He responded with "Nurse!" Every time I tried to disengage, he would say, "Nurse!" Finally I said, "You're a nut!" He looked at me and said, "No, I'm a raisin!" We laughed and hugged, and proceeded to go down for breakfast.

My body was an essential and completely familiar part of their landscape. All the children had their own special words that stood for nursing, the breast, and breast milk. "Nuk" and "Noonie" were favorites. When I had a problem with yeast infections on my breasts and the skin was breaking down, my son matter-of-factly referred to one as "the boo-boo side" and called the other "the like that side."

My youngest daughter loved to rhyme, and her creativity was particularly prolific around nursing. One morning she welcomed me with "Ohhh Noonie is my best kind of juice, Myla Moose!"

She found lots of ways of expressing how valued "noonies" were to her. She could be very dramatic in her choice of words and her intonation. Getting out of the shower one morning, she held a towel tightly around herself and said, "I won't let the gold fall out of my noonies." Another time she said, in a tragic voice worthy of Shakespeare, "My noonie has been robbed!"

As they got older and were in the process of weaning, their sense of humor about nursing continued. I told my youngest daughter at one point that she could nurse "once in a while." Wanting to nurse, she retorted, "Last night was once, and this is a while!" This was the first of many mutual negotiations. As she has grown older, I have had to work hard to match her skill at negotiating.

Nursing had such a powerful effect on my children that at times it could work its magic even without the presence of my body. When my older daughter was two, I was away all day assisting at a birth. When I called home in the afternoon, Jon said she very much wanted to talk to me. I was immediately filled with dread, knowing that as soon as she heard my voice, she would be overcome with sadness and tell me she wanted me and wanted to nurse. As soon as she got on the phone, she started to cry, telling me to come home right away. I told her I'd try to be home as soon as I could. Her response was a plaintive "Nukky me!" I said, "I'll nurse you when I get home." Her voice was insistent, "No, nukky me *now!*" Wanting so much to comfort her, I said very gently, "Okay, I'm nursing you right now. Is it good nuk?" She was silent, and Jon said she was sitting there with her eyes closed, relaxed and meditative, letting me "nurse" her over the phone.

Whether they were angry, or frustrated, overwhelmed, or just ragged, nursing brought peace and contentment. They were their most loving selves when they were receiving love in this form. Nursing my youngest to sleep one night, she looked up at me and said in the lovingest tone of voice, "Mutha, you so sweet." We were both bathed in sweetness.

Even after the children stopped nursing, my body was still a source of comfort and well-being for them. There would be times when they were drifting off to sleep that they would rest their hand on my breast and get this wonderful, peaceful look on their faces. It was as if that was enough to bring them back to a blissful state of being that nourished them deeply. You might call it soul food.

The Family Bed

We have some funny ideas about sleeping in this society. Maybe it's that we are affluent to the point where we can provide children with their own rooms to sleep in. We do this even for babies, and in doing so, we separate them from us. This arrangement is very different from how most families in the world sleep, and from how most families in our country slept in earlier times. Yet our separate sleeping arrangements may be one way in which the "advanced development" of a society deprives rather than nourishes the soul. Parents and children alike may be the losers.

Our pediatrician recommended we keep our first child in his own bed, in his own room, so we could establish from the first that he would have to follow our rules and learn to sleep alone without bothering us. But we went into parenting wanting to be bothered. In fact, we saw it as essential. We felt that our infant baby belonged with us. Sleeping next to us, he could relax into the softness and warmth of our bodies. He was bathed in the security and comfort of our presence. All was right with the world, for him and for us, when he was sleeping between us, usually snuggled right up against one or both of us.

Nothing can really describe the deep contentment we felt, having our baby next to us, not needing to worry about being unable to hear him. Rather than wondering and worrying, "Is he covered, is he cold, will I hear him crying over the sound of wind and rain?", there was no questioning how he might be, because he was right there.

For several years we slept together, breathed together. Even when he slept in his own bed, our bed was often where he started off the night, or wound up by the morning. When we wanted to be alone, we would carry him into his room after he was asleep. More and more as he got older, he wanted to be in his own room, in his own bed. When the girls were born, being closer together in age, there was a time when we had both of them sleeping in bed with us. At some point, we got a larger bed.

We didn't get a whole lot of sleep during those years. Our children woke up a lot at night, not only to nurse but also because that was the way they were. Some children sleep through the night early on without much fuss. Many others don't.

Did we ever think that perhaps we were encouraging them to wake up by being there for them too much, and by letting them nurse when they wanted to? At times we did. But the moments of questioning and wondering didn't bring an end to sharing sleep with our little ones. We worked with the difficulties the way we worked with everything else, trying to find the right balance. There were definitely times when we were getting woken up too much and were exhausted and frustrated. What we tried to do at such times was to make waking up less inviting, mostly by having Jon walk with them rather than letting them nurse.

A greater intention came into play here, one we valued far more than sleep. We intuitively felt that the security and the peace that our physical presence gave our children was nourishing to their whole being. The effect was tangible. We could see it in their open, curious, lively, loving faces. Our presence at night grounded them in their bodies and in the world, and that grounding could be seen in the way they quietly observed the world around them. They were curious without being frenetic, active without being out of control. The well-being and joyfulness emanating from them was wonderfully contagious. They were wholly present—whether it was in a laugh of delight, a shout of anger, or a loving embrace. The purity of their aliveness was enlivening for us and more than made up for the lost sleep.

We were sleep-deprived for many years. There were often times when life invariably intervened in our attempts to get uninterrupted sleep, in the form of teething or colds or stomach upsets. Sometimes it felt like we were playing musical beds. One of us would sleep in an empty child's bed when one of us had to get more sleep. In spite of everything, we managed to function during the day. Along the way we had to redefine for ourselves what felt normal in terms of how much sleep we needed.

We parented this way out of the conviction that deeper things were being fed than our need for uninterrupted sleep, or even time alone together, for which we found creative solutions when we wanted to. We believed that when the children were ready to sleep through the night, they would; and when they were ready to sleep in their own beds they would choose to do so; and of course, they did.

We share our own personal family experience around sleeping arrangements and the philosophy behind it because we felt so strongly—and still do—about the importance of trying to shelter and nourish children's soul needs in this way when they are little. We also emphasize it precisely because it runs so counter to the sleeping practices in families in our society today, although it is the norm in many Asian countries, including Japan. We simply want young couples to know that it is an option, and that it is doable, and that it, too, can be incorporated into a view of parenting as a challenging, disciplined, in many ways arduous as well as deeply satisfying practice. Like everything else, having young children sleep in your bed has its costs; but it can also have very tangible benefits, a feeling of well-being for both parent and child that carries you through the difficult times.

✳

If we ourselves grew up without the experience of intimate, non-sexual touching, or if our boundaries were violated and our trust broken by inappropriate touching, it is natural that there might be a strong hesitation, even fear, regarding sharing a family bed.

Every one of us brings a different personal history to our parenting. For some people, the thought of sleeping together may bring up all sorts of uncomfortable feelings. We may feel some lack of comfort with our bodies, or a need to define our boundaries in a particular way, or fear confusing warmth and love with sexuality. Being aware of such feelings without judging them allows us to work with them mindfully rather than having them automatically control our choices as parents.

Finding ways to meet the needs of our babies and children that we also feel comfortable with requires openness, flexibility, thoughtfulness, and a willingness to stretch and grow against our own fixed, often unexamined assumptions. But it is not so easy, for the same reason that mindful parenting is not easy. It is always bringing us up against what we think are our limits, and showing us the edge beyond which we might feel insecure and threatened. And certainly, trying out any new approaches in parenting can be particularly difficult if both parents don't share the same viewpoint or values. Mindful communication, while essential in any family that cares about maintaining a degree of harmony and goodwill toward adults and children alike, becomes even more important in such situations.

There are many variations and ways to parent with awareness. In no way does a commitment to parent mindfully mean that you have to sleep with your babies or you will not be a good or sensitive parent. Nor does it mean that you have to breastfeed your babies for years. Mindful parenting simply calls on us to pay attention to what we are doing, including the choices we make, and to examine in an ongoing way the effect our choices have on our child. It involves a continual inquiry into what we are doing and why.

We believe that decisions about warmth and comfort, closeness and feeding, and what boundaries and limits might best promote health and happiness and well-being in our particular families are of paramount importance. Mindfulness brought to that very decision making is critical to making parenting a conscious endeavor that is continually sensitive to the changing needs of both the children and the parents. There is no one "right way" to do this. There are many ways to promote healthy children and loving families.

Moreover, choices around sleep may work for a while in a family, and then suddenly, something shifts and a change is needed. If we don't get to see a baby or young child that much during the day, we might find that sharing sleep is a wonderful way to reconnect and nurture her. This might work well with one child, but not so well with another who is a restless sleeper. We may find ourselves too grumpy and short-tempered to be able to function, and will have to try something else.

Fortunately, there are many options. If sharing sleep in the same bed does not work for you or for your spouse or your child, you could put a bed next to yours, or have him sleep in a room next to your own. You can lie down with him as he goes to sleep, or sit with him. Far more important than the choice of sleeping arrangements is finding your own way to foster feelings of trust and connectedness.

In the end, you have to do what feels right to you. Something may be "good" for your child in theory, but if you try it and find you are feeling tense, uncomfortable, and conflicted, how "good" can it be?

It's important for both parents to keep asking themselves and each other what is in their child's best interest, and work together to find solutions to bedtime problems that come up. Sharing insights, examining emotionally charged reactions, trying to see things from the child's point of view, and each other's point of view, are all useful when we try to look freshly at how we spend almost half our lives.

PART SIX

Resonances,

Attunement,

and Presence

Resonances

When a tuning fork vibrates, it will cause other tuning forks in the vicinity to vibrate as well, especially if they are related, that is, tuned to the same wavelength. This process, whereby the activity of one vibrating body brings another body into sympathetic resonance with it, is called *entrainment*. A piano's A strings will be entrained to vibrate when an A is played on a violin across the room.

Parents and children also constantly influence each other's resonances. Our lives orbit within each other's force fields, physically, emotionally, and psychically, and we are continually interacting and influencing each other in subtle and not-so-subtle ways, sometimes known, sometimes wholly unconscious.

Breathing is one basic rhythm that has each one of us vibrating with life. Tuning to this rhythm presents a wonderful occasion to literally resonate with our baby. I (jkz) used to breathe with our babies as part of my meditation practice. I would feel the two of us breathing together swinging in a hammock as the baby slept in my arms, or when I would walk back and forth with a child late at night. Swinging or walking, breathing together, sometimes singing and chanting softly as well, we were resonating together.

If we become aware of the resonances between us, our relationship with a baby can be a continual dance, an exchange of energy of all kinds, sometimes harmonious, sometimes not. It will never be any richer than right in this moment, even though we may have to cook dinner or do the laundry a half hour later, or be interrupted by the telephone. This is a good reason to step into the dance of breathing in whatever moments we can manage it.

✷

Entrainment happens on a lot of different levels in families, but often we are not aware of it, and it can take us places we may not want to go, without us knowing how we got there. If we aren't aware of the energy of the moment, it catches us, ensnares us. It often pulls us down as well as in, such as when we fall into depression, or anger, or anxiety, or any number of other feeling states after spending time with another person. In a family, we are constantly caught up in an ever-changing energy dance with each other, putting out vibrations at different frequencies and interacting with each other's energy in the form of thoughts, feelings, and their expressions—verbal and non-verbal—through our bodies, our actions, and our reactions to events and other people's actions, even tiny ones. If we know we are resonating with forces coming from elsewhere, we can learn to dance skillfully to these rhythms.

Children get into very strong energy states that can affect us in a number of different ways. If we can be aware of their resonances, we can choose our own steps more consciously. If they hit a certain frequency, we do not automatically have to resonate on that same frequency and get caught up in ways that will not be helpful to them or to us.

✷

An outdoor restaurant in summer: A young couple with two children, one about three, the other about four months. The mother nurses the baby, snuggled in her lap. For the longest time, the baby's face is buried in the breast and under parts of her mother's blouse. But her hand is playing with her mother's the whole time. Later, her head surfaces, and she sits on her mother's lap, gazing at her. The mother makes cooing noises, and tilts her head slightly. The baby opens her mouth, making a perfect circle, her blue eyes wide open too, drinking in her mother's face. Her eyes are so open, her mouth is so open, her face so open, she is an incarnation in this moment of pure presence. The eyes are radiating presence. The mouth is quivering with presence.

The mother puts her head down and touches it to her baby's forehead, then moves it back. The baby smiles. There is a complete force field connecting these two. This baby is in the orbit of her mother in this moment, and the two are speaking in a thousand ways, on a thousand wavelengths, across their bodies where they touch, across the air between them.

Later, the father holds the baby in such a way that she can look out over his shoulder. She is settled on his body. Comfortable in his orbit. Her eyes remain hugely open, totally receptive. She sees my (jkz) face, and her gaze comes to rest. I smile. Her face registers it in some way I detect instantly but find impossible to describe. It is alert to novelty. She smiles. It is like a benediction from a purer world. As her older sister sits at the table, I can feel that she too is at home in her body and in the force field of her family. It is not even that they interact that much. They don't. But they form an inseparable whole in which she is completely at home. It shows in her presence, too. The mother tells us as they are leaving that they had just spent many hours in the car, and the kids needed out.

Just an ordinary meal, but it is clear that these children are experiencing that constant give-and-take with parents that forms the bonds of love and announces the benevolence and receptivity of the world to young life, draws out its purity, honors its innocence, and nurtures its being and becoming.

Attunement

Attune: To bring into harmony.

Attuning to our children involves being aware of the messages they are giving us, not just with their words but with every aspect of their being, and adjusting ourselves to resonate in harmony with them.

I (mkz) walk into our local coffee shop and see my neighbor sitting at a table, nursing her nine-month-old as she waits for a friend she is meeting. I say hi, and her baby, curious, stops nursing, looks up, gives me a big smile, and then goes back to nursing. As I wait on line, she begins a game with me across the distance that separates us. She nurses, and then drops her head down so that she is looking at me upside down. She grins and goes back to nursing, and then drops down again, and stares at me. Her mother takes her cues from her, and lets her move her body as she chooses, laughing with pleasure at her daughter's pleasure. This morning in a local coffee shop, one baby is in a state of bliss.

✽

I (mkz) am reminded of when our own children were babies as I take care of my friend's ten-month-old son. Holding him against me as I walk, I try out different things, aware of how he is responding, until

I find the right combination of gentle up and down movements while chanting softly and rhythmically. I slow my breathing down. I feel his body soften and relax into mine. He has no problem telling me without words what he wants. As I sit down with him, he lets me know with his whole body, "No, don't sit down, carry me, walk with me." Then he starts to make little sounds, and I pick up on them, and we make them together. His head on my shoulder, I feel him softening and getting heavier and heavier until he is fast asleep. Slowly I lie down on the couch, feeling his warmth and softness, enjoying the sweet smell of his skin. This clearly feeds him and it is a wonderful gift to me as well. He has had similar experiences many times over with his parents. Each time, his trust grows.

On this rainy day in spring, he is finding out once again that he can rely on another person. He feels a sympathetic responsiveness from me that tells him that what he wants and needs is important, and will be respected. When he gets what he needs, he experiences his power; he feels satisfied, safe, peaceful. All this from a small encounter.

*

When a mother feels out of touch with her toddler and sees him becoming more and more active, to the point of being wild and out of control, she lies down on the rug and lets him climb on her and play with her hair. She is literally letting him get back in touch with her. Gradually, he starts to quiet, to slow down, until after a while, he is lying down on her with the full length of his body, resting, settling into the soothing rhythm of her breath. She sees her child's need for independence and separation and at the same time, his need to hang on to her, to be close, connected. All are played out in this scene on the living-room floor.

*

As children get older, attunement between parent and child becomes more complex. My (mkz) twelve-year-old comes home from school and walks in the door with a scowl on her face. "I'm hungry!" she says in a fierce voice. I see in an instant that school has taken its toll on her. She's feeling overwhelmed. She's been with people all day. Her blood sugar is low. She's about to fall apart. I've learned to have a snack ready for her when she gets home. I've also learned, the hard way, not to ask her questions, to give her space. This is not a time for objecting to her tone of voice or for teaching her manners. After she eats, she usually looks at me in a somewhat more friendly manner and either comes up to me for a hug, or disappears into her room to listen to music.

With an even older child, being attuned might mean being sensitive to their need to be left alone to concentrate on whatever they are doing, especially when they are in the same physical space with us. It might also mean knowing when to reach out and nurture them in small ways.

As I sit in my friend's kitchen, her sixteen-year-old comes in complaining of a pain in her neck. Her mother asks her to point to where it hurts. As we talk, she massages her daughter's neck, periodically stopping her conversation with me to quietly let her know when she feels the knots releasing under her touch. After about fifteen minutes her daughter leaves the room. My friend tells me that this kind of moment together is a rare occurrence now. It probably helped to have another adult present, creating a bit more distance. It is wonderful to feel this mother's sensitivity, her willingness to be open to her daughter unexpectedly reaching out, and her ability to appreciate the preciousness of that moment.

Being in harmony with our children doesn't mean that things will always be harmonious. Attuning in moments of great disharmony and conflict requires everything we have, every ounce of energy and insight, so that even in the midst of struggle, we keep sight of who our children really are and what they need from us in that moment.

Touching

The great anthropologist Ashley Montague observed some time ago that the word "touch" has by far the longest entry in the *Oxford English Dictionary*. No doubt, this is because touch is so basic to the human experience, so fundamental to health and connectedness. Monkey babies don't thrive unless they have constant touching, warmth, and softness. Why think that we would be different? Touch is fundamental to life.

Touch involves being in touch. It can be a unifying experience. We cannot touch without being touched back. It is one way we know we are not alone. Depending on how we are touched, we can feel loved, accepted, and valued, or ignored, disrespected, assaulted.

Touch generates awareness and puts us in touch with the world. We touch and are touched through all our senses, seeing, hearing, smelling, tasting, as well as feeling through the skin.

Being held with sensitivity grounds us in our bodies and awakens a sense of connectedness. It awakens us to ourselves and to the other. A child's whole being is honored when he is touched with awareness, sensitivity, and respect. Learning to be "in touch" with how you feel while you are young grows out of this experience of feeling safe and cared for. Through holding, hugging, cradling, snuggling, smelling, swinging, rocking, humming, chanting, singing, gazing, parent and child both experience the fullness of being alive.

*

Waiting at the Registry of Motor Vehicles, I (mkz) watch a large, soft, woman who is taking care of a red-headed three-year-old boy. She is sitting on a bench, waiting for her license. He is simultaneously using her body as bed, pillow, and jungle gym. He pushes constantly up against her with his body, his head, his arms. When he reaches out and plays with her fingers, she taps his hand, to his delight, with her long fingernails. She is totally accepting of him, never admonishing him to be still, or sit up, or stop what he is doing. There is a sweetness and peacefulness to the scene. The woman has an accent, and I wonder where she grew up, what her childhood was like, and what has influenced her to be so patient, so accepting, so comfortable with touch.

I don't see scenes like this often. What I do see is parents admonishing their children to "behave" in public, and getting angry at them when they behave as the two-, three-, or four- or five-year-olds that they are. I see tired toddler-age children following along behind a parent, crying, without the parent resorting to the simple solution of picking up the child. I rarely see people touching children affectionately and with tolerance for their energy and exuberance.

We seem to be turning into a touch-deprived society. It is rare to see people being physically affectionate, friends holding hands, putting their arms around each other, or lovers embracing. There is enormous loss and isolation that comes from this deprivation, and parents have to work hard to make sure that their children aren't deprived of this essential form of nourishment and communication.

Touch always happens at a boundary that is important to hold in awareness. Otherwise, we may touch unconsciously, and in doing so, be disrespectful. These boundaries are changing from moment to moment. They cannot be assumed or taken for granted. Each moment is new and different. The teenager who yells "No!" when asked if she can be given a good-night kiss, at another time wants to be comforted with a hug. When we are attuned to our children, aware of their energy, their feeling state, we can better sense when they are in need of a loving touch or holding, and when they need to be left alone.

It may help at times to ask ourselves who the touching serves, as a check on our own mindless or invasive impulses. I have vivid memories of relatives pinching my cheeks and kissing me. They had no awareness of how that might feel to me. How often are children asked for hugs and kisses to meet the adult's need for warmth and affection, regardless of the child's feelings or boundaries?

When children repeatedly have the experience of having their feelings respected, are brought up to have a strong sense of their bodies as their own, and are in touch with their feelings, they are better equipped to recognize when someone is acting in an inappropriate manner. Parents can strengthen their child's ability to do this by pointing out and naming inappropriate behaviors when they occur.

*

I (mkz) am moved, and always somewhat astonished, when my children come up to me and hug me. I am surprised, not that they are hugging me but by the *way* they hug me. They hug with a slow, deep, relaxed, quiet, loving touch. As they hug me, I enjoy the nourishment that my children so naturally give in those moments. It feels like a circle of love completed.

Toddlers

Each age and stage, each child, and each moment, provides many opportunities for establishing and then exploring sympathetic resonances. When we are really present with a child, we find ourselves in a special state. It is far more than what it may seem to be from the outside. Inwardly, for the parent, it is a whole universe of mind and rhythm, resonance and connectedness, with sixth senses and intuitions abounding.

With toddlers, the challenge is to stay attuned and to retune quickly. We get this chance over and over again because a child's mind states change so rapidly. One moment he may be one way; the next moment, things are entirely different. If we can be aware of these sudden shifts and transitions, such as his suddenly feeling tired or hungry or frustrated, we can maintain our own balance as we help him move through difficult moments more easily.

This requires being aware of our own feelings, which change almost as rapidly as the child's. Frequently they can be triggered by the child's mood, as when we react with frustration to his frustration. Instead of constricting at such moments and hardening, and becoming ensnared, perhaps we can catch ourselves and respond with greater acceptance and an open presence.

One day, I (jkz) observed a young father in a restaurant trying to eat dinner with his four-year-old daughter. The food had taken too long to come. By the time it arrived, his daughter was no longer able to sit still. She was frustrated, tired, demanding. He just couldn't eat. She was all over the place. It would have been so easy for him to become hard in that moment; to resent her, or to be angry that the food had taken so long to come, or that he couldn't get to eat it even though he was hungry, and probably tired himself. But he maintained his composure and saw what needed to happen. After one or two attempts to have a bite, he had the food packed up, paid the bill with her on his shoulders and pulling on his hair, and left.

I smiled to him as he passed us and we talked briefly about the trials of parenting as I sat there with my girls, old enough now to wait patiently for the food to come, remembering with wistfulness the era when my own mind was finely tuned to "toddler mind" and my choices from moment to moment mainly ruled by their so strong and so rapidly changing needs. That period often feels like it will never end when you are in it. It helps to tell yourself that it is over in the blink of an eye, and that it is worth surrendering to—however trying at times—as a gift to both your child and yourself.

Every age and stage has its own particular dramas. I found it uplifting to watch this father respond so skillfully and so generously with his daughter. It was just a moment. But such moments count. They add up to a childhood, and a life.

*

I (jkz) used to leave work early when I could and go on one-on-one "dates" with my toddlers. I would take them to the playground, or sledding, or for walks along the river, or to hang out in the city center, just watching people and cars and the activity of the world. On the weekend, it was fun to take them with their friends to fairs and farms and lakes. Any occasion with a toddler, even for just a few undivided minutes of play, or wrestling around on the floor, or rolling little cars back and forth, or a ball, is an opportunity for bonding.

The children often did yoga with me on Sunday mornings on the living-room floor, playing at "yoga teacher," where they would guide me in various postures, as we did them side by side. We also did a lot of yoga together, with the children rocking with me as I made my body into a rocking chair, climbing on me or under me when I became a bridge.

As they got older, it became harder sometimes to find ways of sharing moments of concentrated activity and the stillness that comes from them. Even so, we found ways, through playing catch, or sometimes running together, even dancing on rare occasions. The resonances remain; the forms change.

Time

Parents can easily fall into feeling that there is never enough time. We are pressed for it and driven by the lack of it. One morning, I (jkz) heard myself telling one of our daughters when she was about four years old, "Hurry up. I don't have any time," as she was selecting which of three dresses to wear that day. What a message.

There are things we can do to give ourselves more time, and to make the best use of the time that we have. We can wake up early enough and get the children up early enough to have time in the morning without rushing. It can help if they pick out their clothes the night before. We can work at keeping our own time urgency from coloring everything we do. We can do this by remembering to tune in to our breathing and to see that our fears about the future are just thoughts, while the present, what is happening now, is a precious occasion, not to be trampled. We can remember to make eye contact when saying good-bye, to take a moment now and then to hug mindfully.

It is helpful to listen to the tone of our voices as we realize that we are going to be late. As an experiment, we might try lowering our voices and dropping more deeply into right now, into our body, into this breath.

We can also try to not overschedule our children so that they are always going somewhere else. They need down time just to lie around, not watching TV, just being. This kind of "down" time slows time down, and makes room for imaginative play, alone and with friends. Our children need time to be bored, and to find out how to go into boredom and through it, with guidance from us sometimes, and sometimes not.

If we are not aware of the effects of time pressures on the family, we run the risk of living lives of continual acceleration, non-stop doing, and passing that on to our children. This is the trend in our world today. Sometime, somehow, stopping and stillness need to be valued, cultivated, and brought into the home to restore balance and to nurture those aspects of being that are best touched through nondoing.

Many people who have been through the Stress Reduction Clinic say that waking up early and spending time meditating in stillness sets the tone for their whole day, and is worth far more than the same amount of time spent sleeping longer. They are calmer and more intentional in their approach to what they have to do that day, and what they care about. They also observe that other people in the family feel the effects of their meditating. Stress levels in a whole family can be lower when one person is practicing mindfulness.

Sometimes, decisions to opt for more time together rather than for making more money can be extremely healthy for a family. This is a balancing act that always needs to be kept in mind. It is not always possible to do, but sometimes it is more possible than our own mind would have us think. Otherwise, we may wind up, ironically and tragically, missing what may be most important in our lives as we work to "make a living," without examining what this "living" might be.

＊

Ridiculous the waste sad time,
Stretching before and after.

T. S. ELIOT,

"BURNT NORTON," *Four Quartets*

Presence

"Mom, you're not listening!"

Despite my seeming presence, I've been caught with my mind elsewhere. I'm pulled back, only to wander off into creative mental explorations or into obsessive, mostly irrelevant thoughts about future details.

When a child walks in, can we take a moment and really see her and acknowledge her presence? We do that with acquaintances, but we often don't with those closest to us.

The quality of our presence with our children is central to the quality of our relationship with them. As we have seen, presence lies at the heart of mindfulness. To cultivate it requires conscious, sustained effort, attention, a willingness to be authentic, awake, attuned.

When we are authentic with someone, we are being genuine. We are not hiding or pretending. We don't discriminate against certain feelings in ourselves or in our children. But, if we've grown up having to hide our feelings or dissimilate in order to feel safe, being authentic can be extremely scary and difficult. It may be new and unknown territory.

It helps to keep re-minding ourselves—literally to come back to our mind and to our senses. We remind ourselves to come back *into* the present moment, to be aware of how we are feeling. The breath can be our ally in this. Intentionally focusing on the sensations of breathing brings us back into the body. The more we are aware of how we are really feeling in each moment, without judging ourselves, the more we embody authentic presence. The more we live in this way, the more our children will feel it, know it, and embody authentic presence themselves.

Jack and
the Beanstalk

Children want total attention and engagement on the part of adults at key times; at other times they want and can be left to their own devices or with their friends.

For adults, it is hard to give total attention, especially over a sustained period of time. We have drifted from that capacity. Adult minds, as a rule, are filled with conflicting impulses and thoughts, which compete for attention even within ourselves. We have multiple responsibilities. We're very busy. A child may want us to play or to read, and we may do it, but we may do it with only a fraction of our mind, and they sense that easily. Many a time I (jkz) have caught myself reading to one of my children, but thinking about the next telephone call I have to make as soon as the child is asleep. Or reading a story and realizing that I was getting through the story but that I had no idea what it was about. I was thinking universes of thoughts in between each line, if not each word.

Once, when I was so tired I could hardly keep my eyes open, I was telling my daughter a story about a lion, making it up as I went along. But five minutes later, in my tiredness, the lion had become a rabbit. She noticed. We have had many a laugh about that one.

When our son was about four, *Jack in the Beanstalk* was a favorite of his. He wouldn't just let me read it once or twice and then move on to another story. He wanted to hear it over and over again at the same sitting. I loved the story too, but it was hard for me to read it for the seventh or eighth time. Then I realized that he was hearing it each time as if for the first time. The deep theme of the milk running out and having to sell the cow; the tension of hiding from the giant in his castle and observing his covetousness; the challenge of stealing the giant's gold and magic hen and singing harp; the thrill of being chased down the beanstalk, and of getting the ax from his mother just in time to cut it down and destroy the giant—these were real for him every time. His body would tense when the giant came in, and he would smile gleefully as Jack tricked the giant every time.

Seeing the story through his eyes taught me that I, too, could try to be fully present each time I read it, even though part of my adult mind was resisting like crazy. Letting go of that, the story became like a piece of music, repetition of the essence. It is the same each time it is told or read, but it is also never the same. Realizing this expanded my world. *Jack and the Beanstalk* became part of my meditation practice for quite some while, and taught me to be present when I didn't want to be present anymore. Once again, the child becomes the parent's teacher. Fee Fi Fo Fum . . . we lumber about.

Bedtime

It helps to make space in the home for quiet moments, moments when "nothing" is happening. At those times, often just before children go to bed or are in bed waiting for sleep, growth spurts, breakthroughs, creativity, sharing, connecting can emerge. The world has come to a stop. In the quiet, my (mkz) daughter reaches for her sketch pad, sits peacefully, concentrating and creating, completely absorbed in her work. Or, I might read her a simple story that absorbs her imagination, looking into her eyes in moments when the story touches us or makes us smile. Sometimes I just sit with her, and after a time, she may bring up something that happened in school, or something that is bothering her. In the silence of the night, things have a chance to surface.

When our children were little, they nursed to sleep. As they got older, they wanted bottles of warm milk. We sang to them, told them stories, or read to them. As teenagers, some of them still like to be read to. They also listen to music before drifting off to sleep. By bedtime, many different eddies from the day are coming together.

Each child is different. Some children find it easy to fall asleep; for others, the transition to sleep is very difficult. At times we have tried everything possible to make bedtime a peaceful ending to the day, often to no avail. Sometimes, especially when we were tired ourselves, no matter what we did, it was anything but peaceful.

As hard as we both try to protect this time, many things get in our way. Work to be done, phone calls to make arrangements for the next day, more than one child needing us, or children of different ages having different needs, often pulling us in different directions. Older children's needs often get shortchanged, taking a backseat to the younger ones'. It's an ongoing juggling act. Sometimes a peaceful bedtime gets lost in all this. But the nights when I make the physical and psychic space to be fully present and somehow it comes about, sharing a child's concern or feeling her drift into sleep with her head on my chest, I am reminded of how precious this time can be.

*

Now, by the small body of my sleeping son
the hidden river in my chest flows with my son's
and I time my speech to the rhythm of his breath

joining my night with his, singing his night song
as if those waters underground
were secret rivers washing through the soul

bringing out the untold life
which is the stream he'll join in growing old,
in silent hours when his sureness

of his self recedes. There he'll find
the rest between the solid notes
that makes the song worthwhile.

DAVID WHYTE,
FROM "LOOKING BACK AT NIGHT,"
Where Many Rivers Meet

Gathas
and Blessings

Sometimes short poems or sayings are used in meditation retreats or as part of daily practice to remind us of what we already know but so easily forget or take for granted. These poems or sayings are called *gathas* in the Buddhist tradition. There are gathas for waking in the morning, for saying over a meal, for having tea, for remembering to appreciate this in-breath and this out-breath, for almost every occasion in everyday life, all so that we can stay in touch with what is real, and not lose ourselves in thought.

If they are repeated mindlessly, by rote and habit, these verses are virtually of no value. But if they are held, like precious birds, and stroked, and invited to visit, and used judiciously, consciously, they have enormous power. They are very simple, just reminders, but they have a wonderful directional energy. They heal and they soothe. They also point to what we need to remember. Our children learned this little "gatha" in school:

The sun is in my heart
It warms me with its power
And wakens life and love
In bird
And beast
And flower.

The whole class recited it aloud at the beginning of each day in kindergarten and the first few grades of elementary school. The words were accompanied by a series of arm movements that painted a flowing picture: sweeping circle over the head for the sun; the hands tracing lines from over the head back to the heart; palms open to the sky; arms extending out with warmth; to end with the hands being brought back to the chest, closed around each other, and, finally, opening with the life of bird and beast, then forming the petaled cup of a flower.

We very much liked that the children were visiting this little gatha of the heart on a regular basis. We thought it good food for their minds and bodies, and as important, if not more so, as anything else they might be learning. It felt like the daily repetition of this verse was protecting and nurturing something precious in them, reminding them each day of the power and the preciousness of life, and of the central empowering energy of the heart, which we call love. A little morning meditation for the class, to call the heart to awaken and remind the children of interconnectedness . . . sun, heart, life, power, bird, beast, flower, children, love, all one inseparable whole.

We learned many of these gathas from our children. They said one before lunch in school that became our way of moving from the busyness of the day to a moment of silent connection as we sat down to dinner as a family, holding hands around the table:

Earth who gives to us this food,
Sun who makes it ripe and good,
Dear Earth, dear Sun,
By you we live,
Our loving thanks
To you we give.

Then we would keep silent for a moment or two, look at each other around the circle, look at our food and at the whole table set for dinner, and then say, "Blessings on our meal and blessings on our family." If guests were present, and we weren't too shy to do this whole thing, we would say, "Blessings on our guests."

We never said any blessings or grace in my family when I (jkz) was growing up, and I usually felt uncomfortable when I ran into situations in which saying grace was the rule of the house. But as I get older, I understand more and more the importance of intentionally and mindfully blessing what is good so that it doesn't go unnoticed and uncelebrated.

Perhaps that is why I found these gathas of awareness and gratitude so congenial when our children brought them home and taught them to us. They were mindfulness blessings. They seemed so inclusive, so appreciative, so embracing. I like to think that all the years that we said these little verses, and took the time to linger in the feelings they evoked, they were watering seeds within our hearts that continue to flower in our family and in the children, wherever they go. It is good to *know* that the sun is in your heart.

And these gathas may have also planted seeds in the children for loving what is behind the veil of appearance, what great poets know and celebrate so uncannily with words . . .

So great a sweetness flows into the breast
We must laugh and we must sing,
We are blest by every thing,
Every thing we look upon is blest.

WILLIAM BUTLER YEATS,
FROM "A DIALOGUE OF SELF AND SOUL"

PART SEVEN

Choices

Healing Moments

Most of what I (mkz) have learned in my life, I have learned from being a parent. I did *not* learn it in kindergarten. My children are continually teaching me what I need to know, when I need to know it. Over the years I have tried again and again to see things from each child's point of view, and in doing so, often my eyes have been opened to old patterns of relating from my own childhood that were limiting or damaging.

Each time we see and understand something about our own experience as a child, it can act as a guide for us in our parenting. When we sense the presence of something old and destructive, whether it is in the tone of our voice (belittling or minimizing a child's feelings), a look on our face (disdain or contempt), or in our words (e.g., "What's the matter with *you?*" or calling them some kind of hurtful name), we have a precious opportunity to make an important choice. We can choose to continue to go on with our automatic and sometimes cruel behavior, which in some ways may feel familiar and comfortable because we may have grown up with it; or we can stop and try to see more clearly behind our own intense reaction in that moment. We can try, despite ourselves, to see with fresh eyes, to ask, "What am I doing right now? Why am I reacting so strongly in this situation? Where is this going to take me if

I keep going in this direction? What does my child really need from me in this moment? What choices do I have here?"

Clearly it is a lot to ask of ourselves in such moments to consider the possibility of opening our hearts *right there and then*—especially when we are already being carried away by the inner momentum of it all and our own deeply ingrained habits of a lifetime. Is it possible for us to stop ourselves at such times and hold the present moment in awareness, as it is, and observe our impulses without having to automatically act on them?

As our children move through different developmental stages, our own demons from similar periods in our lives can come back to haunt us in particular situations. They can make themselves known with a sudden jolt of recognition, or they may simply be floating around, cloud-like, at the edges of our consciousness. Certain familiar situations can trigger intense reactions on our part that have more to do with us than with our children. The reaction might be a harshness in our response to something a child does; or a pattern of tuning out at particular times; or feelings of discomfort and anxiety.

It can be helpful when one of those disquieting feelings is triggered to pause inwardly, if just for a moment, and listen closely to it. The more upsetting it is, the harder it may be to bring into focus. A clue to how disturbing it really is is how quickly the feeling gets pushed aside. Such moments may be very difficult to capture in awareness at first, especially if our feelings as children weren't accorded much value in our family. We may be used to sweeping them under the proverbial rug.

If we can bring such a feeling back into awareness, it becomes a clue pointing to something deeper. Its significance may not come to us until later, perhaps after repeated experiences that bring up similar feelings. Taking the time to stop, to breathe, to feel, gives us at least a chance to recognize that in some way we are under an old spell, and perhaps to wake from it with a more mindful and imaginative response.

In the moments when we are able to catch ourselves and change course, when we choose to act differently and in a way that is in the best interests of our child, a transformation and a healing take place within ourselves. It becomes a healing moment.

When we choose to honor our children's needs, there is also an honoring of our own unfulfilled childhood needs. When we choose to be kind rather than cruel, we get to experience kindness. It becomes real for us. If we were hit as a child, there is a deep feeling of satisfaction when we choose a better way to resolve conflict when the impulse to hit comes up in us. If we were unprotected as children, when we care for and protect our children, we may find ourselves experiencing feeling safer and more secure as well.

In any moment, we can choose to set aside the armor that has protected us, and ally ourselves with our children, giving them the gift of a more open, compassionate, and understanding parent. In the process, we get a taste of the way it might have been in our own childhood, and more importantly, we get to share the intrinsic freedom and connectedness of this moment not only with our child but with ourself. In choosing to break out of a negative cycle, the magic of a love that is unconditional touches us as well. Each time we are able to do this, we take another step toward wholeness and our own liberation.

*

A young mother recounted the following story:

"I remember a moment of vivid clarity and recognition following the birth of my second child. My parents came over to visit, and my older child was having a hard time and was acting out because the new baby was getting so much attention. I remember my parents reprimanding her, their disapproval, their chiding her to behave better, and I saw clearly in that moment that as long as my children or I were acting nice, or good, we were wonderful in their eyes, but as soon as we started acting human, we were met with judgment. Realizing this, I defended her in their presence. That was a healing moment for me and for her. I was empathic, I was on her side. I didn't betray her. How things 'appeared,' keeping things 'nice,' was not as important as my daughter's well-being in that moment."

Parents and grandparents can betray children with seemingly good intentions. How many moments can you remember when your feelings were dismissed, disregarded, made fun of, belittled, or punished as a child? Each interaction taken by itself may seem trivial and insignificant ("What's the big deal?"; "Why are you so sensitive?"). But they are not insignificant, and when they are repeated over and over again, they can have a devastating effect on the child's self-confidence, self-esteem, and trust.

Such a moment occurred when a mother was driving her nine-year-old son and his friend home from school. The friend was talking non-stop, but her son was uncharacteristically quiet, and occasionally said something back in a grumpy, taciturn way. She reprimanded him for his unfriendliness and reminded him how lucky he was to have his friend coming home with him. After about an hour of playing together, her son completely fell apart, yelling and kicking and crying and she found herself feeling exasperated and angry with him. It was only in thinking about this scene later that she realized that in her own family of origin, being well behaved and polite were of paramount importance. In telling her son how lucky he was in response to his grumpiness, she was basically telling him to stuff his feelings and make his friend feel welcome. She was taking care of the friend's feelings, and her own feelings, but not his.

She realized, too, that she could have done any number of things that would have taken into account her son's feeling state. She could have told his friend that her son was tired and needed some quiet time in the car and for a period when they got home; or she could have shortened the play date and brought his friend home. Instead, she had switched into a mode of behavior that was repeating the old and familiar pattern of denying feelings when those feelings were not "positive," polite, and friendly.

At another time, she had taken her son to visit her mother, who hadn't seen him more than two or three times in his life. The grandmother decided to invite one of her friends over at the same time and proceeded to ignore her nine-year-old grandson and engaged in a lively chat with her friend. Meanwhile, trapped in an environment that had little to interest him, he became bored and restless, and proceeded to run around the room and knock into the furniture. Embarrassed by her inability to control her son's unruly behavior, the mother angrily dragged him out and took him home. She was furious, and admonished him for behaving rudely and not listening to her when she told him to stop. He looked at her with a pleading look and said, "But Mom, Grandma didn't even *talk* to me!"

Suddenly, a veil fell from her eyes and she saw that she had put her son in the same situation she had always been put in when she was a child. No matter how much her mother had ignored her feelings and needs, she was always expected to be polite, friendly, and thoughtful. Here, her mother had not made any effort to reach out to her grandson, to engage him, to think about what would be fun for him; yet when he reacted in a totally normal way for an active, energetic child, he was blamed. Instead of being angry at her mother, she had become angry at her son and replayed the familiar scene of her own childhood. Her son could see that his grandmother was ignoring him, but she had been unable to see it until he pointed it out. Another example of how our children can teach us, if we are open to listening and learning.

In thinking about all this later, the woman said she felt that it would be unrealistic to expect her mother to change, but that the next time they visited, she would bring some things for her son to do, or meet in a park, or insist that her mother come to her house. She also did something that was very important in rebuilding trust. She acknowledged that she was wrong, and apologized to her son for getting angry at him for having a difficult time in a difficult situation. In being able to communicate her understanding and acceptance of his experience, she was strengthening his trust in her and also supporting him in trusting his own feelings. The opposite of this—denying, minimizing, or belittling his feelings— would have been what we like to call "crazymaking" behavior toward her son, making him feel there was something wrong with him for feeling as he did.

No matter how hard we try to be mindful and present, there are inevitably many times when automatic behavior simply takes over. When that happens, our child needs to hear us apologize and acknowledge how hurtful it was, although sometimes apologizing becomes too frequent and too easy. There are times when it may be more helpful to acknowledge what happened silently to ourselves, and inwardly renew our commitment to be more mindful. We can also, if we catch ourselves, stop and say to our child, "Let's begin again," or, "Let's try again," and do it over differently. In this way, we nurture—or begin to heal and rebuild— a trusting, caring relationship.

Becoming aware of limiting or destructive patterns of behavior in our own family as we grew up, of our own experiences of sadness, anger, and alienation as children, is both a painful process and a tremendously useful one. We can use this awareness to help us make wiser choices in our parenting.

Who's the Parent,
Who's the Child?

The demands of the age we live in, its time pressures, economic pressures, and social pressures, all coalesce to rob our children of some of the most precious qualities of childhood. There is a dreaminess to childhood, a moving slowly from one thing to another, that gets torn away under the pressure of time. Children now are prematurely pushed to be independent because the parents need them to be. They are growing up more and more in a physical and emotional vacuum, raised by TV and their peers rather than with the guidance and support of adult men and women.

There is certainly enough anguish in the circumstances that befall families, through age and through disease or accident, not to compound it by creating unnecessary emotional burdens and prisons for those we love out of the automatic habits of a lifetime, and to fulfill our own unmet emotional needs. To bring this domain into greater focus, we might ask ourselves what the unwritten and unspoken emotional rules were in our family of origin.

A friend once described only being visible to her father when she spoke with him about his work, which was in science. Only when she failed her pre-med courses did she realize that she was on a path that wasn't hers, and began to focus full time on her art work, incurring the strong disapproval of her father. The tacit rule was, "I am happy to ap-prove of you as long as you do what I want."

These tacit understandings are different in different families. In some, the parents' emotional needs dominate; in others, emotional needs are ignored completely. Unspoken patterns are set up for the benefit of the people with the most power, usually one or both parents. Appeals based on guilt, shame, devotion, duty, responsibility can all be used to manipulate and coerce children to maintain such tacit patterns, leaving little room for the child to have and express his or her own feelings and needs.

Some parents only know how to feel close and connected through their wounds and their pain. They unconsciously want their children to feel their pain with them and, sometimes, to carry it for them. A subtle entraining may take place between parent and child—wholly beneath the conscious awareness and intention of the parent—in which the child learns to tune in to the emotional needs of the parent, often without anything being said. Rather than the parent being empathic and com-passionate, the child takes on that role and is expected to empathize with the parent's feelings, troubles, and stresses. The child becomes predom-inantly "other-oriented," acting as the parent's confidant, a sympathetic ear. The child's own feelings, needs, desires get buried. The son may be-come a "good boy," the daughter a "good girl," at the expense of their own feelings, their own inner selves. The only other choice they may feel they have in order to hold on to who they are is to do something ex-treme, such as reject their parents completely, get into self-destructive behaviors, run away, or become isolated and remote.

Children have to develop their own sense of self before they can be aware of others in a balanced and healthy way. They need to know how *they* feel, what *they* need, what *they* want. They also need to learn how to communicate appropriately in this domain, and to feel a sympathetic emotional responsiveness from those around them. As we have seen, this is a major responsibility of parents: to actually behave as adults, and respond to and meet the needs of their children.

When this happens, over time children naturally learn to be more aware of other people. They begin to experience what it means to engage in dialogue and have a sense of "the other." They speak, the other listens; the other speaks, they listen. Hopefully, they begin to have direct experiences of reciprocity. Through having their feelings and needs listened to, responded to, and by being able to put their trust in others, they develop the skills needed to have full, reciprocal relationships of their own. In general, this takes some time to develop. For some children, it may be a process, unfolding over many years. For others, it may happen at an early age.

When children feel the latitude and safety to say how they really feel and how they really see things, it is only natural that they will challenge their parents a lot. One of the most frustrating things for us in our family has been our children's skill at certain ages in turning any situation around and making us into the bad guys—making it our fault—making us wrong. Being able to acknowledge their own involvement and responsibility takes children a long time, and a lot of patience on the part of parents.

A man writes to his father about the things that have pained him and troubled him about their relationship. The father writes back, "I forgive you for those terrible letters." He disavows that there might be any truth in what his son wrote. Instead of asking his son to forgive him, he is dispensing forgiveness as if his son had committed a crime by telling him his true feelings. How much less damaging, to say nothing of healing, it would have been if he could have heard his son's pain and felt some compassion for him, even though he was unable to understand it. Then he might have replied, "I feel for you deeply and regret any pain I might have caused you. I am willing to get together if you would like to and try to understand what happened."

*

A woman who turned her back on a "perfect marriage" and came out as a lesbian said: "I didn't want to lose my mother, but my choice was to lose her or to lose myself, and I couldn't do that."

*

Two grown sisters, speaking of their mother: One said, "We don't think of her as our 'real' mother because she doesn't act like a mother. It feels more like we're *her* mother. She is constantly letting us know that we are not doing enough, that we can't love and appreciate her enough."

*

What did your parents expect of you? What were you responsible for emotionally in your family? In what ways were your parents child-oriented? What basic needs were met and in what ways? How much room were you given to act in different ways? Who in the family was responsible for the quality of the relationships? Who had to make things better? Who fed whom?

Sometimes as adults we find ourselves carrying a heavy emotional pack on our backs. This pack holds all sorts of things that may not really belong to us, but that over the years we have been in the habit of carrying—our parents' pain, their expectations, their disappointments, their secrets, their anger, their wounds. Sometimes, even thinking about putting down this load can fill us with such feelings of inadequacy and guilt that we are paralyzed emotionally, unable to make a move. If we put down the burden, we will be a "bad" son or daughter. How could we do that?

When we finally do try to put it down, when we try to step out of a role that was imposed upon us a long time ago and that we have been playing primarily through force of habit, guilt, and fear, when we refuse to play by the old unspoken emotional rules of the family, all hell can break loose.

Disengaging from the old, comfortable familial patterns of relating and moving toward greater emotional independence may be seen as a major betrayal. We may be met with ferocious resistance and criticism. Creating new emotional patterns in our lives takes tremendous courage and persistence.

It's never too late to say, "Enough!", to put down the load we are carrying, and try to create new patterns of relating that are more appropriate and balanced. This process in turn may help us to see more clearly the expectations that we have of our own children, allowing us to free ourselves and them from unnecessary emotional burdens. Everyone becomes lighter, more spacious, more authentic, and emotionally healthier.

So, perhaps it's a good idea from time to time to ask ourselves whether our children are here to meet our needs, or whether it is the other way round. And at what point in their lives do we start acknowledging that they have more and more responsibility to identify and meet their own needs?

Even with grown children, there are times when they need us to give them support, understanding, and to the degree that we can, assistance. If there is a disagreement or a rift between us, it is our responsibility as parents, if we can find the courage to assume it across all the pain and the gulf of time and hurt, to reach out to our grown child, to find ways to heal, to reconnect. It may not be possible in all cases, but a truly open heart can melt a great deal of hurt and anger. We can only try, and perhaps never give up our willingness to reconnect in healthier ways. But sometimes, we have to wait for our children to want to again.

If we didn't get our emotional needs met by our parents, as much work in psychology has shown, we may find it particularly difficult to give to our children or to ourselves, and the cycle may be repeated over and over again, from generation to generation. We have a chance to stop that truly vicious cycle, to turn parents into parents and allow children to be children. It's an ongoing process. We give to our children, and they in turn give to their children.

This requires a degree of selflessness which can be especially difficult if we are feeling grievously wounded and incomplete ourselves. But to be selfless is not necessarily a huge sacrifice, for the irony is that we may come to experience completion, wholeness, and a healing of our own emotional wounds precisely by tending to the needs of our children in appropriate ways.

As our children get older, there will be ways in which they will continue to need our support. And as we age, there will be times when we will need their support. A circle of life, an ongoing giving and receiving, changing over time, can nourish us all.

*

My hands reach down, trembling with anger, reach toward the needy child, but instead of roughly managing her they close gently as a whisper on her body. As though I am somehow physically enlarged, I draw her to me, breathing deeply. The tension drops away. At this moment, I am invested not with my own thin, worn endurance, but with my mother's patience.

This is a gift she has given to me from far away. Her hands have poured it into me. The hours she soothed me and the deep quiet in which I watched her rock, nurse, and comfort my younger brothers and sisters have passed invisibly into me. This gift has lain within me all my life, like a bird in a nest, waiting until the moment my hands need the soft strength of wings.

LOUISE ERDRICH, The Blue Jay's Dance

Family Values

What we value most in our family is a sense of connectedness, of being part of a larger, loving whole that shelters and nourishes us and allows us to be known and accepted for who we really are. This doesn't just magically happen. It takes a certain kind of inner work, and its complementary outer work, to build and maintain such a family culture within the home. The form constantly changes as the family changes in size, as children grow, as we grow and change as parents and as people, and as changes take place in the society that have a profound impact on us. And at some point, the children have to break away from the family culture to create their own.

Every family develops a unique culture, whether it is aware of it or not. The challenge of mindful parenting in part involves bringing the qualities of this family culture into awareness and making conscious choices that reflect and embody our values as parents.

Much has been made of the whole question of "family values." Often this is done in a highly politicized or moralistic framework that holds a narrow view of what constitutes a "good" family. Anything other than the standard two-parent, husband-wife family is considered suspect. It doesn't seem to matter what kinds of parents people are or what kinds of values they hold as much as whether they are in the correct "form."

The word "value" means that which is accorded priority through its worth (worthiness) and its intrinsic strength (valor). What is valued in a family can be seen in its priorities. If the parents' needs are put first in the family, that is one kind of family value. If the children's needs are accorded sovereignty, that is another kind of family value. What we make a priority will set the whole tone for the family culture and its values. So "family values" is not a theoretical concept. It doesn't matter what we think or believe, or what our principles are, if none of it is being actualized in the way we live.

Our individual and collective values speak volumes through how we conduct ourselves in the ordinary, everyday unfolding of our lives. We embody our priorities, whether we like it or not, and whether we know it or not. So it can be very helpful to look into them, to bring awareness to the whole domain of what we are already embodying, in a spirit of inquiry and acceptance, rather than judgment. If we don't feel comfortable with particular aspects of what we see in our own behavior or in our own priorities within the family, perhaps, in the spirit of mindfulness practice and of mindful parenting, we might look at the whole question of what it would take to incrementally establish different priorities that reflect more deeply what we care about. We might ask ourselves, "What *is* most important to us? What *do* we value most as parents? Are there basic principles we can point to that are priorities for our family, that we actually put first in our choices and in our actions?"

In our own family, we value sovereignty, empathy, acceptance, and awareness as fundamental avenues for expressing love and caring. As parents, we try to live in accordance with these values, giving them our highest priority from moment to moment. Out of these come other values, such as respect, truthfulness, responsibility, flexibility, autonomy, and privacy. We value peace and harmony as well, but we don't want them at the expense of what we value more, such as sovereignty, truthfulness, and autonomy. As a result, sometimes our family life is anything but peaceful. We are convinced peace and harmony cannot be imposed, just as values cannot be imposed. They have to be nurtured along, cultivated, drawn out by example and through trust and patience and by the whole atmosphere within the family.

Many families put a premium on outer appearance over everything else. Yelling and screaming are never tolerated. What seems to get highest priority is being "well behaved," looking "presentable," and being "accomplished." It is made very clear that only certain emotions are acceptable.

The inner work of keeping in mind the importance of what lies underneath the world of surface appearances, in the feeling realm, in the domain of the soul—and a willingness to try to communicate honestly and encourage the same in our children—embodies a way of being that recognizes that the inner life of an individual is more important than how that person appears on the surface to the outside world.

The emotional and physical atmosphere the parents create within the family sets the stage on which the ongoing development of a family's values unfolds. The more that mindfulness can be brought to this dimension of family life, the more likely it is that the deep inner values of the family will be held in awareness and accorded priority in parenting decisions.

One aspect of family atmosphere and culture that we value highly is a sense of the home as a haven, a refuge from the bombardment of outside stimuli, a place in which our own values set the tone and can have a tempering, broadening, and deepening effect on what we perceive as the often superficial, frenetic, and materialistic values of the dominant culture.

Family rituals can be an important part of the fabric of this home culture. Rituals create a comforting atmosphere that grounds the family members in space and time, and strengthens the feeling bonds between parents and children and among the children. It is the quality of our intentionality and the consciousness that we bring to them from moment to moment that give family rituals their meaning.

Anything can be made into a family ritual, from waking up the children in the morning, to tying their shoes, to brushing or braiding their hair, to having a bath, to having dinner together as often as possible, to lighting candles at the dinner table, to saying a blessing, or singing a song together, or sitting around the fire in winter, or telling stories before bedtime. All can serve to enrich family life.

It is also important to have some awareness of the physical environment in the home. While this may not be the highest of priorities, when the home is dirty and in chaos, everyone's energy is affected. This goes beyond keeping the house orderly for appearances' sake.

Mindfulness can be directed to reestablishing order in the house in many different ways. The simplest activities, from clearing the table to vacuuming to doing the laundry, can be occasions for moment-to-moment awareness. As children get older, it helps to make organizing and cleaning the house another family ritual so that the work is shared by everyone. The home is made ready for new beginnings.

In our family, we find we both need to take responsibility for an overarching awareness of the family as a whole. The family is nourished by being held in our consciousness and having its needs considered in much the same way that we ponder the needs of our individual children. There are times when the family needs attention. We have to bring everyone together, sometimes for family meetings to name and solve particular problems, sometimes just to tune in to each other and reconnect, sometimes just to have fun. Over time, a collective sense of being part of a larger whole develops in the children as they get older and begin to share in the responsibility for the family's continued well-being. This will take different forms at different ages and even with different children.

We believe that children form their own broader societal values out of the atmosphere and culture of the family and from their expanding interfaces with the world. Just as we cannot impose values of peace and harmony in the family, we cannot inculcate values, such as generosity, compassion, non-harming, equality, and appreciation for diversity through moralizing or coercion. We can advocate for them, however, but ultimately, it is through embodying these values ourselves that our children come to have a direct experience of them and absorb them into their view of themselves and the world.

A positive family culture can provide children with a strong framework for moving out into the world and finding their own way. Our role as parents is to come to know what we most deeply value, and to embody that as best we can in our own lives and in our parenting.

*

"My son had grown up in the outer boroughs of New York City. His father and I having divorced when he was rather young, I felt it was up to me to instill in him the values which I believed were important in life. Among them was respect for all people regardless of their heritage or life circumstance.

"Since his childhood, much had changed in New York City. Many areas, including the neighborhood he now lived in, were inhabited by homeless men and women—sometimes aggressively begging and sometimes more passively sitting or sleeping in doorways.

"One cold winter evening I was eager to meet my twenty-three-year-old son at his apartment to take him out to dinner in his new neighborhood. My visits with him were precious moments to me—all too infrequent as far as I was concerned, but at the frequency that suited him. I knew that it had to be that way in order for him to be successful in establishing his adult life on his own terms.

"As I approached his building, I noticed a woman sitting on the sidewalk, begging, just to the right of the doorway. I felt tension building in my body as I averted my eyes from hers, pretending not to see her as I entered the building. I didn't want any awareness of human suffering to interfere with my intention of spending an evening enjoying the company of my son.

"Soon my son and I were on our way, down the elevator and out the door, to choose from among the wide variety of local restaurants. We would visit with each other that night over a leisurely meal.

"As we stepped out of the doorway of his building, he walked over to the woman sitting on the sidewalk—in the same spot where I had made a concerted effort to avoid seeing her just a short while before. As he gave her the change from his pocket, to my surprise he said to her—in introduction—'this is my mother.' As I looked in her direction I was greeted by a warm open smile—and we acknowledged each other with 'hello.'

"He knew it was O.K. to see her as just another person—in a terrible situation—to whom to be kind.

"I had wanted him to learn to see the common humanity in all people without exception—and so he had. I felt deeply moved as I realized that now he was re-teaching me a value that on that evening I had lost track of. It was a value that I had taught to him so many years before."

Good Consumers
or Healthy Children?

In the overwhelmingly consumer-oriented culture of today, parents can easily be seduced into making decisions and choosing lifestyles in which their babies come to experience the world more through objects than through sustained contact with people. Instead of the huge array of "child-oriented" products enhancing a parent's relationship with a child, the products that are supposed to make parenting easier can easily become a replacement for the essential *human* interactions a child needs so much.

For example, a baby might be carried for a minute and then put in a car seat, then carried from the car in the car seat into the store, then back home, where she may be placed in a crib or a baby seat, and later put into a stroller for a walk. Most of the baby's day could be spent passively contained and touching lifeless objects. The ambient sounds that dominate her world might very well come from the TV or radio. At naptime and bedtime she may again be left alone and untouched.

If the parents are not mindful of the world of experience *from the point of view of the baby,* the child's environment can easily become adult-centered, utilitarian, chaotic, disembodied, and disjointed. Whether the objects the baby touches are made of plastic or natural materials, they are still objects—cold, unmoving, disconnected from the warmth, the stimulation, the responsiveness of a parent's body, soul, and spirit.

When we continually put our children aside while we do something else, relying on objects to hold them and entertain them, winding up the swing, playing a taped story, turning on the TV, we inadvertently encourage them to be passive, powerless recipients rather than active participants in a living, responsive, reciprocal world.

In addition, because of the time pressures that parents are experiencing as we pursue our careers, provide for our family, and try to manage all the different demands being placed on us, our children, at younger and younger ages, are often expected to do more and more for themselves and by themselves.

There is even a style of parenting babies called *self-soothing*, which, according to William and Martha Sears in *The Baby Book*, " . . . emphasizes techniques of teaching babies how to comfort themselves—by leaving them alone or setting them up to devise their own methods— rather than allowing babies to rely on mother or father." They go on to say why this philosophy of parenting is so potentially damaging: "This school of thought ignores a basic principle of infant development: A need that is filled in early infancy goes away; a need that is not filled never completely goes away but recurs later in 'diseases of detachment'— aggression, anger, distancing or withdrawal, and discipline problems."

As a consequence of such trends, with sometimes seemingly minor and innocuous changes in our lifestyles, little by little we run the risk of losing precious interactions with our children, and they, of losing a certain kind of nourishment from us. Rather than getting caught up completely in what is "the best" product to buy, we might bring a degree of mindfulness to how these products will affect our child's experience of the world and her relationship with us.

For instance, we may put an infant in a carriage without giving it any thought. But, if we consider what it might be like for her, we might see that in a carriage, she will be squarely facing out to the world, with no protection from all the stimuli, bodies, noise, and energy that are coming directly toward her. We might also see that, while all these unpredictable stimuli are coming, unfiltered, at this very new being, she is physically removed from what she knows best and from what helps center her in her world—her parents.

As an alternative, we might decide to hold her in our arms, or carry her in a sling or cloth carrier close to the body. Here, she is in the world and yet protected from it at the same time.

When children reach a certain size and weight, carriages are very useful, and by that time, the child is ready for that kind of interface with the world. But for a one- to two-year-old, while a carriage might be useful at times, the child's experience will be far richer if he or she is also worn on the back in a child carrier. In that way, she gets to feel the movement and warmth of her parent's body, and can reach out and touch his face and hair. In this position, people's faces are right at eye level so that she can communicate with them over her parent's shoulder, or lean into his body if feeling shy. All the while, the child's feet ride the foot bar, push against it, moving her whole body up and down, stretching. A sense of security and a whole world of sensory stimulation and responding come just from being carried.

Making these kinds of choices may entail somewhat more work for us in the short run. However, there are wonderful gifts and pleasures that come to us from parenting in this way, that mirror what our children are receiving from us. We are closer, more in touch, and more in tune with them. Feeling them close to us, we also feel more secure. We are less likely to miss a child's subtle communications, whether a smile or a sound, or the light touch of a hand . . . moments of pure pleasure.

Walking my (mkz) dog along a bike path with a friend, we are passed from behind by a woman wearing a Walkman and walking fast, pushing a toddler in a carriage. She passes us and is about ten steps ahead when I hear her say in a loud, commanding voice, "Dog!" Listening to her Walkman, in her own world, her timing is off. By the time she is identifying this "dog" to her child, we are well behind her and the dog is a complete abstraction, out of context, disconnected, disembodied.

*

Products are created to "free us up," so that we can do other things. They are acquired with the expectation that they will make our lives easier or entertain us. But if we are not paying attention, we may overuse them, and find they have become barriers and substitutes for human interaction and presence. They can end up isolating and depriving our children, or overwhelming their nervous systems. We may find ourselves paying many times over for the time that was freed up, when we are faced with children who are acting out because they are hungry for attention, physical contact, and human warmth, or who crave constant stimulation. Children in this needy state are tremendously demanding, as they should be. Repairing the damage is much more difficult and much less satisfying than meeting their needs in the first place.

When our son was in nursery school, his teacher was struck by something that happened one morning. She recounted to us the following story. As the children sat on the floor in a circle, she asked each of them what they liked to hold when they went to sleep at night. Some children mentioned stuffed animals, others, their baby blankets and the like.

When our son's turn came, he looked at her and said simply, without embarrassment, "My mommy."

There are certainly times when objects of convenience are both useful for parents and fun for children. But as parents, we have to keep looking at the whole of our child's daily experience. The key is to find the right balance. We might use a carriage when we need to, and yet make sure there are many other times when we hold or carry our baby or toddler. We might play a story tape in the car, and read or tell stories to our children before they go to bed. Stuffed animals and baby blankets can be wonderfully comforting, but they shouldn't be the only or the main source of comfort in our child's life.

We might ask ourselves, is it healthier for our child to be bonded to objects or to people, to be reaching for blankets and toys when they are distressed or reaching out to human beings? Each object that takes the place of a human interaction has the potential of robbing us and our children. Relationships are built on shared moments. If we're not careful, the child with "everything" may end up being a child with nothing.

Body Madness and
the Yearning for Intimacy

Sometimes, unbeknownst to ourselves, we give our children negative messages about their bodies—not only in what we say, but in the tone of our voice, the look on our face, the tension in our own body. Negative messages about something as basic as one's body can deeply wound a child's self-esteem, and undermine his natural exuberance and feelings of pleasure in his body and in himself.

A friend observed the following scene. In the bathroom of a large department store, as a woman was changing her two-year-old's diaper, she kept saying to him in a very disapproving, disgusted way, "Oh you stink! Oh phew! You smell bad!" Her little boy protested, saying, "No I don't! I don't smell!" Ignoring his response, she continued her negative commentary. At a certain point, the little boy couldn't stand the shaming any more and insisted to his mother: "The kitty did it!"

This little boy had to dissociate himself from his body in order, against great odds, to maintain his positive feelings about himself. The simple act of having his diaper changed had become an act of emotional cruelty and degradation. If he continues to be shamed in this way, how will he view himself and his body as he gets older?

How different it would have been had his mother, looking into the lively and interested face of her two-year-old, been able to recognize and accept her feelings of revulsion, and at the same time empathize with what it must be like for him to have to lie still in that strange and noisy public place while she cleaned off his body and changed his diaper. Working with her own feelings with more awareness, she might have seen that she could feel disgusted by the smell *and* feel empathic toward her son at the same time.

*

In our increasingly touch-deprived society, much of our time is taken up in disembodied, non-interactive activities. As a culture, less and less are we together with others, talking, playing music, singing, dancing, fishing or playing basketball, cards or chess, cooking and eating together. Hugging, snuggling, holding hands, being together in silence, watching logs burning in a fireplace, looking at the stars, listening and being listened to, gazing at our loved ones, are all in danger of being lost to us.

At the same time, true solitariness is also being lost. We are constantly bombarded by noise, people, things, activities, phone calls, mail, and an avalanche of electronic images. We have less nurturing time within the family and with others, and also less nurturing time alone, for silence, for contemplation. Family time is now dominated by television. Even dinner is often eaten in front of the TV or with it on. The home computer and video games can also consume hours of what used to be family time.

Such increasingly ubiquitous and powerful elements of the broader culture continuously threaten to erode family connection and community, and time and space that might be devoted to knowing our inner selves. We are at greater and greater risk of losing our children to the enticing values and images of the peer culture, the mall culture, and the various media.

With violence, alcoholism, drug use, and sexually transmitted diseases on the rise among youth, perhaps we should ask ourselves if addictive behaviors are in some way related to these huge changes in the culture, as well as our society's move toward a more commercialized, object-infatuated, and disconnected style of parenting.

With children experiencing a lack of connection in so many fundamental ways, it is not entirely surprising that there are so many teenage pregnancies and so many teens who turn to drugs, alcohol, and cigarettes to try to achieve a sense of well-being and connectedness. By having their needs met in appropriate ways, at each age and stage within the family, children can develop inner resources and strengths that make them less susceptible to the destructive quick fixes that are so ubiquitous as they get older.

Deprived of intimacy in the family, increasingly younger teens are seeking intimacy in sex. "Intimate" is defined as "pertaining to the inmost character of something; most private or personal; closely acquainted; very familiar; very close." Its use alluding to a sexual relationship is far down the list of meanings, and yet it is frequently what first comes to mind in these times. Rather than having the experience of feeling close emotionally, of being able to ask for a hug, or to be held lovingly, teenagers may feel that sex is the only avenue available to meet their tremendous need for love and closeness.

Adults and children alike swim in a sea of sexual images. They are everywhere: on magazine covers, in newspapers, on billboards, in movies, and on TV. Perhaps the obsession our society seems to have with women's breasts, especially large ones (which are the closest to what breasts look like when filled with milk), is in part a frustrated yearning for nurturance, closeness, and connection, for being fed on the deepest level. Perversely, while it is considered totally normal to be sexually preoccupied with breasts in our culture, it is not okay for toddlers to touch their mothers' breasts in public in a non-sexual, loving way. In some states, anti-nudity laws have been used to prevent women from nursing in public, a flagrant contradiction of the supposed importance of "family values."

With the priorities of our society so skewed, it becomes even more important that children be healthy and balanced within themselves, with a strong positive sense of their bodies and a strong inner sense of who they are. They need to experience themselves as whole human beings, neither disembodied intellects nor sexualized objects. They need huge doses of unconditional love and non-sexual forms of physical closeness within the family.

If children grow up in an environment in which their emotional needs are held in awareness and responded to appropriately, they will gradually come to be more aware of their own feelings, whatever they are, and learn to recognize for themselves what they truly need. When they are better able to identify their own needs and choose healthy ways to fulfill them—whether it is with hugs, or time alone, or a hot bath, or to let out their energy in some kind of sport, or in dancing or listening to music, or to express their feelings in painting or writing or to share them with a close friend or mentor—they are not as vulnerable to the allure of addictive activities. For that allure is nothing more than the false promise that their natural longings for intimacy and connection, an experience of feeling whole, and of belonging, will be satisfied.

Media Madness

We live in a time when things are changing more rapidly than ever before in history. We have more information available to us than ever before; but perhaps much of it is not what we most need. As part of the information revolution, our children now have access to veritable worlds of experience that go far beyond network television, which is mind-numbing enough. We have moved irreversibly into an age of laptop and ever smaller computers of enormous and increasing power and versatility, of the Internet and the World Wide Web, video games, computer games, countless cable channels, videos, movies and more movies. If we're not careful, our children can spend most of their time relating to the world via machines and technology, spending more time inhabiting "other realities" than the one in which they live and breathe.

There's no question that the world we live in is transforming before our very eyes. These technological inventions and those yet to come, both in hardware and software, are making a new world; and by the time they are adults, our children will have to have learned about it and be able to relate effectively to it, whatever that might mean. All the more reason for them to be strong and balanced in body, mind, heart, and spirit, and not lose their connectedness to the real world.

Fully embodied human beings cannot be nurtured through technology, no matter how clever or wholesome, but only through soul time and the nurturance of the human heart by human beings who feel and who care. Technology, overused as electronic baby-sitters when parents are busy, or as a convenience when children are bored, or as a potentially seductive virtual information community, can too easily displace important childhood experiences and face-to-face human interaction and activities.

Parents will be facing increasingly difficult questions that they are ill equipped to answer, as most of us will know so little of the details of this electronic world compared to our children. This world is exploding into ever more complex levels of existence. It is almost as if we are giving our children the assignment to go off to another planet without guidance from the family, trusting that they will be well and that the world they are visiting is benign. This may be just a little naive. Are we to give our children unlimited access to this new world just because it exists? Are we examining and thinking about potential positive and negative aspects? How can we maximize the positive and minimize the negative? We often have far more questions than answers. But the questions and the questioning are very important; they keep us thinking about the effects these technologies are having on our children.

Parents might ask themselves, when children are playing video or computer games, what state are their bodies in? What parts of their bodies are they using? What kind of movements are they making? What images are they absorbing? How much violence is there? What might its cognitive, emotional, and social effects be on children who repeat this process over and over again, and live inside this virtual world? What are the messages they are getting? What are the values that they are absorbing?

As with video games and computers, when children sit in front of a TV, we think it is important for us as their parents to ponder similar questions. Studies have shown that, on the average, a child watches twenty-five thousand hours of television before reaching the age of eighteen, and witnesses more than two hundred thousand acts of violence, including sixteen thousand murders. Preschoolers are now watching twenty-eight hours of television a week. In its *Physician's Guide to Media Violence* (1996), the American Medical Association reports that the amount of time spent in front of a television or video screen is "the single biggest chunk of time in the waking life of an American child." The average family in America has the television set turned on for seven hours each day. Sixty percent of families have the TV set on during mealtimes.

As parents, we need to be mindful of the effects of such exposure on our own children, and to observe carefully the relationship our family has to this dominating force in our society. We need to be asking ourselves questions like, what is happening in our children's bodies and minds as they watch television, and in the aftermath of watching? What messages are they absorbing? How passive are they? Are they in a hypnotic trance or conscious? How many hours do they do this each day, each week? What are they not doing while doing this? Do fights start when the TV goes off? How much cruelty are they witnessing? How is all this affecting their attitudes and behaviors, and views of themselves and of society? Just asking such questions and observing carefully will help us to make choices that might significantly increase the quality of family life and enhance the soul lives of our children.

Similar attention needs to be brought to other avenues through which our children are affected by the media and entertainment industry. What does it mean that children are taken (or go by themselves) to see movies with grotesque, horrific, terrifying images that sear into their minds and their memories, when they have no way to filter them, put them in perspective, or to understand them? It is hard enough for adults to do that with such mind-numbing and frightening images. Some parents bring children as young as one or two into such movies. The sound track alone is an assault on the nervous system, designed to elicit intense physiological reactions. Many of the images in violent movies are unthinkable, and it is unthinkable that children would see such things. It is unthinkable, and yet it has become the norm; and as a culture, we have become inured to it.

Both movies and television can promote tremendous paranoia and distrust. They can make children feel that the world is full of crazy people who are out to get them. In fact, the homicide rate in the United States is at epidemic proportions, two to three times as high as it is in the second-highest-ranked country, and among those perpetrated by people under twenty-four years old, it is almost eight times as high. An overwhelming number of studies have shown that increasing rates of violence of all kinds are directly connected to violence in the media and entertainment industry.

We find we have to keep reminding our children and ourselves that, in spite of this level of violence in our society, it is still a relatively small percentage of people who are violent and dangerous. Our children need to know that even in the most dangerous neighborhoods, there are many people who are good and caring. Helping our children to feel safe and to see the world in a realistic way that allows them to feel hopeful is a difficult, ongoing task. The more violence they witness in the media, the more difficult this task is.

In many homes, the television is on almost all the time. The images that come from the news bombard even very young children daily with all the horrible things that are happening in the world each day. Whether they are actively "watching" the news or not, young people are growing up immersed in a particular, highly skewed, view of reality synthesized out of what corporate network executives decide is "newsworthy." This process tends to focus selectively on the most violent and terrible things that are happening locally and throughout the world. Conversely, huge areas of human generativity and creativity, which are equally or more important and "newsworthy," are virtually ignored.

We feel that, as parents, we need to work at consciously making the home more of an island of sanity and soulfulness for our children in the face of this media onslaught and its values, the rising tide of technology, the commercial exploitation of everything, and the resolution of all human emotion in half-hour TV sitcoms.

It is a lot easier to start out parenting without a TV than it is to regulate its use once you have one. You avoid a lot of struggles when the children are little. More importantly, you are protecting your home from an invasion from a powerful negative force that takes a tremendous amount of energy to control once it is inside. Children can get along fine without a steady diet of cartoons and sitcoms, no matter how engaging or clever. The presence of television dramatically alters the atmosphere in the home. It looms as a constant and seductive offering, against which all other activities children might engage in are measured. In this way, it can subtly or not-so-subtly interfere with their experiencing their own rhythms in the day.

Children are developing greater familiarity with characters on TV than they are with real people, and they get attached to them. Real-life experience gets put on hold, so that they won't have to miss an episode with their TV friends. Many experiences are lost to TV: time spent in imaginative play, in contact with the natural world, playing outside, sports, time for musing and introspection, creative time, time with the family, time spent connecting with and giving to the larger community.

It is possible to provide experiences that are not bound by this two-dimensional world. When our son was five, he had a monarch caterpillar that he put in a jar with some milkweed. He fed it and watched it day after day as it ate the leaves, then miraculously spun itself into a chrysalis, and then, after a long latent period, emerged as a butterfly, which he then set free. It is from such integrated, participatory experiences that children learn about the world. They are also living metaphors that point to the meaning, order, and interconnectedness underlying the world and living things. Such experiences stimulate the imagination and delight children with their magic and mystery.

When we look at our children after they have been engaged in a creative process, such as drawing or painting or singing, or they have been on an inner journey via listening to us read from books that transport and elevate and excite, that create and populate whole worlds in their minds with beautiful language and finely developed characters and relationships—books such as *Ronia the Robber's Daughter, Roll of Thunder Hear My Cry, Huck Finn, The Hobbit,* the *Arthurian Legends,* and fairy tales and myths from different countries and cultures—there is a sense of them being enlivened, their eyes shining, their faces awash with pleasure.

We don't see that look on their faces after they have been watching TV or movies. The process is too passive; no imagination is required. All the images are pre-created for them, many numbing the nervous system in their attempts to keep them engaged. There is no time for mulling, for pauses, to connect the story to other things of meaning in their lives, or to share moments of deep feeling when something touches them.

In the face of the constantly changing and growing technological revolution that we are inescapably in the midst of, and in the face of its multiple effects on the home and on our children, parents have to begin to sit up and pay attention. We will need to examine, as best we can, its positive and negative implications and effects, and create some kind of balance that supports a healthy family environment and the full development of our children. With some children, at certain stages in their lives, this can be a continual struggle, requiring constant negotiation. For instance, regarding television, we may need to think deeply and negotiate seriously around about how much our children are watching, as well as when, what has to be done first before they can watch, which programs they can see and which ones they can't, and plan alternative activities to spark their interest, imagination, and participation.

We have found that getting rid of the television altogether, and the VCR, although a radical step given their ubiquity in American life, is a viable, in fact, a wonderful option. It is not until they are out of the house entirely that their most pervasive and insidious effects on family life can actually be seen in the contrasting peace and creative uses of time which only become options and a way of being in their absence. What is lost in terms of entertainment for both children and parents is more than compensated for by the renaissance in relationships and imagination within the family and in the children that then have a chance to emerge.

✳

This is not
the age of information.
This is *not*
the age of information.

Forget the news,
and the radio,
and the blurred screen.

This is the time
of loaves
and fishes.

People are hungry,
and one good word is bread
for a thousand.

DAVID WHYTE, "LOAVES AND FISHES"

Balance

We are continually seeking balance in our parenting. To a large degree, it is a very personal matter. What feels balanced to us might feel completely unbalanced to you, and vice versa, and what may feel right to you may feel wrong to someone else. Moreover, what may feel right to us now may not feel that way at some other time. It's a continual process, since the balance point keeps changing. Each of us has to work at defining what balance means for us, and creating it from moment to moment for ourselves, for our children, and for the family as a whole, as best we can.

When our children were babies, the struggle for balance took the form of continually tapping our inner and outer resources as we went through a period of intensive giving. With so much energy pouring out, both physically and emotionally, we needed infusions of energy and support from family and friends.

Our infants' inner balance was dependent on our responsiveness to their needs. When they fussed, or cried, or seemed uncomfortable, we responded, and balance was restored sooner or later. When we were dealing with colic, there were times that nothing we did worked; but we kept at it, meaning we continued to work at being present, even in this very trying situation.

When our children became toddlers, balance was maintained with a watchful eye on their movements and providing them with what amounted to guided, healthy choices. When they were having a hard time, we tried to help them to restore balance by being sensitive to the cues they were giving us—whether it was that they were hungry, or tired, or overstimulated. There were times when balance could be restored by giving them a chance to let their energy out in active and noisy play, and times when they needed to be held, soothed, and comforted.

When we sense that our children are out of balance in some way, a thoughtful reexamination of a child's schedule may help. Is there a balance between activity and quiet time? What foods is she eating? How much sleep is he getting? Young children thrive on consistent daily rhythms and rituals; they need plenty of time to do things, and adequate time to make transitions from one thing to another. We need to be aware of this and to make decisions that promote balance in the child's day.

At times, especially with younger children, it is helpful to follow the principle of "less is more." Simplifying their day as much as possible, giving them more of a routine, having some quiet, alone time with them may be just what is required. In the busyness of our scheduled lives, the nurturing, soul-feeding moments can be squeezed out and lost without noticing that this has happened.

Nourishing, restoring moments can take many forms. It may be a quiet, dreamy time in the bath, or playing a game with a child while remembering to be fully present. Or it might be telling a story or singing a song, or doing something together like drawing or baking muffins, or skipping stones on the water. Renewal can come from something as simple as the quiet reassurance of being held in our arms, or in our laps. Putting aside our agendas, we can bring our awareness to the breath, keeping it slow and deep, feeling our child relax, his breath naturally slowing down, finding its rhythm, in harmony with our own.

We can make our mind
   so like still water
That beings gather about us
   that they may see,
It may be, their own images,
   and so live for a moment
With a clearer, perhaps even with
   a fiercer life because of
   our quiet.

SOURCE UNKNOWN, ATTRIBUTED TO W. B. YEATS

Every situation we find ourselves in is different. Each moment is new. What was needed yesterday may not be helpful today. Discovering what our children need involves being sensitive to them, not imposing our will, picking up on their cues and responding intuitively and creatively in each moment. Our own stillness and patience clear the mirror in which such reflections can be seen.

*

School-age children experience their autonomy and their individuality through their friends, their activities, and how they dress. They feel their power as they discover their own unique interests and talents. They need privacy and lots of psychic space, but they still need support and guidance as they move out into the world. They are better able to self-regulate, but at times we may need to help them restore balance by stepping in and setting limits either for them or with them. Finding balance during this time often involves maintaining meaningful connections with them as they strive for freedom and separateness.

Particularly as they enter adolescence, those connections can feel like thin threads compared to what they were when they were younger. Maintaining those threads, seeing that they endure, doing what we can to strengthen them, even if sometimes it means just staying present, is itself a monumental undertaking and at the very heart of being mindful. Those connections grow stronger at certain points only when we are willing to give our children the freedom to discover their own unique selves in spite of our anxieties, reservations, doubts, dislikes, and even our grieving for a more idyllic time now seemingly gone.

At the same time, to maintain some balance, we need to provide limits when appropriate—limits that reflect our values and show our care and concern. The questions of how much freedom, and what is harmful and what is harmless, are ones we continually find ourselves asking as we try to strike the right balance between freedom and limits.

When we sense that a teenager is suffering from a lack of balance, we might first want to encourage him to examine for himself what is working and what is not working in his life, and to find his own creative solutions. At times, however, it may be necessary for us as parents to step in and initiate either major or minor changes. This may take the form of advocating changes in his program at school, finding the right outlets for his energy and creativity outside of school, and ways to connect with the broader community so that he may feel a greater sense of belonging and purpose. To advocate and initiate change in ways that do not diminish our teenager's confidence in his own inner resources takes great skill and attention. We have to be aware of our own impulses to be intrusive, dominating, all-knowing, or patronizing. At other times there will be nothing we can do to make things better.

Parenting older children can feel very lonely and empty at times. It may be hard to maintain our own balance, especially if we are not supported in our efforts by our partner or friends. Even if we are supported, the challenge sometimes requires us to stand "inside" the feelings of the loneliness and the worry, mindfully embracing them in awareness and accepting them without trying to do anything about them at all, except recognize them. Through acceptance and awareness, they may transform into feelings more akin to solitude and not-knowing. These feeling qualities, so different from loneliness and worry, can nourish rather than deplete us in times of difficulty, and sometimes give rise to new openings.

More and more we find ourselves trying to balance out the negative influences of the culture on our family. In doing so, we often have to make decisions that are in conflict with what our children want, and what their peers are allowed to do. School-age children can benefit from consistent but reasonable limits on their exposure to the deadening and destructive aspects of the culture—from malls to movies. Our position may make them angry in the moment, but there is a feeling of security in knowing that your parents care enough about you to stick to an unpopular position based on their values, even if you temporarily "hate" them for it. As adults, we have to be prepared to hold their anger without feeling hurt and angry ourselves and showering it back onto them.

Arriving at such decisions and working to help our children identify alternative activities and outlets for their energies in such moments takes considerable time and effort on our part. It's hard work to find solutions that we can live with and that are not totally depriving or punitive. We are always working in the force field of peer conformity, which sometimes exerts an extremely strong pull on our children. It is important to work with this wherever possible rather than against it; to respect their need to fit in and be accepted and be "like everybody else," and at the same time, to encourage them to find ways to express their own individuality. As they struggle to define themselves, we can provide a reassuring framework that they can bump up against and that helps ground them. Finding the right balance requires us to provide healthy limits, while not being so rigid and restrictive that we create forbidden fruit and, in the process, push our children away.

Some friends told us the following story: Their eleven-year-old daughter was invited to a birthday party at which the children were going to have cake and ice cream and then go out to a movie. Our friends learned that the movie had grotesque scenes with violence and cruelty that they didn't want their daughter to see. A crisis ensued. "But *everyone* is going, why can't I?" The parents felt strongly that they did not want their child to see that movie and took a firm stand. In speaking with some of the other parents, they happened to find one for whom the pickup time at the end of the movie was difficult. Together, they came up with a plan to have both their daughters go to the party, skip the movie, and have an overnight together. This solution satisfied the girls and the parents as well. A happy ending, but only after a lot of work and negotiating.

"All my friends get to watch as much TV as they want!" "Why do we have to eat so healthy?" "Lauren gets to stay up and talk on the phone as long as she wants, why can't I?" "All my friends have their own TVs." It takes a lot of inner strength to stand up to this kind of often relentless pressure. Yet, to allow our children to do all the things they want to do, or to give them all the things they want, to make them "happy," is not always in their best interest.

Possessions are power in our society. A child who feels lost or powerless can easily turn to objects, thinking that they will make him feel better. The development of a child's inner life, his sense of himself and his own unique being, requires something more complex than the latest "cool" sneakers. Helping our children find soul-feeding activities—whether martial arts, dance, sports, playing a musical instrument, backpacking, drawing, fixing or building things, journal writing, singing or rapping, or whatever speaks to who they are—is a needed balance to the quick fixes of our consumer-oriented culture.

In doing this we are challenged to find the right balance between overscheduling our children's lives, giving them too many choices, too many activities, on the one hand, and neglecting our children, not putting in the time and energy needed to help them find outlets for their creativity and their unique gifts, on the other. Overscheduling can be another form of neglect if setting them up with non-stop activities replaces spending time with them ourselves, or contributes to severe imbalance in their lives in other ways.

Some children find their own balance easily, naturally seeking activities that interest them as well as knowing how to take time alone to be quiet and introspective. Other children need a push, sometimes a strong one, to get them to do things, to try new things, to be active at all. Some need help in slowing down, in redirecting their energy into more quiet activities. Assisting children in creating some balance in their lives can take considerable effort, encouragement, and action on our part. To do this without forcing or dominating our children is its own challenge. Out of our own unique experience and out of our willingness to work mindfully with situations that arise, we can find creative ways to help them discover new possibilities for inner balance.

*

Our youngest daughter, at the age of eleven, comes back from an art class with a sketch of a model's face. It looks like a real person in her thirties. It has caught the uniqueness of an individual and uses colors that I (mkz) would never think to use—yellow, blue, olive green—to give form to her face. She has always been very matter-of-fact about her drawing ability, but I can see that she is proud of this particular sketch, and she actually tells me that she feels proud of herself.

Later on I see her looking at it as she walks by. She has gone from the non-thinking mode of pure looking and sketching to seeing the result with more distance. At one point she is troubled that the eyes look so different from each other, and she asks me what I think of them. I tell her that that is what makes it so real, so interesting. People rarely have perfectly symmetrical faces. She seems satisfied. All the storms and disruptions, the struggles and difficulties of the past few days and weeks are swept aside. There is a natural feeling of balance and well-being in her and between us in this moment. Like a plant, she is growing toward the light, expressing her deepest nature.

*

It's late at night when I (mkz) pick up our older daughter from school. Almost fifteen, she's had a full day of classes, rowed hard for crew, and has just been to Boston with her English class to see a play which they have recently read. She wakes up early and is usually tired and grumpy by ten o'clock. Tonight, though, she's full of energy and good spirits. Dark days of emptiness and boredom seem far away. She's fully engaged now—blisters on her hands from rowing, appreciating the quality of the acting she just saw, planning her strategy for getting done what is due the next day, asking my opinion about her course selection for next year.

As we talk about what she wants to do next year, I cherish the feeling of balance in this moment. Having lived through some difficult times with her, I am soaking in this moment in spring, almost midnight, this quiet give-and-take.

*

Another challenging area in which we struggle to strike an appropriate balance is in teaching our children the difference between trusting other people and having a healthy distrust of people under certain circumstances. We encourage our children to trust their own feelings and intuition, as part of trying to see the situation as clearly as possible. This is one way we can begin to teach our children to be discerning.

While childhood is a time of innocence and naïveté, and that innocence needs to be protected and never betrayed, as children get older there is such a thing as being too naive. At appropriate ages and in appropriate ways, we can encourage them to be aware of how other people are behaving toward them. We can model this in our own behavior, letting them know when we see people acting in ways that are disrespectful, deceitful, or strange, or asking them how they felt in certain situations and supporting them in their feelings. Naming behavior as we see it is an important life lesson, and developing a discerning eye to see how others are behaving toward us is a learned skill. In being less naive, our children may be more cautious and wary, even distrusting, in certain situations. This is more than balanced out by the loving relationships they hopefully have with their family and friends, bonds that have been built over time on a foundation of trust, honesty, and acceptance.

*

Mothers particularly struggle to find a balance between nurturing where it is appropriate and necessary, and knowing when to put on what Clarissa Pinkola Estes, in her book *Women Who Run with the Wolves,* calls "the brass brassiere." This includes knowing when to say no as in, "You need to take care of this yourself," or, "I can help you with this later, right now I need to finish what I am doing," or, "I need to lie down for fifteen minutes and then I'll be ready to discuss this with you." It also includes knowing how to clearly convey this message without it being hostile or rejecting. This is a major challenge. So is figuring out when it's appropriate to give support or help, and when it is important for the child to do it himself.

Another challenge is to find ways to take care of ourselves without it being at our child's expense. But, especially when our children are little, we need to extend ourselves as much as possible to give them energy and attention, nurturance and caring. As our children get older, more and more we need to balance the giving, nurturing, available mother with what Estes calls the "moon mother." I picture the moon mother as compassionate and supportive, but providing a spaciousness that is empowering and freeing.

Mothers and fathers both may find themselves conflicted, as they try to balance their need to be engaged in meaningful ways in the world, and supporting the family financially, with their children's needs and desires to have them at home and available for them. It is a continual process of striving for inner and outer balance, of examining our options, of making choices, of observing the effect of our choices on our children, and of making adjustments, fine-tuning as much as we can.

When we ourselves are balanced, we can be child-centered without being child-obsessed. There is a big difference between an ongoing appreciation of our child's unique qualities, and being overinvolved and overinvested. When we feel balanced, we are able to appreciate what is positive without becoming attached to having to have it always be in evidence. We are able to relate to our children from our own strong center, in touch with our own wholeness, connected in our own ways to the world, experiencing our own pleasures and meaningful connections.

We are always amazed and awed whenever we see parents who have been able to transcend the limits of their own childhood and the era and mores of the time in which they were raised, and create—sometimes out of nothing—a different model of parenting. Somehow they have managed to create more balance in their own parenting, to provide softness where there was only hardness, or to provide healthy boundaries where there were none, or are able to give support and encouragement when they themselves were neglected and ignored. Seeing this gives us hope that a new way of parenting is possible, one that is more balanced, and more whole, if we can begin to pay attention and see the choices we really have in each moment.

As parents, we are continually walking the tightrope between freedom and limits, trust and distrust; between activity and stillness; between junk and substance; between connection and separation. It's a worthwhile balancing act, a practice just like any balance pose in yoga, but much more challenging.

PART. EIGHT

Realities

Boys

The elemental exuberance of boys, their endless fascination and won-der at the world, and the thousands of ways this energy expresses itself in play and in times of quiet and stillness, offer countless challenges and opportunities for fathers to reconnect with this same elemental energy in ourselves as we nurture them and provide them with guidance and models as they grow to manhood.

As a father, I revel in a special joy that comes in and from the times I have spent with my son at different ages, encountering the world to-gether and watching him grow day by day as he explored it on his own. His exuberance made everything an adventure.

When he was fascinated with dinosaurs, we would go to the sci-ence museum and stare at the huge *Tyrannosaurus*, so ferocious-looking, first at eye level from the second floor, then from the bottom, looking up. Then we would explore the rest of the museum. When I went out for a run, I would sometimes take him along when he was little, hold-ing the handle of a toy motorcycle as he rode alongside around the big pond where so many people went to run or to walk their dogs. Later, on occasion, we ran together. I loved to read to him in the evenings, or on camping trips we took, and to tell him special stories involving him, which I made up as I went along.

We wrestled a lot, rolling around on the living-room floor grappling like lions until we were exhausted. We did that for years, until he became a wrestler in high school and the risk of an accidental injury to me got significantly higher.

When he was very young, I trained regularly in Zen sword fighting (*Shim Gum Do*—the "Mind Sword" Path) and he would come to the *dojo* with me and watch us work out. Later, I stopped training, but for years he and I would sometimes practice stylized fighting forms with wooden swords, bowing to each other before and after each bout. He had a short sword that he could wield easily. It was exhilarating to block each other's strikes with our swords, to see that we could protect ourselves from scary blows coming from different directions while remaining calm and stable, grounded in the movement, the rhythm, and the sounds of the sticks clashing.

On rare occasions, we clashed in anger, not with swords but when our strong wills pushed or pulled in different directions. Gradually, I learned to control my own fiery temper and make more room for him— lessons I learned with difficulty as I struggled to grow beyond the vestiges of my own childhood. I worked hard at being as present as possible when I was with him. It was made easier because we loved so many of the same things. As he got older, more and more he did things with his friends.

Different boys, according to their temperaments and interests, need different things as they are growing up. One thing they need a lot of is space to grow on their own, and to find things out away from their parents. As a boy growing up on the streets of New York City, I learned incomparable lessons I could never have learned from my parents by spending countless hours in the streets playing ball, or just hanging out, which we developed into a fine art, watching the underbelly of city life.

But I also came home for dinner every night, and learned other things from my parents.

In addition to all their various activities and pursuits, solitary and with their friends, boys have an abiding and overriding need for their fathers, and also their grandfathers and other men, to be present, to care about them, to show interest and share time with them, and to tell them stories and listen to theirs. I sometimes encounter the poignant longing for adult male attention and energy from small boys who do not see their fathers much, if at all, for whatever reasons, when I go into schools or playgroups. I have noticed that for boys who do not live with a man in the house, my presence and proximity is of interest, and they tend to gravitate around me like inner planets hugging a sun. They climb on me or just touch my arm or hold on to my leg. They want to play, or just be close to a man.

Boys need male guidance in exploring their own power and its limits, and in how to use it for their own good and the good of others. Boys need to learn how to know and respect their own strength, and yet not exaggerate it or flaunt it. They need to learn how to listen to the world and know its power and their own limits; how to listen to their own feelings and respect them, and how to express them, to find their voices, and to know the importance of honesty and of keeping one's word. They need to learn how to listen to and respect the feelings of others; and to know the sacredness of life, and its interconnectedness.

These lessons are all picked up by exploration and by example over time, by doing things with them, or spending time together in non-doing, which sometimes looks like fishing, or playing catch, or hanging out in a field, looking at the clouds; not by lectures or sermons. Such lessons take time, and can only come from fully embodied adults, fathers or other men who care and who make it a point to be around.

Is it possible for us as fathers to commit ourselves, inadequate as we may sometimes feel about the task, and hamstrung, even imprisoned by our jobs and by material and professional obligations and attractions, to support our boys in knowing their strength, in finding meaningful expressions for their desire for power and mastery, and also to create an environment where feeling things deeply is not only acceptable but seen as important, and respected? Such an orientation is not fundamentally different from what we believe girls need as well.

The prevalent culture seems quite polarized around the question of how men should be, and this polarization is damaging to fathers and sons alike. One ubiquitous stereotype, premiered in beer commercials, is the tough, macho, beer-drinking, fun-seeking, happy-go-lucky, womanizing, perhaps alienated and misogynistic male. Another stereotype is the sensitive, in-touch-with-his-feelings, considerate, and somewhat wimpy-with-women male. Fathers need to help their sons become aware of and interpret the various subtle and not-so-subtle messages and images the culture puts out, many of them demeaning of women and girls, so that they are less likely to get caught up in such stereotypic images and thinking—and the behaviors that follow from them—and can find their own ways of being.

Many of these images of men and women are products of what Robert Bly calls the "sibling society," a world in which the father is absent physically or spiritually, and where the prevalent role models are synthesized by the media. In this world, there is precious little mentoring by elders and initiation into adulthood and into the collective knowledge and wisdom of those who came before. It is a world in which the past is rejected and condemned without even being known. Deep mutual alienation leads to the young attempting to raise and socialize themselves. Much of the dominant culture has an exploitative and predatory feel to it, even as progress is being made to protect the rights of children and women.

We have to ask ourselves what a boy (or a girl) will need in order to survive (for it *is* a matter of survival, survival of the soul, as well as of the body) and to live wisely in this world that is emerging at the turn of the millennium. In the absence of a culture that honors and values children and takes some collective responsibility for their spiritual growth and their entry into the world of adults, parents are going to have to do yeoman's and yeowoman's work to guide their children.

As fathers, we need to be strong ourselves—and wise, and present. We may have to look deeply into our very cells and genes in order to find our human strength and our own sovereign nature, and what is best of our lineage, whether Native American, African, Asian, European, Christian, Jewish, Muslim, Buddhist, Hindu, "none of the above," or "other." The alternative is a living death for ourselves and for our children, the death of not knowing who we are, and perhaps not caring, the death of having no "people," no community in which we are known and have a place.

Boys need the presence of competent, embodied men in their lives, men who *do* know who they are and are not afraid of or numb to how they feel, men who are empathic and accepting, playful, wild and soulful, who are not enslaved by their work, and don't fear or hate women. The presence of a strong, empathic man in the role of father, grandfather, or mentor is always important for young boys, but it is needed more and more as boys move into adolescence. The transition from boy to man requires a vision, a new way of seeing, and a new way of being in the body.

Boys need elders, and rituals led by elders, to help them make this transition. They hunger for the close proximity of their fathers and of other trustworthy men they can respect as guides and role models. Boys have a deep need to feel loved and valued by men and to understand how these men see the world, so that they will be able touch their creative energies and learn to channel and use their own power wisely. They need to come to appreciate mystery and the unknown, including other people and customs, and not be swept up in a tribal mentality that makes absolute distinctions between "us" and "them," and then, out of fear and prejudice, plunges into war and violence to vanquish "the other," not realizing that "them is us."

*

Boys receive essential sustenance from a loving, nurturing relationship with their mothers. Being held in the aura of a mother's love, without being controlled or having to take care of her emotional needs, creates a foundation of inner security and emotional grounding needed for the separations and adventures into the world that have to come as the boy gets older. But they need fathers from their earliest moments as well, as do girls. And the fathers need their sons. If we are not present at key moments in our sons' lives, we will not know them. If we see them born, hold them constantly when they are little, dream dreams with them as they sleep on our shoulders, walk with them in the world and speak with them of what they see, offer them tools to work with and projects to bend their arms and their minds to, get down on the floor with them and play and invent games, watch the sun go down and the rain fall, dig in the mud and build castles at the beach, throw rocks in the water and carve sticks, climb mountains and sit by waterfalls, mess around in rowboats and canoes, sing songs, get together in groups, watch them sleeping and wake them gently—then our souls will know their souls; our spirits will know their spirits.

Fathers and sons can help each other grow and find beauty and meaning. And as the sons grow, they will find other sons who share their passions, and form friendships that endure and that are based on getting high on life. Music and drumming, wilderness and woods and fields, city life, sports, literature and the arts, all beckon, through periods of light and darkness, offering worlds of meaning and value, serving as mirrors in which boys and men can see themselves and continue growing, living their moments fully, trusting their own power, grounded in their bodies, and becoming full, planetary adults as they participate in the mysteries of generativity and the generations, and of finding their own paths and their own places in the world.

*

"When they were four or five we would go over to Bald Mountain on foot and we could look back and see our place. When they were seven and eight, we went up to Grouse Ridge on foot and we could look down from Grouse Ridge and see Bald Mountain from which you can see our place. A few years later we went on up to the High Sierra and got up on 8,000 foot English Mountain from which you can see Grouse Ridge. And then we went on over to Castle Peak which is the highest peak in that range which is 10,000 feet high and climbed that and you can see English Mountain from there. Then we went on north and we climbed Sierra Buttes and Mount Lassen—Mount Lassen is the farthest we've been out now. So from Mount Lassen, you can see Castle Peak, you can see English Peak, you can see Grouse Ridge, you can see Bald Mountain and you can see our place. That is the way the world should be learned. It's an intense geography that is never far removed from your body."

GARY SNYDER

Pond Hockey

When the temperature rises for a day or two and then freezes again without a snowstorm, the winter ponds in New England beckon for a good game of ice hockey. At times like these, if it was on the weekend or over vacation, my son and I (jkz) would put on layers of warm clothing, grab our sticks and pucks and skates, and head down to the pond below the hill. There we would don our skates, struggling with the long laces with freezing fingers until they were pulled tight enough; waddle over the remaining feet of snow; and touch new freedom at the ice edge.

We would skate around for a while, inspecting the ice all over the pond, adjusting to the feeling of being on skates once again. Then we would carefully select a spot and set up a goal with a pair of boots a few feet apart.

We played one on one . . . one of us defending the goal while the other tried to come at it with the puck. The defender had broad latitude to come out of the goal and try to take the puck away from his opponent, so there was lots of fast skating all over the pond, clashing of sticks, racing to get to the puck first. There were fakes and lots of shooting, chases, and bumps, as we maneuvered around each other with exhilarating swiftness and laughter. And of course, there was lots of scoring, and the sheer joy of sensing the puck sail past the defender and through the boots, sometimes on highly improbable trajectories that made us laugh.

As we played, we generated heat. No matter how cold the day, how biting the wind, after a time the hats would come off, and the gloves, then the coats and sweaters. Sometimes we would be down to just shirts on top. As long as we kept skating, we stayed warm. We played for hours. There was never a time that wasn't the best time. Every time was just now, beyond thought, caught up in the joy of sharing what always felt like a particularly male energy in going up against each other time and time again, coming in with the puck, chasing one other, blocking shots, protecting the goal.

Sometimes we played at night, in the orange gloom of one tall floodlight put up by the town, hardly able to see the puck in the shadows. But most of the time, we played in the afternoon, on and on, as the winter sun moved toward its early exit. At times, we had to stop and catch our breath. Lying on our coats spread-open on the snow at the edge of the pond watching the clouds against the deep blue of the sky, or the strands of pinks and golds beginning to show themselves in the west, our breath visible in the air above us, we would revel in silence and perfection.

I would like to say we did this every weekend for years and years, but we didn't, and those days now seem long past. And I would like to say that my girls and I had similar feelings when we played pond hockey, and we did on rare occasions. The girls were drawn to other things. They loved to skate, and skated better than we did, but they lacked interest in the game of stick, puck, goal, and pursuit.

Most of the time, the pond was covered with snow or rough ice and was unskatable. Some winters, it wasn't frozen enough when we wanted it to be. And we had other things calling us as well, and other chances to be together. But none was ever better than playing hockey on the winter pond.

Wilderness
Camping

As much as we can, we have tried to take time with our children individually, one parent alone with one child, rather than always doing things together as an entire family. Children need a dose of full attention from a parent from time to time, and to do special things that are their unique undertakings, without having to compete with siblings or the other parent. Such outings are special adventures, whether they last a few hours or a few days, whether in the wilderness or in the city, whether we are alone together or at some special event with lots of other people. They afford new opportunities for closeness and seeing each other in a new light.

＊

One of the things I (jkz) have most enjoyed doing with my children is to take them camping in the wilderness, one on one. In a day or two, we have experiences that can give new shape to our relationship, and memories that can last a lifetime. There is nothing like being in the wilderness for a few days to remind us of what is important, and to get down to the basics of living, and staying alive.

I took one of my daughters when she was nine years old to the Wild

River in the White Mountains. We parked at the head of a trail and walked along the river for about five miles. She was missing her mom from the start. The stultifying heat didn't make our going any easier. At a certain point, in response to her unhappiness, I suggested we get into our bathing suits and soak in the river to cool down. She loved being in the cool river in the heat, but she still cried a good deal as we walked on. I carried her pack as well as mine. She alternated between wanting to be home, wanting to be where we were going, and not knowing what she wanted . . . just feeling horrible.

At one magical point, we ran into a train of llamas going the other way. That added an exotic touch to our adventure, if only briefly.

It was the usual story. We had to keep going so that we would get to the place I had planned to make camp before the sun went down behind the mountains. Of course, she didn't understand that, and didn't see why one place wasn't as good as another. But I had a special place in mind, a large flat place perfect for pitching the tent, and close to a small waterfall, which I knew would delight her.

With much crying and missing her mother, she walked along, while I tried to maintain my composure, struggling with feeling inadequate, worrying that maybe this was going to be a disaster, feeling like a failure for not being able to allay her fears or "make" her happy.

Finally, we got to the place I had in mind, a place I had passed through with her brother several years before on one of our adventures that had taken us over South Baldface and down into this valley. The shadows were already long. As soon as we arrived, her mood changed. She enjoyed pitching camp, setting up the tent, stowing our sleeping gear, getting a fire going, and cooking dinner. The little waterfall was our companion, singing to us as we worked and cooked and ate sitting on logs by the fire. The sky was full of stars as you never see them in or near the city, their shimmering light filtering down on our heads through the dark openings in the treetops surrounding our cozy clearing.

We got into our sleeping bags early, and fell asleep to the singing of the river. She fell asleep first. I lay on my back looking out at the sky, breathing with my whole body, so happy to be with my daughter, listening to her breathing, feeling the joy of adventuring together.

We awoke to a crisp blue morning light, the mountaintops just turning golden. We got warm, had breakfast, and sat around the fire, making plans for the day. My idea was to hike to the top of the ridge. But that was not her idea at all. She wanted to stay put. She had no interest in going to the top of anything, view or no view. She didn't want to walk, hike or climb, especially with a pack. She had her home now. So stay put we did, as I stowed away my own strong expectations and desires, realizing she had to choose her own way.

We explored along the river, and when it got warmer and the sunlight descended into the valley, we explored *in* the river. Noon time found us sitting on a high rock with the river streaming around us on all sides, boiling and roaring. There, I read *Ronia the Robber's Daughter* to her, Astrid Lindgren's wonderful story of a strong girl in olden days living in the forest with her young friend, Birk, as they try to sort out the craziness of their feuding families' lives. It was good to be in the woods together, alone, far from civilization. We could be happy with very little: sun, water, forest, each other, this moment.

Softball Breaks
Through the Gloom

Sunday of a three-day weekend—the start of school vacation week. I (jkz) have been away so much of late that when I'm home, I feel like a stranger. Myla and the girls develop their own rhythms in my absence. To reconnect, I sometimes ask dumb questions, like "What are you talking about?" when they are speaking together.

They don't like this. It feels intrusive. I stand in the doorway to my daughter's room while Myla is having a conversation with her. I'm seeking closeness, but it feels off to them, like I'm waiting for something to happen, filled with unvoiced expectations. In such moments, I feel like a stranger in my own home.

My practice in such moments is to be present without imposing myself and my needs. It is not easy. In fact, it's quite a struggle. Just being present, doing what I need to do, but not succumbing to resentment or isolating myself further by leaving the breakfast table early, or working, or being on the phone, these are my challenges. If I do these things, it feels like I'm still traveling, fundamentally away, even though my body is around.

✳

The morning was gloomy with low clouds, a mid-April chill, communications with distant family, and the need to catch up on work. But rather than isolate myself in my study, I came in and out of the kitchen, making sure that I was around and not giving in to the impulse to pick up the Sunday paper.

Trying to get my daughter out of the house is not easy, but I try again today, in the late afternoon. At this age (eleven), she usually rejects anything I propose we do together. But her softball coach had called a few days earlier and told her she should play catch to prepare for the team's first practice. After dinner, she agrees to play in the backyard with me. We go outside. The setting sun is shining now beneath the clouds which have kept the day gray and gloomy, matching my mood. Now low evening light from the west floods the side yard, setting everything aglow.

We start throwing the ball back and forth. At first, we can't find a left-handed glove for her, so she throws rightie, claiming to be ambidextrous. And she is. She can throw accurately with her right arm and catch beautifully with her left hand. We play with intensity, the ball rocketing back and forth. I direct my throws first to one side of her, then to the other, so she will have to backhand a fair number of balls. Then we expand to include pop-ups and low line drives, mixing up everything.

She catches about 90 percent of everything I throw, this after a year of not playing at all. We are in synch. I can feel her enjoyment of this, and her recognition of her own grace and mastery. She is good, a natural. But I know she should have the one left-handed glove we have somewhere. We take a break and I look for it in the one place I haven't looked yet, and find it.

Now her catching is shakier for a time, as she adjusts to the new glove and the opposite positioning. But her throwing, competent with her right arm, is three times more powerful and accurate with her left. Back and forth, back and forth, high, low, catching backhand, catching on the open side. I haven't done this in ages. I am fast revisiting ancient rhythms from my own childhood. The pattern hasn't entirely disappeared in forty years. It amazes me that the glove knows where the ball is so much of the time.

She is warming to this. Her cheeks turn red. She is fine in the chill air without a coat. She is also warming to me. I feel it. Finally, finally, we are doing something together out of doors that involves some exertion, something we can both enjoy and talk easily around.

I have waited months for such a moment. I have invited her to bike ride together. "No." To rollerblade. "No." To go for a walk. "Are you *crazy?*" To drive someplace nice and sit by a pond. "No way." Yet right now, it is happening, and I feel that the effects of my having been absent are being washed away. Right now we are truly together, doing something that is rare for us and that we can come back to all spring if she likes. Now that we are on Daylight Saving time, we can play after I come home from work.

We are also rediscovering that it is still possible for us to have fun together. I feel her strength as the ball goes back and forth, and see her experiencing her own strength in the most natural of ways. I am enjoying this playing catch immensely, and can feel the same from her. And the enjoyment is richer for bringing father and daughter back to closeness. We dwell so much apart, and in such different worlds, that we can become estranged from each other. But here is at least one way, at least in this moment, where we are being shown that we are still deeply connected, and can enjoy doing something together. As we throw the ball back and forth and listen to the thud in the gloves, and the sharp crack when it goes over my head and hits the wooden fence behind me, it feels as if we've been doing this forever. Time falls away.

I am careful not to find ways to stop or interrupt these moments for anything. I know they will not last. The light is fading. She is expecting a phone call from her friend about when the friend and her mom will be coming by to pick her up for a sleepover. The phone call comes. She must get ready. But we have met once again, she and I, and that counts for a lot with both of us.

Afterward, we sit around waiting for the doorbell to ring. We are alone in the house. Out of the blue, she offers (this never happens, I can hardly believe that it is happening now) to tell me how she made the larger-than-life sketch of herself in her art class. She explains that the exercise was to do the whole thing without lifting the pencil from the paper, looking in the mirror and only rarely at the drawing. I could have asked her a hundred probing questions and never gotten her to talk about something like this. She doesn't answer probing questions. But she does respond to presence. I see that it is my job to know this and to be accessible, even when it seems like there are light-years between us.

Girls

When our girls were little, I (mkz) took great pleasure in the wide variety of qualities that surfaced in them at different times. They showed enthusiasm and delight in the simplest of activities: picking strawberries and carefully tasting each ripe berry before putting it into their basket; dressing up in old clothes of mine and remnants of cloth, and transforming themselves into queens and princesses; pretending to be baby dolphins, as they swam around me in the ocean. When they saw deeply into things and shared a sudden insight with me, or showed kindness or compassion in some way, I would delight in those wondrous and warmhearted aspects of their being. There were also times when they were fierce, angry, and completely unmovable. Even as I felt thwarted by their indomitable wills, I would find myself cherishing their strength, their power, their one-pointedness.

In those years, both home and school were, for the most part, havens from the broader culture. Their world was simple, with few pressures, expectations, or external distractions. As they got older, of course, things changed. Slowly I became more and more aware of the numerous messages they were getting from the prevailing culture—messages that were ubiquitous and limiting, and that put all sorts of expectations and pressures on them just because they were girls.

*

Everywhere girls turn, at every checkout counter, in newspapers, magazines, TV, and movies, they are met with sexualized images of women that can deeply affect how they view themselves. These images subtly or not-so-subtly suggest that the greatest power they have is as sexual objects. This message is tremendously limiting and damaging to girls, particularly as they approach adolescence.

Such images are used to sell all manner of products. Not only is the focus constantly on buying and consuming, whole industries are devoted to convincing women and girls that they need to make their bodies more beautiful and more "perfect." Yet most of the images are of bodies that few women naturally have, or only have for a brief time. This "ideal" look, synthesized by the advertising world, can foster in girls a strong dissatisfaction with their own bodies, their hair, their clothes, their skin—virtually every aspect of their physical being.

Appearance is accorded supreme importance. The focus is on cultivating a look, on sculpting a surface. As a result, many girls spend an inordinate amount of time and energy preoccupied with how they look, or don't look. This often happens at the expense of honoring and developing their physical prowess and strength, their creativity, and their inner selves. Parents face a constant struggle to provide an authentic, supportive, balanced view of being a girl or young woman in the face of this very alluring, ever present, enticing media barrage. As difficult as this may be, there are some things we can do.

We might start by becoming aware of the pervasive influence of this industry, so that it is not missed entirely, or taken for granted as an inevitable part of the cultural landscape. Awareness is a first step. Once we start to pay attention to potentially negative influences on our girls, we can begin to see the effects they may be having on their self-image, their self-esteem, their interests and goals. Rather than just continually trying to repair damage that is already done, we can try to prevent damage by limiting their exposure and consumption. We can also discuss with them what we are seeing, in a hopefully non-heavy-handed way so that they can see what lies behind these images of women. They can begin to be aware of the implicit messages and how the desire for buying is fueled in the minds of viewers, readers, and consumers.

A girl who grows up watching all there is to see on television is going to be saturated with many more narrow and demeaning images of women than a girl whose exposure to the media is more limited. Limiting exposure has the added benefit of freeing up time and space for real-life experiences, which hopefully will broaden her view of herself as a whole person with valuable strengths and skills, and many unique qualities. Girls often have such experiences playing sports or engaged in activities or projects, whether artistic, intellectual, or community-oriented, that challenge and develop their creative powers.

At the same time that we try to create some sanctuary from the culture and encourage an awareness of the power of the media, we of necessity have to balance our restrictions and even the expression of our views, or we may end up creating a gulf between ourselves and our children. After all, they are drawn not only by the surface allure of this world of advertising, TV, movies, and music videos, but also by its artistic and entrepreneurial creativity.

This is one reason why mindful parenting is so difficult. As parents, we have to continually work with our fears, our own limitations, our own feelings of powerlessness at times, as we strive to provide some degree of balance in the lives of our children. The fine line we try to walk in our family is to protect and limit at the same time that we stay open and flexible. As the girls get older, this involves more and more negotiation and compromise, and, ultimately, encouraging them to make their own choices thoughtfully.

Children want so much to feel "normal" in what they can do and see, and they compare themselves, naturally enough, to what their friends are allowed to do and watch, and how they behave. What is considered "normal" in our society is often violent, cruel, and much of the time, demeaning to women. It is so ever present that we can become inured to it and hardly see it at all. In the face of this deluge of imagery—which continually connects sex to violence, objectifies girls, and virtually ignores or makes invisible older women, large women, strong women, dark-skinned women, women who don't fit in with the classic, light-skinned, vulnerable, thin-bodied ideal that "sells"—anger would be an appropriate response. But of course women are not supposed to get angry. When we do, we are labeled all sorts of unpleasant and degrading things. We are met with: "What's the matter with *you*?" or, "Why do you take things so seriously?" or, "Where's your sense of humor?" or, "Is it *that* time of the month?"

In parenting girls, we have to continually counter this narrow view of women. When we silently accept the dominant view, we are basically colluding in our society's denigration of women. We have to find and use our own voices as women and as mothers if we are to support our girls so that they don't lose theirs. As their mothers, we need to embody an alternative for them, a different way of being, a different way of viewing the culture they live in. Our girls truly need us as their allies in a culture where their way of seeing things—and what may be most important to them—is often not valued or even acknowledged.

As our daughters experience all the different and sometimes difficult physical and emotional transformations of pre-adolescence through the teen years, fathers need to be particularly mindful of unconscious or habitual ways they may have of relating to women that might influence how they relate to their daughters. This may take the form of being disrespectful or flirtatious, or continually putting their own needs first. A father's need to be loved and adored by his daughter can keep him from seeing what it is that she really needs from him.

Concerned for the well-being of our girls in a culture such as ours, we both feel we have to be fiercely protective of their strengths, their aliveness, and sense of who they are. At the same time, we also have to examine how our own expectations might unwittingly limit their range of expression and their autonomy. We have to ask ourselves, over and over again, are we attached to their being a certain way? Do our girls have to be nice, thoughtful, sensitive, kind, quiet? Do we expect them to smile a lot? Are we taking into account their temperaments, at the same time that we are open to changes in them? Has a sanguine, shy daughter become a fiery, energetic, outgoing, vocal teenager? Do we allow our girls to be angry, to be loud, to be obnoxious in the ways we sometimes *expect* boys to be? Do we allow them their own interests, whether it's quantum mechanics, engineering, clothes, or movie stars? Are we supporting them in finding ways to express their unique abilities, creativity, and strengths?

Our responses to these questions and others like them might change from day to day, or even from moment to moment. But asking them is an essential part of our own work as parents.

A large part of this process is working with other people's expectations of our girls. When we or our daughters become aware of messages that feel inappropriate or limiting or denigrating on the part of an authority figure or their peers, including sexual harassment or sexual stereotyping, we can help them identify and name the troubling attitude or behavior, and support them in their feelings. By doing so, rather than minimizing the problem or denying the validity of their feelings, we are letting them know we are their allies and that when they are unjustly treated or subtly demeaned, feeling angry or hurt is not only okay but a healthy response.

Too often, they are made to feel that it is *their* problem and that there is something the matter with *them* for having the feelings they do. We can support them in learning how to stand up for themselves and speak assertively, giving clear and confident messages that define their boundaries and name unacceptable behaviors on the part of others.

*

To keep my mouth shut. To turn away my face. To walk back down the aisle. To slap the bishop back when he slapped me during Confirmation. To hold the word *no* in my mouth like a gold coin, something valued, something possible. To teach the *no* to our daughters. To value their *no* more than their compliant yes. To celebrate *no.* To grasp the word *no* in your fist and refuse to give it up. To support the boy who says *no* to violence, the girl who will not be violated, the woman who says *no, no, I will not.* To love the *no,* to cherish the *no* which is so often our first word. *No*—the means to transformation.

LOUISE ERDRICH, *The Blue Jay's Dance*

*

When one of my daughters was eleven, for months she related incidents to me in which she felt her teacher was being disrespectful to her or her classmates. One day she told me the following story. She was talking and laughing exuberantly with her friends at an evening school event when her teacher came up to her, called her by name, and said in a chiding voice, "Be a *lady!*" She told me that she looked her teacher straight in the eye and said, "I *am* being a lady, just a *strong* one!"

✻

Through the experience of having their feelings validated, slowly, over time, girls are better able to see and name attitudes and behaviors that are troubling to them. They can learn to be more readily in touch with what they are feeling, to trust those feelings, and to express them effectively. In this way, they learn to empower themselves and build a repertoire of emotional competencies that will be critical to their further development. Such strengths will be particularly important when they are living on their own in a society that can be deeply disempowering, predatory, and exploitative.

✻

I was in a small store that sells Oriental rugs with my then eleven-year-old daughter. The storekeeper was from another country, and related to us with an exaggerated smile on his face. It made me uneasy, but I quickly proceeded with the business at hand, which was to look at a few rugs. When we got outside, my daughter told me that she felt really uncomfortable because whenever I looked away from him, she noticed he was looking at her in a "weird" way. I made some comment to her about cultural differences. Later, I realized how inadequate my response was and how my focus had been to explain away and excuse his behavior rather than validate her feelings of discomfort.

That evening, as I was saying good-night, I told her that I had been thinking about what happened in the store, and that I didn't want something like that to happen again without our having a signal we could use so that she could let me know when something was making her un-comfortable. I suggested that if it happened again, she take my hand and give it a squeeze, and I would know that something wasn't right and we should leave right away. Her eyes lit up and she smiled as she thought about this.

✶

At a certain point, one of my daughters became enamored of a female rap group called Salt N Pepa. At first listening, I was taken aback at how overtly sexual the lyrics were. As I listened more, I heard women who were unapologetically strong, self-assured, sassy, *and* sexual. Their energy felt healthy and life-affirming, the antithesis of weak, passive, afraid, vic-timized. Behind the label of "rap group" were modern-day Amazons, and in their own unique way, unexpected role models.

More and more we have to work to ensure that our daughters stay in touch with what is strongest and most vital in themselves, and are not—as so often happens between the ages of nine and fourteen—socialized to surrender their voices and their sovereignty, submerging what is best in themselves. In the following chapter, we share with you a Norwegian tale about a girl who remains true to her own nature.

Tatterhood—
"I Will Go As I Am"

Once upon a time there was a king and queen who had no children, and this grieved the queen very much. She was always bewailing their lack of a family and saying how lonesome it was in the palace with no young ones about.

The king remarked that if it were young ones she wanted running about, they could invite the children of their kinswoman to stay with them. The queen thought this a good idea, and soon she had two little nieces romping through the rooms and playing in the palace courtyard.

One day as the queen watched fondly from the window, she saw her two lassies playing ball with a stranger, a little girl clad in tattered clothes. The queen hurried down the stairs.

"Little girl," said the queen sharply, "this is the palace courtyard. You cannot play in here!"

"We asked her in to play with us," cried the lassies, and they ran over to the ragged little girl and took her by the hand.

"You would not chase me away if you knew the powers my mother has," said the strange little girl.

"Who is your mother?" asked the queen, "and what powers does she have?"

The child pointed to a woman selling eggs in the marketplace outside the palace gates. "If she wants to, my mother can tell people how to have children when all else has failed."

Now this caught the queen's interest at once. She said, "Tell your mother I wish to speak to her in the palace."

The little girl ran out to the marketplace, and it was not long before a tall, strong market woman strode into the queen's sitting room.

"Your daughter says you have powers, and that you could tell me how I may have children of my own," said the queen.

"The queen should not listen to a child's chatter," answered the woman.

"Sit down," said the queen, and she ordered fine food and drinks to be served. Then she told the egg woman she wanted children of her own more than anything in the world. The woman finished her ale, then said cautiously that perhaps she did know a spell it would do no harm to try.

"Tonight I want you to put your bed out on the grass. After it is dark, have two pails of water brought to you. In each of them you must wash yourself, and afterward, pour away the water under the bed. When you awake in the morning, two flowers will have sprung up, one fair and one rare. The fair one you must eat, but the rare one you must let stand. Mind you, don't forget that."

The queen followed this advice, and the next morning under the bed stood two flowers. One was green and oddly shaped; the other was pink and fragrant. The pink flower she ate at once. It tasted so sweet that she promptly ate the other one as well, saying to herself, "I don't think it can help or hurt either way!"

Not long afterward the queen realized she was with child and some time later she had the birthing. First was born a girl who had a wooden spoon in her hand and rode upon a goat. A queer-looking little creature she was, and the moment she came into the world, she bawled out, "Mamma!"

"If I'm your mamma," said the queen, "God give me grace to mend my ways!"

"Oh, don't be sorry," said the girl, riding about on the goat, "the next one born will be much fairer-looking." And so it was. The second twin was born fair and sweet, which pleased the queen very much.

The twin sisters were as different as they could be, but they grew up to be very fond of each other. Where one was, the other must be. But the elder twin soon had the nickname "Tatterhood," for she was strong, raucous, and careless, and was always racing about on her goat. Her clothes were always torn and mud-spattered, her hood in tatters. No one could keep her in clean, pretty dresses. She insisted on wearing old clothes, and the queen finally gave up and let her dress as she pleased.

One Christmas Eve, when the twin sisters were almost grown, there arose a terrific noise and clatter in the gallery outside the queen's rooms. Tatterhood asked what it was that dashed and crashed about in the passage. The queen told her it was a pack of trolls who had invaded the palace.

The queen explained that this happened in the palace every seven years. There was nothing to be done about the evil creatures; the palace must all ignore the trolls and endure their mischief.

Tatterhood said, "Nonsense! I will go out and drive them away."

Everyone protested—she must leave the trolls alone; they were too dangerous. But Tatterhood insisted she was not afraid of the trolls. She could and would drive them away. She warned the queen that all doors must be kept tight shut. Then she went out into the gallery to chase them. She laid about with the wooden spoon, whacking trolls on the head or shoulders, rounding them up to drive them out. The whole palace shook with the crashes and shrieking, until it seemed the place would fall apart.

Just then her twin sister, who was worried about Tatterhood, opened a door and stuck out her head to see how things were going. *Pop!* Up came a troll, whipped off her head, and stuck a calf's head on her shoulders instead. The poor princess ran back into the room on all fours and began to moo like a calf.

When Tatterhood came back and saw her sister, she was very angry that the queen's attendants had not kept better watch. She scolded them all around, and asked what they thought of their carelessness now that her sister had a calf's head.

"I'll see if I can get her free from the troll's spell," said Tatterhood. "But I'll need a good ship in full trim and well fitted with stores."

Now the king realized his daughter Tatterhood was quite extraordinary despite her wild ways, so he agreed to this, but said they must have a captain and crew. Tatterhood was firm—she would have no captain or crew. She would sail the ship alone. At last they let her have her way, and Tatterhood sailed off with her sister.

With a good wind behind them, she sailed right to the land of the trolls and tied up at the landing place. She told her sister to stay quite still on board the ship, but she herself rode her goat right up to the trolls' house. Through an open window she could see her sister's head on the wall. In a trice, she leaped the goat through the window and into the house, snatched the head, and leaped back outside again. She set off with it, and after her came the trolls. They shrieked and swarmed about her like angry bees. But the goat snorted and butted with his horns and Tatterhood smacked them with her magic wooden spoon until they gave up and let her escape.

When Tatterhood got safely back to their ship, she took off the calf's head and put her sister's own bonny head back on again. Now her sister was once more human.

"Let's sail on and see something of the world," said Tatterhood. Her sister was of the same mind, so they sailed along the coast, stopping at this place and that, until at last they reached a distant kingdom.

Tatterhood tied up the ship at the landing place. When the people of the castle saw the strange sail, they sent down messengers to find out who sailed the ship and whence it came. The messengers were startled to find no one on board but Tatterhood, and she was riding around the deck on her goat.

When they asked if there was anyone else on board, Tatterhood answered that, yes, she had her sister with her. The messengers asked to see her, but Tatterhood said no. They then asked, would the sisters come up to the castle for an audience with the king and his two sons?

"No," said Tatterhood. "Let them come down to the ship if they wish to see us." And she began to gallop about on her goat until the deck thundered.

The elder prince became curious about the strangers and hastened down to the shore the very next day. When he saw the fair younger twin, he promptly fell in love with her and wanted to marry her.

"No, indeed," she declared. "I will not leave my sister Tatterhood. I will not marry until she is married."

The prince went glumly back to the castle, for in his opinion no one would want to marry the odd creature who rode a goat and looked like a ragged beggar. But hospitality must be given to strangers, so the two sisters were invited to a feast at the castle, and the prince begged his younger brother to escort Tatterhood.

The younger twin brushed her hair and put on her finest kirtle for the event; but Tatterhood refused to change.

"You could wear one of my dresses," said her sister, "instead of that raggedy cloak and old boots." Tatterhood just laughed.

"You might take off that tattered hood and the soot streaks from your face," said her sister crossly, for she wanted her beloved Tatterhood to look her best.

"No," said Tatterhood, "I will go as I am."

All the people of the town turned out to see the strangers riding up to the castle, and a fine procession it was! At the head rode the prince and Tatterhood's sister on fine white horses draped with cloth of gold. Next came the prince's brother on a splendid horse with silver trappings. Beside him rode Tatterhood on her goat.

"You're not much for conversation," said Tatterhood. "Haven't you anything to say?"

"What is there to talk about?" he retorted. They rode on in silence until finally he burst out, "Why do you ride on that goat instead of a horse?"

"Since you happened to ask," said Tatterhood, "I can ride on a horse if I choose." At once the goat turned into a fine steed.

Well! The young man's eyes popped open wide, and he turned to look at her with great interest.

"Why do you hide your head beneath that ragged hood?" he asked.

"Is it a ragged hood? I can change it if I choose," she said. And there, on long dark hair, was a circlet of gold and tiny pearls.

"What an unusual girl you are!" he exclaimed. "But that wooden spoon—why do you choose to carry that?"

"Is it a spoon?" and in her hand the spoon turned into a gold-tipped wand of rowanwood.

"I see!" said the prince. He smiled and hummed a little tune as they rode on.

At last Tatterhood said, "Aren't you going to ask me why I wear these ragged clothes?"

"No," said the prince. "It's clear you wear them because you choose to, and when you want to change them, you will." At that, Tatterhood's ragged cloak disappeared, and she was clad in a velvet green mantle and kirtle. But the prince just smiled and said, "The color becomes you very well."

When the castle loomed up ahead, Tatterhood said to him, "And will you not ask to see my face beneath the streaks of soot?"

"That, too, shall be as you choose."

As they rode through the castle gates, Tatterhood touched the rowan wand to her face, and the soot streaks disappeared. And whether her face now was lovely or plain we shall never know, because it didn't matter in the least to the prince or to Tatterhood.

But this I can tell you: the feast at the castle was a merry one, with the games, and the singing, and the dancing lasting for many days.

*

Sovereignty and authenticity are the key to every ounce of Tatterhood's life energy and to everything—on the surface so strange, even repulsive—that she did or said. Tatterhood is not afraid to be herself. She was born raucous and queer; you might even say "ugly" from the point of view of conventional thinking. She is loud, dirty, fearless, strong. She knows her own way and goes her own way, regardless of what others think. There is not a passive bone in her body. She has sailed her ship as both captain and crew, stolen her sister's head back, and seen something of the world to boot. She is a wild woman who is also capable of love and devotion to her "perfect" sister, a sister who has all the outward, conventional attributes that society adores in women. Tatterhood is as dark as her sister is light. Her appearance, perhaps not so pleasing, requires, even demands acceptance on its own terms, an honoring of the underlying essence of her being, deeply and always beautiful, although hidden to the unseeing eye.

Tatterhood's sister tries to get her to change her ragged clothes and wash her dirty face. She wants her to look her best. How many of us as parents have struggled with wanting to protect our children from the criticism of others, wanting them to be seen as beautiful, as we see them? But Tatterhood stands firm. "No, I will go as I am."

As the prince rides next to Tatterhood, he is silent. When he finally speaks, at her insistence, he doesn't make small talk. He speaks honestly and asks a straightforward question: "Why do you ride on that goat instead of a horse?" When her goat is transformed into a horse, the prince notices. He becomes more attentive. He proceeds to ask other questions, but stops short of asking about her clothes. It is for her to choose to show him. You feel his acceptance of her in his silence. She has to ask him, "Aren't you going to ask me why I wear these ragged clothes?" He refuses, saying that it is clear that she has chosen to dress as she is, and that when she wants to change them, she will. It is in that moment, when the young prince acknowledges her sovereignty—"That, too, shall be as you choose"—that she is transformed, and in the process, teaches him what is most important about love.

This complete acceptance and recognition of sovereignty, important for all children, is especially critical in parenting girls. For to be healthy and whole in a society that is continually constricting them with narrow expectations and limitations, they must be able to find their own way and express their own unique natures.

Advocacy, Assertiveness,
Accountability

At one point, a friend and I (mkz) had similar experiences being called in to discuss incidents that happened in school with our daughters. The themes were the same: strong-willed girls say how they feel about something, and are seen as "disrespectful."

One afternoon, I was called into the elementary school principal's office. The principal, a woman in her early sixties, said that my daughter and a group of fifth-grade girls were told by an aide that they shouldn't be playing soccer with the boys and that they had to stop. My daughter told the aide she was being sexist, that the girls had just as much of a right to play as the boys. The principal imitated for me my daughter's angry, defiant body language by crossing her arms and putting her head to the side, in a manner that suggested she assumed I would agree that her behavior was not acceptable. She went on to tell me that she had had my daughter brought in to a meeting with the recess aides, and told her that she was not allowed to behave in a manner that was disrespectful, that the aides had to ensure the safety of the children, and that the children had to listen and obey them. The principal assured me that she had asked my daughter for her side of the story and told her she needed to write a note of apology to each of the aides.

I agreed with her that my daughter did need to learn to say how she felt in a more respectful manner. But I said that it sounded to me as if my daughter had felt angry about what she perceived to be an unjust situation and was trying to communicate her feelings to the aides. It also sounded to me as if her concerns and point of view were ignored and she was being labeled as "bad" for expressing them. I asked the principal if she thought that, had a boy crossed his arms and spoken up for himself in a similar way, it would have been seen in such a strongly negative light.

Later on, I told my daughter she needed to learn how to stand up for herself without being disrespectful, that saying someone was being sexist could feel like name-calling if other people didn't understand what she was trying to say. Also that she had to be aware of how she spoke, of her body language and tone of voice, and that not just what she said but *the way* she said it was important. I wanted her to see that her actions affected other people and had consequences, one of which was to influence their ability to hear what she was saying.

Learning how to say how we feel and how we see things in a respectful manner is not easy. It takes lots of practice. We have to give children room to do this, to learn from trying, from making mistakes, and from trying again.

The courage it took for her to speak out was never acknowledged. The message she was given was that she should be quiet and compliant. If my daughter keeps getting this message when she tries to stand up for herself or for others, and if she didn't have parents who accepted her anger and tried to see her point of view, she might start to turn inward, stop speaking up, and perhaps begin to feel badly about herself and lose her self-confidence, as happens to so many girls. At nine they are vital and confident; by the age of fourteen, somehow that strength can become hidden, tentative, unseen, even lost.

✻

My daughter's friend is an extremely gifted student, perfectionistic, demanding of herself. She also has clear ideas about things. Her fifth-grade teacher had told her to leave project pieces (puppets she had made and books from the town library) in school over the weekend. She had brought them to class as part of a report she was going to give. She didn't feel that they would be safe left at school over the weekend, but instead of telling her teacher that, she just said, "No, I want to take them home." The teacher felt she was being disrespectful and called up her parents. Although this girl never "acts out" or "misbehaves" in school, her teacher chose to see her behavior in a very limited framework and interpret it as disrespectful of him, rather than as a sign that she felt secure enough to say what she felt she needed to do.

It is true that she could have communicated more effectively and perhaps been seen as more respectful, had she explained her concerns to her teacher. But again, the fine art of communicating requires practice and experience. Even so, as the adult, her teacher could have been more respectful of her by asking what her reasons were for wanting to take the project home.

As parents, we need to help our children to identify their concerns, to express them in an assertive and respectful manner, and to stand up for what they think is right, even when they are not understood, or when their feelings are not taken into account. To do this, we must be willing at times to advocate for our children, and to help them make sense of the difficult situations they sometimes find themselves in.

If children sensed that their feelings counted, that there was an attempt made to understand their point of view, that the adults were sympathetic and inquiring rather than judging and closed, so many more essential life skills might be learned in school.

Mindfulness in the Classroom—Getting to Know Yourself in School

In South Jordan, Utah, at the Welby Elementary School, a fifth-grade teacher named Cherry Hamrick has been incorporating mindfulness into her teaching to support her students, not only in being themselves but in knowing themselves better as they learn. She has made time each day for the children to focus inward. She speaks of it as a time to become "intimate with yourself."

Each day, a different child is in charge of ringing a bell to signal the beginning and the end of this quiet time. The rule is, the child decides how long the class is to sit quietly and follow their breathing, with an upper limit of ten minutes. The children choose how long they practice, and in what ways. In addition to sitting meditation, they sometimes practice a body scan meditation and mindful stretching, walking meditation in the schoolyard, and standing meditation on line before they go into the classroom. Their stress reduction exercises went from seeming "weird" and "strange" to them in the beginning, to being an important part of their day to them, and something that many of them love and enjoy sharing with their parents and siblings.

In the process of focusing on their breathing and watching their thoughts come and go, they learn that they don't have to react to every thought that comes into their minds, that just because the mind is jumping around and agitated at times doesn't mean they have to jump with it. With practice, they become more comfortable with silence and sitting still. One boy with ADHD (attention-deficit hyperactivity disorder), after years of problems in the lower grades, was able over the course of a year to learn to sit still and be relatively comfortable, and to focus on the flow of his breathing for up to ten minutes at a time. His ability to concentrate in the classroom changed dramatically, and for the first time he was accepted by his peers and teachers. His mother told me this one day when I (jkz) visited the classroom. This boy led a ten minute sitting meditation for the class, including some visiting parents, giving the instructions himself as we sat in silence.

Learning at a young age to touch silence and stillness within oneself, especially if it is taught in school in an open and non-manipulative or coercive way, can be valuable in balancing out and dealing with the stimulation and outward orientation of the school day. Among other things, children can discover how to tap into their innate ability to go into deep states of concentration, and use it to focus on the task at hand.

One of Ms. Hamrick's students, an eleven-year-old girl, wrote to me, saying:

"Doing meditation has become more of a habit at home for me, and I will be doing this for the rest of my life. While I was doing meditation at first, and an itch came, I would say, 'feeling, feeling,' to myself, but after one minute, I would find myself scratching it. But now I don't scratch it because now I can be with it long enough that it just goes away. In my meditation, I've also noticed that my breathing has become deeper and I'm more focused on it. In yoga, I've noticed that I get more energy than before, and I think it's because I'm more mindful on what I'm doing. Because of meditation and yoga, I don't rush everything I do like I used to."

Ms. Hamrick has not only brought mindfulness-based stress reduction into the classroom. She has integrated mindfulness in one imaginative way or another into virtually every aspect of the curriculum, including math, English, science, and geography. She encourages her students to use their whole selves in their learning. They approach a subject so that they develop not only their cognitive and information-processing skills but also their intuition, their feelings, and their bodies. In this way, they are learning the basics of what is now called *emotional intelligence*, as well as developing greater enthusiasm for learning.

A teacher in the school wrote, describing his experience of sharing an open classroom with Ms. Hamrick:

"The attitude and climate in her classroom was very impressive, especially as I had not heretofore experienced anything like it before. I became aware of certain vocabulary she used to describe things. . . . She referred to what she was trying to attain as a 'functional classroom.'

"I noticed a peaceful atmosphere in her classroom with the students cooperating and discussing their work together. Talking was encouraged; but only work-related talk and 'feeling' talk was allowed. There was genuine interest and concern among the students and the teacher. They practiced talking about feelings and processing them on a daily basis. I noticed the students grow in their self-esteem and their regard for human life as well as all life in general.

"The students seemed genuinely happier and more content in the classroom setting than I had ever observed or experienced myself. They expressed their love with appropriate touching (hugs), and they knew how to resolve conflict and problem solve in a loving, caring fashion rather than in a hostile or abusive fashion.

"Ms. Hamrick also taught the students how to focus and how to get in touch with their own breathing, and how to control their own lives with that technique. They seemed to be able to work better during the day after a few moments of meditative preparation in the morning. We taught in an open classroom situation, and their ability to focus and not be distracted by all of the noise in that type of environment is a tribute to Ms. Hamrick's application of her training and drive."

Ms. Hamrick herself described in a letter to me a trying time when her class had to move temporarily to a new space while renovations were conducted during the school year:

"The fifth grade teachers have all been commenting on the disruption of this move and the radical behavior changes in their students. Actually, the comments about poor behavior can be heard throughout the school. The first day was chaotic for most teachers. I found our daily [mindfulness] practice to have paved the way for some simply beautiful days [in the new environment]. . . .

"Our first day of the move was peaceful, with attitudes focusing in on working together as a classroom. . . . While the school was going crazy with teachers and students making efforts to tour their surroundings to find out where everything was located, the Rainbow Riders simply wanted to break in their classroom with what they refer to as 'their feeling.' They wanted to sit together in the 'feeling' they experience when they meditate together. They love the saturated serenity they experience together. They are cute about saying it is something that is hard to explain. They insist that it isn't 'words,' which is frustrating for most adults if they want an explanation. The students say it is something that has to be felt, and 'it didn't come to them for a while and it happens best when they are together.'

"That first day of the move, I just sat back and let them lead the way. I do that a lot because it gives me the sense of where their understanding and process is really at. They were not interested in knowing where everything was located, just the essentials like the restrooms and drinking fountain. They simply wanted to connect with each other and get involved with our own classroom. I waited until 11 A.M. and I asked them to let me know when they wanted a tour of the school. They simply smiled and said they were all OK. They said I could show them the cafeteria at lunch, but that we weren't there yet. The students continued to explain to me politely that I was 'using my forecasting talent' and that for now it would be better to stay in this minute of time. I said, 'Oh, okay,' and wondered what they must think of me. One boy [the one characterized as having ADHD] was upset at the explanation and said, 'Don't rescue her thinking. She will figure it out.' . . .

"We are on our second week [in the new space] and they still have only wanted to see the essentials and the rooms they need at the time. I am loving the results of our practice. I have continued to ask them to tell me when they want to go on a tour and they have said that it might be nice to tour the school upon leaving. They have commented on what they see as 'the other classes are caught up in a lot of things that they really don't need and are not focusing in on being and working with themselves or each other.' P. said, 'They do a lot of running around always trying to get something and it never stops.'"

These children, under the guidance of a highly skilled, deeply motivated, imaginative, and daring teacher, are learning to focus inwardly, and are getting to know themselves better and to experience working together in ways that are meaningful and deeply authentic.

*

This is not to say that, as parents, we should teach our children how to meditate in any formal sense, although there are times when useful applications of meditation may naturally arise. In those moments, drawing on our own experience and practice, we might, for example, suggest to our young children to be aware of and look very closely at what "color" their pain is and how it changes from moment to moment when they have hurt themselves, or show them how to "float" on the waves of their breath as if in a little boat when they are having a hard time relaxing or going to sleep, or to see if they can think of times when their minds "waved" because of what other people did or said when their feelings have been hurt.

It seems wise to take our cues from our children and their expressions of interest at different ages. Ultimately, the best teaching we can do is by example, through our own commitment to be present, and our sensitivity to them. When we practice formally, either sitting or lying down, we embody silence and stillness. Our children see us deeply focused and become familiar with this way of being. Many of the insights and attitudes that develop from our mindfulness practice will naturally filter into the culture of the family and affect our children in ways that they may in time find useful in their own lives.

PART NINE

Limits and

Openings

Expectations

Expectations can easily govern how we see things and our behavior without our really being aware of them. They can either be useful and positive and catalyze important openings, or they can be cruelly limiting and cause a great deal of suffering for both parents and children. For this reason, it is critically important that we bring mindfulness to our expectations and their consequences.

We all have expectations of ourselves, and of others, and we are especially likely to have them of our children. Usually, we don't undertake anything without having expectations about what it will be like, what it will do for us, what its value will be. Our expectations often get us where we need to be; but they also can seriously impede our ability to experience anything freshly because we insist on measuring it against those very expectations. They create the most problems when we hold them rigidly and when they are unexamined, or unconscious.

If we start by examining our expectations of ourselves, we may find that we harbor many different ones and judge ourselves severely when we don't meet them. One common expectation is that we will do things well, or "right." We expect to do well in school, to succeed in the workplace, to be a good parent and a good son or daughter, to be liked by other people.

Judging ourselves harshly when we feel that we don't "measure up" can elicit a range of feelings: shame, stupidity, disappointment, embarrassment, anger, humiliation, inadequacy. These are the same feelings that our children can experience when they don't meet either our or their own expectations. For this reason, it is important to be aware of our expectations and ponder their value, the purposes they serve, and the ways that they affect our children.

Our expectations often lead us to want something from our children that we haven't gotten, or are used to getting from them. Expecting certain behaviors can be a guise for controlling or ordering our children to do certain things. When our expectations are examined and clearly stated, they can be helpful to everyone in the family in clarifying either what we want or what we don't want, and what is completely unacceptable to us. Each family has its own expectations based on its values. We believe that, as parents, our expectations of our children should be in the interest of their growth and well-being.

Our expectations will be different for different children and at different ages. They may also be different for boys and for girls. We have expectations that have to do with the day-to-day workings of our lives, like who is responsible for what, and we have much more loaded, problematic, often unconscious and unspoken ones, such as that one child will always be obedient, no matter what, and another will always be defiant. Some parents don't praise their children when they do well because it is taken for granted. It is what is expected of them, so why bother acknowledging it? It's only when their children *don't* meet their expectations that something is said.

To increase our awareness of our expectations so that we do not project them onto our children unconsciously and unwisely, it can be helpful to ask ourselves specific questions: Are our expectations realistic and age-appropriate? Do they contribute to a child's growth? Are we expecting too much or too little? Are we setting our child up to experience unnecessary stress and failure? Do our expectations enhance our child's self-esteem, or do they constrict, limit, or belittle the child? Do they contribute to a child's well-being, to his or her feeling loved and cared for and accepted? Do they encourage important human values such as honesty, respect for others, and being responsible for one's actions?

We need to examine whether our expectations take into account the many facets of our children's natures and whether they afford them the room to try out different behaviors. For instance, can we value nonviolence and still allow our children to express their angry or aggressive feelings as long as they don't hurt others? Can we see that expecting a child to always be compassionate and loving, and then expressing disappointment when he or she shows anger or self-interest, can be hurtful to our child and is neither compassionate nor loving? If we are not careful, we can easily maintain a double standard, expecting one thing of our children and something else of ourselves.

Mindful parenting asks us to embody what we believe in in the conduct of our own lives, and to do so, as best we can, without being harsh and judgmental toward ourselves when we don't meet our own expectations, and without falling into self-righteousness when we do. Living this way, we can let our children learn from our way of being as they chart their own paths and develop their own expectations of themselves.

Some expectations we have of children are basic, bottom-line aspects of a healthy relationship. Wanting them to be generally respectful is one. But what does that mean? Does it mean that they are polite, saying "please" and "thank you"? Are we insisting they be that way all the time, sometimes, most of the time? What do we expect on the physical level, like chores, participating in the work of the house? What do we expect them to do for themselves, and for others? Do we expect demonstrations of affection and caring? Do we expect them to share our pain, our unhappiness, to fill the emotional gaps in our lives? Can we allow our children to be children and have their own inner lives?

In the spirit of inquiry and discernment, we might attend to whether we are seeing our children clearly in each moment and modifying our expectations according to the circumstances. We might ask ourselves if we are harboring expectations, like old belief systems, that our parents had of us, and automatically projecting them onto our children. It would be good to ask whether some of our expectations are merely disguised attempts to get what we want, to have our own way, and to control things.

We might ask whether our expectations limit the full range of expression of our daughters and sons. Whether we expect boys to be loud, assertive, and self-centered, and girls to be sensitive, caring, "other-oriented," and "nice."

In a meeting with one of our daughter's teachers, a caring person and dedicated to teaching, he turned to us and said, "What happened to the smiling, happy, eager-to-please girl that came to school at the beginning of the year?" This same teacher stopped her in the hall one day and asked her why she was looking so serious. He expected her to act a certain way, and assumed that if she was not smiling, there was something wrong.

Our daughter doesn't want to have to smile. We expect her to be respectful of others, but we don't feel she has to look a certain way, or smile or be "eager to please." Outer-oriented, "eager-to-please" children may find themselves more vulnerable in many situations, unable to say no, doing things they don't really want to do. Their response to the expectations of others may be to put on a face that is not theirs, a smiling mask that they hide behind. In the process, if this behavior becomes a generalized way of coping with the world, they may lose touch with their own true nature since they do not feel that it will be accepted. Not having to smile when you don't want to is what sovereignty is all about.

Children need to be supported in developing their own expectations of themselves that are both realistic and healthy rather than being straitjacketed by the expectations of their parents and others. It can take decades of therapy to undo the damage that is caused when children embark on journeys driven by expectations that they unquestioningly adopt but that are not truly theirs.

✳

I (mkz) remember very clearly that my expectations for our first child changed when we had another baby. The older child suddenly was expected to be more responsible and independent in ways that were not expected of him before the arrival of his younger sister. The child who had been our "baby" was suddenly seen in a different light compared with a new infant, and our expectations for him started multiplying, until we saw what we were doing. Perhaps this common phenomenon comes about in part because it makes our life with a new baby easier; or, it may be a byproduct of some kind of biological species protection where we fall in love with the new baby and the older sibling loses his magical aura because he doesn't need us in the same way a baby does to survive.

When I see other parents having similar expectations of their "older" children, I wish I could remind them that their two-year-old is still a "baby" in many ways; that their four-year-old is just that—a four-year-old; that their six-year-old still wants to be held, to feel their adoration and loving energy; and that their eight-year-old still needs hugs and time alone with them and not to be always in charge but free to be a child.

Our children also have expectations of us, and it is helpful to be aware of them. They might expect us to be on time, or they might expect us to always be late; to be reliable or to be unreliable; to be available for them, or not to be available; to immediately get angry, or to be understanding. Their expectations of us are based on their experience of how we have acted in the past. They can reveal to us our own behavior, to which we may be blind. This gives us a chance to change in ways that may be healthier for them, and for us as well.

For example, when a child breaks something, she may expect her parents to get very angry about it. It may be that in the past, her parents have gotten angry at her in similar situations. However, on this occasion, the parents respond with understanding and acceptance, because they are trying to be more aware of their own behavior and its effects on their child, and also remembering what is most important. In doing so, they are embodying kindness and respect for her, and in breaking out of the limited realm of expectations that they had for their daughter, they have helped create new and broader expectations in her.

It's not always necessary to change our behavior. Sometimes it is important simply to acknowledge it. When we suddenly become grumpy or short-tempered and speak in a sharp manner, it can be confusing or upsetting to our child. If we can acknowledge in that moment that we are tired and having a hard time, without blaming him, we give him a framework for understanding what is happening. When we act in an unexpected way and we are able to name it for what it is, we are making an unpredictable and confusing universe more ordered and understandable. Then children are not as likely to blame themselves or to feel tense and anxious when a parent's mood changes abruptly. It also teaches them something useful about people in general, and they may eventually come to see aspects of their own behavior more clearly as they get older.

Our expectations of our children will vary to some degree depending on the pressures we are under, and the depth of the resources we feel we have to draw on in that moment. We can't *expect* compassion or understanding from our children. That doesn't mean that they will not be compassionate or understanding at times. Sometimes children respond with tremendous kindness and sympathy; but usually they just want what they want and they aren't interested in our problems. Nor are they interested in long explanations, with lots of words. But it does help them to know that our actions are connected to how we are feeling, just as their behavior is connected to how they are feeling.

We all have certain unwavering expectations of our children. For example: "You're not allowed to cross the street without an adult"; or "No matter how angry you are, you're not allowed to hit people." Making clear what we feel is unacceptable behavior and what our expectations are is another way of nurturing our children. Small children, particularly, feel safe and secure, and experience a sense of relief when a parent steps in and sets a clear boundary.

As children get older, they start to assume more responsibility—both for the things they need to do, and for the ways in which they behave. It helps them when we hold them accountable for their actions, and respond in ways that both honor their sovereignty and give them natural and appropriate consequences for what they have done. We have to constantly reexamine what are appropriate expectations to have of them as they grow and change.

We may find that we have to struggle with our own expectations when we least expect to. When one of our children didn't want us to be present at a school event, we were shocked and disappointed. We wanted so much to go, and our child wanted to experience it by herself. She wanted it to be *her* experience.

When our son was going off for the first time to college, I (mkz) wanted, I *expected* to drive him there. As his mother, I wanted to see his new home and be a part of this important transition. He wanted something different. He wanted his friend, with whom he had traveled across the country, to drive him. He wanted to arrive at college as an independent person, not as a son being taken to school by his parents. After he told us this, for some moments I was torn between strong feelings of disappointment and the effort to see it from his point of view. Ultimately, understanding why it was so important for him to go in his own way helped me to let go of my long-held expectation and be able to say with sincerity and acceptance, "I understand why you want to go with your friend, and it's fine with me."

In such situations, children are asking parents to see things from their point of view. They are asking for understanding and acceptance. Too often, parents are operating only out of the framework of their own needs and desires, not their children's. It is our job as parents to look at what is best for our children within the context of what is possible, and when necessary, to let go of our own strong attachments to how we want things to be. This requires a degree of selflessness from us.

We give our children a great if unseen gift when we wrestle with our own expectations and are able to consciously let go of those that are destructive to their well-being. This is the inner work of being parents, and being grown-ups. When we are able to do this, the atmosphere in the family becomes lighter, there is a feeling of spaciousness and balance, and room for everybody to grow.

Surrender

Just when I've (mkz) been through several particularly high-pressure, jam-packed weeks, my youngest gets sick. Her face is flushed, her head hurts. I'm straining to be free and suddenly I'm on an even shorter leash.

I'm angry and frustrated, feeling pushed to the limit. I don't want this to be happening. I want to withdraw, crawl into bed myself and shut the door, but she's feeling bad, she wants me, she needs me. My heart goes out to her. She's not doing this to torture me. She can't help it, she's sick. I feel myself take a deep breath. I feel myself surrendering to what is needed, and put aside my expectations and lists of things I had planned to do.

The fever intensifies her experience of everything. Her eyes are bothered by the light, so the curtains are pulled, her room dark and peaceful. There are none of the usual diversions: music, phone calls, TV. Occasionally she sleeps. When she's awake, she doesn't want to be alone. I sit with her. I get her a cold cloth for her forehead. I bring her tea and toast, I read to her. And as I do these things, there is a comfort in being able to do what I can to make her feel better. The moments of reading to her, or just sitting with her, holding her hand, have a quiet richness. She'll look at me with pleasure as I read to her, or she'll say, "I'm happy we're together." Her eyes are especially bright, her face almost translucent. I think about how different her day would be if she were in school, and I'm struck by how this "sick" time can be so nourishing. I've often noticed my children emerge from illness with a different look to them, as if they've somehow grown, changed in this crucible of intense heat we call fever, and in their retreat into quiet and nurturance.

Of course there are moments when she is irritable, angry, and demanding. Those moments are my laboratory. They put me to the test. Will I take it personally and get mad at her, or will I remember how it feels to be sick, and be sympathetic and receptive to her? Can I let her show frustration and misery without judgment, without criticism? Can I let go of my own expectations for what I wanted the day to be and surrender to the necessity and the beauty of what has emerged?

Limits
and Openings

Some studies suggest that when parents are either very permissive and provide few if any boundaries or limits, or else are very authoritarian, rigid, and domineering, the children suffer from low self-esteem. When children are treated with respect and are accorded a good deal of latitude within a clear framework of limits and boundaries, which can be flexible and at times negotiable, they tend to grow up confident and secure in themselves. Within the context of a caring, connected, and engaged relationship, limits can be seen as defining openings for our children, and not merely as barriers we throw in their paths.

Setting limits in our family is not something we do just to feel our own power. We try not to act in an authoritarian manner, which demands unquestioning obedience. Our limit-setting is usually around things that we feel have a negative impact on a child's well-being, things like bedtimes, TV, junk food, movies, video games, and around behaviors that affect the well-being of others, such as disrespect, hitting, and name calling.

When we set limits, we have to do so in ways that feel right to us and fair to our children. This of course varies with age. When they are young, by being too rigid, we may inadvertently encourage their preoccupation with whatever they are not getting, whether it's toy guns or candy. As they get older, the stakes get higher. If we are too rigid, they may stop trusting us, or lie to us, or they may completely withdraw.

If we are too loose with them, at any age, we soon start to see the negative effects on them as well. This can take the form of exhaustion, tension, irritability, fearfulness, anxiety, aggression, poor judgment, and disrespectful behaviors.

When our children were little, we tried to give them freedom to explore, to pursue the things they were interested in, to try on different behaviors. When they did things that were harmful or dangerous, we tried to keep our responses limited to those specific behaviors, letting them know without overwhelming them, that what they were doing was not okay. At the same time, they could feel from us that *they* were okay, that our love, and our acceptance of them was a constant.

At times our limit setting came out of anger, the feeling of "That's the last straw!" But more often, it came out of simple common sense, out of concern for how much sleep they got, or for what they were eating, or for their safety. Over time, gradually, they learned by encountering such limits how to take care of themselves, and eventually how to make their own healthy choices.

With older children, sometimes flying in the face of strong peer and societal pressures, at times we have had to step in and impose some kind of limit on their activities. This requires considerable perseverance and skill at high-level negotiating, and can be exhausting. This effort is as necessary and as demanding as getting up in the night with them when they were babies.

The older our children get, the more we may find ourselves wanting to say, "I won't tolerate this!" in certain situations in which our expectations and their behaviors are wildly divergent. Our protestations can come out with a strong self-righteous tone, which only compounds the problems. At the same time, underneath that, we may be feeling completely helpless to influence the situation. For after we pronounce that we won't tolerate the particular behavior, then what? All of the relatively simple strategies that may have worked when our children were little, like distraction and redirection, or physically removing them from whatever, just don't work with older children.

We often find that we have to wait till our older child is not angry and is more receptive before we can work out solutions and compromises in problematic situations. We have to rely on a combination of their own innate good sense, their respect for our feelings and concerns, and the use of concrete consequences, like losing the use of the telephone, or when they are older, the use of the car.

Whatever we decide to do or say, it helps when we are able to be grounded and in touch with our own energy and feelings, perhaps by bringing our attention to our breathing, intentionally slowing it down and making it deeper. We might also be aware of the tone of voice we are using. We might try putting aside the stern, often loud, hard edged voice that seems to come so naturally in such moments, saying the same thing more quietly, yet with firmness and clarity.

Ultimately, our children's responsiveness to any limits on their behavior depends on how connected they feel to us or the family as a whole, how much they can see the limits coming from our concern and caring, and how fair they feel we are being.

Like many parents who have a child in middle school, there was a time when we were suffering the negative affects of one of our daughters spending all her free time on the telephone. What had started harmlessly enough developed into a situation, where from the second she came home from school to the moment she went to bed, she was either on the phone, or anticipating a phone call. Anything she did could be interrupted at any moment, including her homework. Eventually, despite her assurances that her homework was not being neglected, she just didn't have the quiet space to really concentrate on the difficult work she had, and her schoolwork suffered. But the worst effect that the phone had was that it pulled her out of the family so much that she began to relate to us as if we were strangers and in an angry and distant manner.

We realized that just telling her that her phone time would be limited would have been very autocratic, and would have made her extremely angry and precipitated a huge scene that would have created that much more distance between her and us. We decided instead to call a family meeting in which everybody in the family got to speak, uninterrupted, to say how we were feeling about the phone issue. Hearing each other, we were all better able to understand each other's point of view. We each said what we could or couldn't live with, and we eventually came up with a phone schedule that was a compromise with which we were all satisfied.

After a few days of having uninterrupted time at dinner and an hour afterward to do her homework, she admitted that she "kind of liked" the new phone schedule. We could see she felt a certain sense of relief at having a quiet, uninterrupted time for herself. It was something she wouldn't have initiated. That had to come from us.

After another week or two, she inevitably started to try to bend and change the compromise we had come up with. She told us she wanted to start on the phone a half hour earlier and we said she could if she ended a half hour earlier. Not being willing to do this, she went back to our original agreement. Being aware of the positive effect of the new phone limits on both our daughter and the family as a whole made it much easier to stand our ground.

There will always be special situations and times when we need to be flexible, and it is important to be sensitive to them. In some ways, this makes parenting harder, because our children know the possibility exists for negotiation and at times they will look for every window of opportunity to bend the rules. They can be masters at arguing their case, veritable trial lawyers at times, and it is hard not to take this in as an admirable trait, even as it threatens to thwart our position.

Every child is different. Bedtime for an early riser will be different from the child who is naturally a night owl. A child who is a good reader will have more resources on "no TV" nights than a child who finds reading difficult. Children who are less impulsive and more thoughtful will naturally need less limit setting from their parents.

Even as we notice changes or shifts in our own tolerances and limit-setting with different children at different ages or in different circumstances, part of mindful parenting is to continually re-examine whether what we are doing and thinking is in *this* child's best interest, and to ask ourselves if there might be a better way that we are not seeing.

*

As our children become teenagers, the road we travel as parents twists and turns, the visibility decreases, and things are not always what they seem. Signs of distress in older children can be easier to ignore or deny than the cries of a baby. Teenagers need their privacy, but that privacy also means we don't always know what's going on, what they are really doing, what they are involved in. It may be tempting for them to lie to us so that they can do what they want. Their focus can easily shift to "What can I get away with?" rather than "What is in my best interest?" We may find ourselves tempted to say "yes" to things we really want to say "no" to, both to avoid a fight and because we may fear that saying "no" will just push them further away.

Teenagers, like younger children, need us to provide periodic reality checks for them. They need us to be honest about how we feel, and clear about what we perceive as the dangers to their well-being. At the same time, we have to be careful not to push them away, not push them into closing up, walling off, discounting us, disconnecting from us. Very often, when we feel we have to say "No" to things they want from us, if we are not mindful, that "No" may carry many other tacit messages such as "We don't trust you," "You're bad," "You have no judgment." We need to be aware of these feelings in ourselves, if they are present, and the automatic reactions they trigger, so we do not fall into creating more unnecessary distance and alienation in moments that are already difficult enough.

If a parent says to a teenage daughter, "No, you can't be alone with this boy at his house," the response may be, "Don't you trust me?" The parent might, with some thoughtfulness, respond by saying, "I don't trust the situation. It's too easy to feel pressured into doing things that may be harmful or that you may feel badly about afterwards." This response has at least the possibility of being seen, not as an arbitrary exercise of power but as a respectful and non-naive assessment of a situation, one that does not impugn the integrity of the child. She may not see it as we do, or she may reject what we say completely, and be resentful and angry. Nevertheless, in that moment, the parent is pointing to something real, and understands that this one interaction, however it turns out, is bound to be one of many such encounters. Choosing, with some degree of wisdom, what situations we place ourselves in is one of those life lessons that it takes time and experience to learn.

*

A friend of ours got a call from her daughter saying "Mom, I'm in New York City." This occurred after several discussions with her daughter as to why she did not want her, at sixteen years of age, to go to New York on her own to visit a school in which she was interested. Her daughter proceeded to tell her that she hadn't been able to reach the person she thought she would stay with and had called another young woman who she met recently, and was now staying with her. How might this mother react to such a *fait accompli*? How can she work with what she is given?

She took a moment and assessed the situation. She realized that her daughter was trying to take care of herself and had been thoughtful enough to call her so that she wouldn't worry. Her daughter was already in New York. No amount of anger about it would change that. She told her daughter, wisely and honestly, "I'm not angry right now, but I reserve the right to get mad later." In this way, she left her options open for dealing with her emotional upset at another time, and proceeded to ask her daughter questions about her safety and if she had the things she needed to complete her trip and return home. She realized that her daughter was trying to do something that was very important to her. Although she disagreed with what she did, at the same time, she was able to appreciate her daughter's courage and resourcefulness. By remaining clear about her own feelings, but also thinking deeply about her daughter's needs, she was able to be supportive and not let their conflicting positions come between them.

✳

The inevitable challenge of parenting is that the older our children are, the scarier things can become for us as they move out into the world and encounter potentially dangerous situations over which we have little or none of the control we had when they were little. One important aspect of our inner work as parents during this period is to be mindful of our own fears and anxieties. This at least gives us a chance not to get so caught up in them that they completely cloud our vision and sensibilities and make it impossible to see what is really going on with our children, or to communicate effectively with them. We can use the motivating power of our concerns to call on our ability to be present, to be empathic rather than adversarial, to know or sense the problems our children may be facing, and to explore ways to support them in growing in healthier and more soul-satisfying directions.

This is a time when we can build on the work we have done in the past to create trust, and most importantly, a shared feeling of connectedness within the family. With this as a foundation, it becomes possible, if not always easy, to talk with our children about such things as the costs and risks of alcohol, drugs, and unprotected sex (emotionally as well as physically unprotected).

Having more and more freedom and faced with all sorts of choices, some of which are destructive and dangerous, and sometimes with strong pressure from peers, it becomes essential that older children develop their own capacity for self-awareness. This includes the ability to be in touch with what they are feeling in any given situation, including highly conflicted feelings, and to ask themselves what it is they really need. With some self-awareness, they are more likely to make healthier choices and better able to set their own limits and boundaries.

Many activities naturally build self-awareness, along with self-discipline and self-confidence. It is critical that parents, schools, and communities collaborate in providing such opportunities for children and give them mindful guidance as they encounter these challenging situations. Activities such as martial arts, sports, dance, painting, rock climbing, wilderness camping, journal writing, and many more provide occasions for children to experience limits, real and imagined, and the satisfaction of openings and breakthroughs. An inner experience of self-efficacy and mastery in one area will inevitably spill over into other areas of their lives. Ultimately, our children reach an age when they have to rely on their own awareness and good sense and past experience as they go out on their own and encounter the challenge of continuing to grow as their lives unfold.

Minding
Our Own Business

Don't draw another's bow;
don't ride another's horse;
don't discuss another's faults;
don't explore another's affairs.

WU-MEN,

THIRTEENTH-CENTURY

CHINESE ZEN MASTER

"Where did you go?"
"Out."
"What did you do?"
"Nothing."

FAMILY DIALOGUE

It is easy for parents to fall into thinking that we need to know everything that is going on with our children, including what is going on in their inner lives. It's only natural that we feel this way since we are so close to them when they are little, and take so much joy in and so much responsibility for their learning new things and expanding their horizons. But as they get older, it is very important that we leave them psychic room for privacy, and for sharing with us what they choose to, when they choose to, all the while generating a field of loving kindness around them in our own hearts. When they do need to share something with us, perhaps then they will feel that they can trust us and that we might understand their concerns.

This requires presence and availability on our part. It also requires a healthy respect for *interiority*, for the inner life we can never know of someone else, and are lucky if we can recognize in ourself, and, as a consequence, a healthy resolve to mind our own business. It is a delicate balance, requiring a high degree of sensitivity, discernment, and patience.

Of course, since every child is different and every parent is different and no two circumstances are the same, we have to be continually aware of the current situation in the family and in our own minds. In order to mind our own business, we will have to know what our true business is as a parent, and what it isn't.

It's not just a matter of knowing, either. It is also a matter of style. Patience and presence without prying or probing or being overbearing, and without judging them when our children do share something with us, can make for a much happier relationship than if the children experience us as always minding their business, wanting to know more than they care to share, and broadcasting hurt feelings when we might feel left out or cut off.

This widening of the psychic space between us can catalyze our own inner development as well as theirs. We might find it enlightening to think back to when we were adolescents. At some point, were there not things that we needed to keep to ourselves, things that were just not our parents' business, and never would be or could be because they were emerging experiences in our own private inner world?

There are things that can never be shared. Our child may tell us at some point that he is in love, or is going to get married. We may know something of the outer and have a sense of the inner, but we can never fully know the inner, and rightfully so because it is not ours to know. Our job is to take care of our own inner business, the business of our own mind, our own body, our own relationships, and our own life, according the same freedom and respect to our children as they make the transition from total dependency as small children to independent and interdependent adults.

The quality and warmth of our connections with our children will be proportional to how much we continue to do our own inner work and keep a sense of appropriate boundaries, our willingness to have our older children find their own ways, and keep their own council. They may be more inclined to communicate, the less we hunger to know. Presence and openness, love and interest, and a willingness to respond are all that is necessary. This kind of spaciousness is the basis for respect and trust between parent and child. This is part of the business that it *is* ours to mind.

It's Always
Your Move

After watching a movie with both girls, the older one goes off to sleep, but the younger one needs something else before bedtime. She gets into her pajamas and asks for a story, then changes her mind and asks whether we might play chess on her bed. One game, we agree, and then lights off and to sleep.

We will have to be very careful not to upset the pieces on this roll-out board on top of the mattress. But first, she asks me (jkz), princesslike, if I will get her a tangerine (she loves tangerines), "and also, Daddy, a hot water bottle" to warm up her bed on this cold November night. I am happy to get them for her, once I can find the stopper for the hot water bottle. Then I go and get the chess set.

We have been playing chess again for a few weeks now. Sometimes she asks me, sometimes I ask her. For the longest time, I couldn't get her to play, but Myla thought to get a bigger board and a set of bigger pieces than the ones we started with, and also one of those dual chess clocks that you hit each time you make a move. The clock definitely adds an extra something to the game. It's as if you sign off on each move, affirming that it is really what you mean. She loves playing with the clock, and so do I, although we never do look at the time elapsed. It's that definitive banging of it after each move that appeals.

We settle into our nocturnal game. She has black. She "always" has black. I checkmate her early. We are both surprised. I myself didn't realize it was checkmate at first. She had castled and I brought my queen right down to her king, with my bishop backing it up, and somehow, none of her pieces could take me or interfere. It happened so fast, we decided to play "just one more."

I tried to set up a similar opening in this game. She soon saw what I was doing, with no talk between us. I could tell, because she moved just the right pawn to just the right place to make my attempt futile. With the tiniest bit of help at a few crucial places, she checkmated me just one move away from my checkmating her. It was so much fun, we decided to play just one more.

I am tired by this point, and there is a major current of reluctance in me to play anymore, that is, until we start playing. Then that falls away in the energy of the moment.

This time, we wound up with an elaborate endgame in the center of the board involving both queens in adjacent positions with both kings backing them up, with some rooks and bishops right in close and our kings fleeing through openings here and there as we pursued each other, checking and then losing the checking advantage back and forth. It was wonderful, and like nothing either of us had seen before. She was playing lying down by this time, her head on the water bottle at board level.

We sometimes make amused or suspicious eye contact while playing, silently catching what the other is attempting, or experiencing the sheer joy of engaging over this funny world of elegant archetypes in plastic on sixty-four squares. She never wants me to point out anything, but I like to let her take back a move if it means losing something important, like her queen, or missing a great opportunity which I know she isn't seeing. And she sometimes lets me do that . . . and then won't want to hear another word.

She wants to figure things out herself, and in each game I see her perceiving more and making better moves. She learns so fast from her experience—much faster than I am learning. She catches me in mindless mistakes and is sometimes gracious, sometimes less inclined toward forgiving. She is learning to see my moves and where they might be going, and how she might interfere with them, as well as forming her own strategies for pressuring my position and moving the game along. There is a spatial wisdom growing here. I can see it in her. Perception is challenged to expand. Risks need to be seen and weighed. Plans need to be formulated but also changed over and over again, in response to changing situations on the board. Strategy and tactics develop of necessity.

Every game is an infinite number of possibilities narrowing themselves slowly down to one inevitable end, the one that we get. But we can and do sometimes replay different possible ends. It's like role-playing alternative scenarios in a personal dilemma. We see the elements involved and their combinations and our own power to make choices and direct the flow of things. We visualize and actually explore different approaches, and see the consequences that unfold from each. All sorts of psychotherapy make use of role playing to sort out emotional dilemmas and the different ways we might navigate through difficulties. Imagine beginning to learn this while playing a game, and developing the inner repertoire of seeing alternative openings and moves that will further the unfolding of our lives in ways that might embody an element of wisdom.

After this game ends, the flow of things is definitely into sleep. She asks if I will stay with her. I shut off the light and sit on her bed. She is asleep in moments. I know it from her breathing, which suddenly deepens and gets quieter.

Most of the time at this age, if I ask, "Can I put you to bed?," she says, "NO!," so her invitation is very special for me, and I feel that it is special for her as well, a chance to revisit a move she used to make a lot.

I breathe with her for a few more minutes and then leave quietly, closing her door.

*

Sometimes we won't mind looking for the stopper of the hot water bottle . . . or its counterpart in our lives when it's our turn to make a move. At other times, usually lots of other times, well, we *will* mind looking for the stopper of the hot water bottle, we won't want to get a tangerine, or put ourselves out . . . it's too late, we're too tired, we just want our child to go to bed . . . and we *won't* want to play chess, or anything else! And sometimes it's right not to.

But if we choose, just as an experiment, to give to our children right at that moment that we are most inclined not to, and instead of clamping down and closing up, we make ourselves entirely available and either willingly engage them or gently redirect them, if that is possible, we may find that a whole world opens up for them *and* for us, a shared world, that in retrospect, we would not want to have missed, could not have predicted, and which might be more important to us than anything else we could have done, in spite of our fatigue or how busy and pressed for time we thought we were.

In making generous choices to attend to a child in that kind of moment, we are not acting like her servant (even though it may feel that way sometimes), but more like a true king or queen, a sovereign, rich with time and generous of heart.

But let's face it. Although we are a sovereign in our role as a parent, at some stages more than others we also *are* a servant—just as a wise king or a queen or any leader is a true servant of the realm. And it is worth being one in that sense.

It is a tricky business. Giving ourselves fully to our children, limit-lessly in terms of our being, which in its deepest nature, as we have seen, is limitless, runs so much against the grain of our society that it is vir-tually taboo even to talk about it. And yet, it is important to talk about, examine, and experiment with as part of our own practice, making new moves on our chessboard, sometimes bold moves we may never have con-ceived of before, and learning from what comes of them, as the world—as it so often does when we take the initiative—opens to make room for our offerings.

*

You are the notes, we are the flute
We are the mountains, you are the sounds coming down.
We are the pawns and kings and rooks
you set out on a board: we win or we lose.
We are lions rolling and unrolling on flags.
Your invisible wind carries us through the world.

RUMI

Branch Points

Did you ever stop and think of how things might have turned out differently in your life had it not been for the remarkable confluence of unfathomable, minuscule, seemingly random events that so influence our lives and proffer momentous potential openings, as well as limitations? Had I (jkz) decided to go to lunch five minutes earlier or later than I did one December day, or had Myla not run into a friend and fallen into conversation in a particular place, in all likelihood, we would never have met. We wouldn't have had the children we did or wound up living the lives we are now living. This points to something precious and mysterious about living itself that may be worth pondering.

Had things not unfolded the way they had, other things would no doubt have happened, and we would now be living other, very different lives. It would also have been a very different me, for the me that I am now is in large measure due to the texture of our relationship together and our love for each other.

Life may be generic, but love and beauty are specific. The world continually calls us to celebrate those specifics, in the places where we truly belong and feel most deeply at home. It calls us to celebrate the children we have, the life that is ours to be lived, if we can be here for it and awake to its texture and images and sounds, so that these intimate and always present aspects of our lives are not merely confined to memories stored away with the photograph albums. Our present actualities are true blessings, and their emergence every day nothing short of miraculous in their particulars.

This observation continually reminds me to hold the virtual "pregnancy" of each and every moment with great reverence and respect, reminds me that its potential is always momentous, even if we cannot know or foresee the next moment until it arrives, and even if for the most part so many of our moments seem at first blush only humdrum and bland, and each day seemingly more or less like the next. It is easy to miss the ways in which every moment contains the enormity of the entire universe, can be full of surprises and unthought-of possibilities, and forget that we can watch them unfold, and are called to participate in their unfolding. Young children are native to this magical world, where everything is fresh and new and possible.

Seeing each moment as a potential branch point can be an exceedingly useful way of looking at our lives as they unfold. If, in our own lives, we desire the future to be different in any way, as so often we do with great passion—whether it is to have a better relationship with a child or make something new happen in our lives—the only time we ever get to act to make it so is the present. For isn't the present actually the future? Isn't today yesterday's future? Here it is already. We have it now, right here.

Seeing the present in this way, we might ask ourselves, How is it? Are we at home here, in this actuality? In this, or any moment of our lives, do we actually know, feel, sense where we are and how we got to this place, to this moment?

The only way to know is to keep our eyes open, and that means all our senses. Even then, knowing may not mean knowing, but rather knowing that we don't know, and yet persisting in keeping the question itself alive because it is interesting and we are curious, and because, however our lives are right now, they are unfolding now, in this moment. This truly is it.

We know that each moment unfolds out of the preceding one, which colors it in some way. The present moment has a momentum of its own. Our actions always have consequences. If we hope to learn anything, or grow, or express our feelings, or improve the quality of life in the future, *this* really is the only time we ever get to affect the course that the incessant stream of actions and consequences we think of as our lives follows. If we take responsibility for attending to the quality and the possibilities of *this* moment, whether with a child or by ourselves, the next moment will be affected by that awareness, and therefore different.

Mindfulness may thus provide openings that may not have been accessible even the moment before because the mind is now seeing differently. These openings may have always been here as potential, but their actualizing frequently requires our wholehearted participation. So, when it is time to do the dishes, we do them in that way, with full presence of mind. And that opens up the next possibility. It is the same with everything.

The challenge is to see if we really can embody, fully, the life that is ours to live, with the children that are ours to nurture, right here, right now . . . and now, and now, and now, each moment, day, and night a new beginning, as we move through light and through darkness.

PART TEN

Darkness and

Light

Impermanence

Paddling a canoe across the lake in early morning July in northern Maine, looking for moose while my family sleeps in a lakeside cabin, I (jkz) observe the whirlpools coming off the paddle in the otherwise still water, one from the outside edge of the blade, another off the inside. They spin in opposite directions for a time, slipping behind me as the canoe moves forward. They are just water in motion, separate for a time, their distinct form due to the swirling of the water. As I look back to stay in touch with them, I see that they are soon gone. Their energy of motion passes back into the lake. Others appear with each stroke, each different, unique. They are mesmerizing. Form appearing for a brief moment out of emptiness, due to certain conditions which the lake and my paddle obligingly provide.

To me, these whirlpools are as fascinating as the moose I search for but do not find this morning, and in some ways, not too different. Living things too appear for brief moments in seemingly separate entities we call bodies, dance in the light of day for a time, and are soon gone. We know life appears in its distinct forms because of certain conditions. We know it is soon gone from those distinct forms and will appear elsewhere, anew. We know about death. But we see this particular moose or person as more or less permanent, and its passing takes us by surprise and frequently fills us with horror, as it should. Yet we know that its passing is as much a part of the way things are as its arrival. We know that all things are impermanent and fleeting, but hide from this aspect of things until it is right in our faces.

Several weeks later, I am reminded of these musings as I look at the pale, emaciated body of my friend dying of lymphoma at fifty, surrounded by his friends, a shocking almost-skeleton with his muscles and tendons exposed in ways we don't see except in death, still able to summon up from somewhere, in spite of his pain and diarrhea and fear-racked, medicated body, the energy to come to a party, lie on the couch, and play with breathtaking virtuosity on the guitar, sending currents of beauty off the strings and into our very souls. His wife and eleven-year-old daughter, so full of life, sit nearby.

I am struck dumb by the poignancy of it all. My children are seeing something they have never seen before. It is not pretty, but it is awe-inspiring, and it is transcendent. We, including his longtime doctor friend at whose house this is taking place, can do little for him other than make him comfortable and honor the life that is still in him.

We cannot stop the process. We find we can hardly even name it, so strong is the impulse to deny or turn away. As his thin fingers pick the strings while the other hand defines the notes, his face contorts with effort; or is it pleasure? He seems to ride in these brief moments beyond time, even as it feels to me that he is showing us, sharing with us, perhaps most for his daughter, the power he still has and the beauty of what he has known in his life and heard in his ear.

I met a woman recently whose son, in his last year of college, was killed when the car he was driving at night in the desert went off the road and crashed. Perhaps he had fallen asleep. She will never know. What explanation would suffice? A life snuffed out in its prime, a hole rent in the fabric of this woman's life, the life she had given birth to and nourished, with all its connecting threads, suddenly no more. How to hold this? How to come to an acceptance of the unacceptable? And yet this, too, has been part of parenthood since the beginning of time.

Perhaps the best we can do is feel the fleetingness of life and of our present moments, and live inside them, one at a time, as fully as possible, hugging our children and rejoicing in their life, and feel at the same time the certainty of death, of life arising *and* passing away. The breath can remind us of this, as it arises and passes away, as can our moments, our friends, the weather, and our thoughts. Can we find ways to ride these currents mindfully and let life flow through us? Can we honor those mysteries beyond our knowing, which shape our frail humanity and give it surprising strength and wisdom?

*

BOUNDARIES OF LOVE

Beyond and before
the inequities of passion,
the four halves
are secretly braided.
Dispositions of our truth;
possibilities are born and
in time, buried.
Hidden galaxies and
futile losses,
our impatient hearts forbid this.
Places where the unknown
are exquisite and elusive.

RYAN JON ROBINSON,
AGE SIXTEEN, OCTOBER 1995

This poem was written several weeks before Ryan Robinson died of an accidental gun shot wound to his head at an unsupervised teenage party where alcohol was involved. The boys had found a handgun, which they thought was unloaded, in the parents' bedroom. It happened to have been a Russian gun. Unlike American models, the safety on this gun allowed the trigger to be pulled back and clicked. The boys had removed the clip and had "dry-fired" the pistol many times into the fireplace. The safety must have accidentally been switched off right before it came to Ryan. None of them had any inkling there might be a bullet in the chamber. His father, who had attended a mindfulness retreat I had conducted the summer before, wrote to me:

"Ryan had just transferred to a new, much larger high school. On his first day, he insisted on wearing a T-shirt his friends at his former school had made for him. On the front it said, 'Hi, my name is Ryan,' and on the back, 'I'm new here, be nice to me.' I was in the kitchen as he raced out the door, late again. Frantically he came running back in. 'Where's my cape? I forgot my cape.' I said, 'No, you don't really want to wear your cape. Not on the first day. Why don't you just check it out, get the lay of the land.' Cautiously, he replied, 'Is that what you think I should do, or is that what you would do?' Well, the answer to that was obvious. He had the ability to really see what was going on with people, although perhaps unspoken, and tell the truth about it. Sometimes that ability could feel confronting. But it was always truthful.

"Ryan's death, shortly after his sixteenth birthday, forever ruptured the fabric of our cozy little family. The resultant separation divided a life that I had previously taken for granted from the extraordinary pain of each subsequent day. The grief

I experienced in those first two months was far greater than any appreciation for being alive that I could relate to. Being alive simply hurt too much.

"A huge part of me died with Ryan that cold October night. During the past four months, my life has felt like a prison sentence; something to be endured, no longer enjoyed. For so many weeks after the accident the thoughts and pictures that raced through my mind were uncontrollable. They consumed my sleep and my waking hours. I would attempt to observe them, notice them, breathe with them, but it was hopeless. Everywhere I turned, I was reminded of him. It was like a thousand wild stallions stampeding out of control. . . .

"I am thankful for my mindfulness practice. It has become a road map that guides me over very rough, very painful and yet uncharted terrain. It is interesting, I used to believe my thoughts were who I was. Now, my thoughts are what I have, not who I am. My life seems to have become the context within which all my thoughts occur, within which my emotions run. Throughout the day the thoughts and emotions arrive as always. Some, the most wild of the stallions, continue to run unrestrained, out of control, with me at their mercy. Most of them, however, I am able to observe, experience and let go of, while returning to my breath. With the majority, I can now grab the saddle and hoist myself up before being dragged along behind at the end of a rope, bouncing off of my own rocks called 'victim' and 'self-pity.' For this I am very grateful.

"During the day I observe a variety of thoughts. 'I can't do this anymore . . . My life isn't worth living; I failed as a parent.' During my sitting meditation, I observe these and other considerations . . . All the while I attempt patiently to return to my breath. I forget, and return. I go away with my thoughts, and return. I notice my impatience, and return. I can see now that underneath the thoughts and the emotions, underneath the sorrow, the emptiness and all of my grief there is something else. It is the absolute unconditional love that I have for a beautiful young man whom I simply miss very much.

"Perhaps the greatest lesson I have learned from this tragedy is the arrogance I had maintained in my relationship with time prior to the accident. I have learned how important it is to tell people when you love them, because tomorrow is just a concept of our minds."

The River
of Buried Grief

I (jkz) have been in a room with seven hundred men of all ages, every one in tears over his lost relationship with his father. Before they walked into the room and spent time talking and listening together, most were barely aware that they carried such grief, and hardly any would have shared it with other men.

I have been in groups of hundreds of health professionals where, during intensive training in mindfulness, immense personal sadness from childhood poured out of person after person, men and women. At these retreats, we let such emotional expressions of grief, and the stories that contain them, occur and go on for some time without any reaction or comment other than our full and silent attention. People have a hard time realizing that making space for deep and unpleasant emotions is as much a part of mindfulness as following the breath.

A veritable river of grief seems to flow through us. Its subterranean course is not always in evidence, so we may have no idea it is there. But this river of grief is never as far from us or as foreign to us as we might think when we see it coursing though the heart of someone else. Seen or unseen, it can color an entire life journey, including our character, choice of profession, and how we parent.

I am convinced that this river runs through us all, carrying deep, perhaps archetypal feelings we rarely come in contact with or even know exist. When we are out of touch with our own grief, it can feel more than a little awkward and strange when someone else gets in touch with theirs. It is easy to feel embarrassed for them, or aloof and a little judgmental, like, "Why are they making such a big deal about something like that?" "It happened so long ago?" "Haven't they dealt with that already in therapy?" "I'm certainly beyond that."

We are all to some degree defended against the deepest feelings we carry. If we weren't, we would no longer be carrying them in quite the same way. People who are less defended against their own grief are not so judging of others'. The real work of mindfulness is making room for whatever is happening while it is happening, with openness, equanimity, empathy, and compassion. It means being patient with ourselves and with others and not jumping to move on prematurely to something else because of our discomfort.

But in those rare moments when we do connect with our own grief, when it's *our* feelings that surface in this moment, for whatever reason, the situation is all of a sudden very different. Then the whole world is in pain, our whole universe colored by a grief that we feel extends far beyond the personal.

Perhaps we wouldn't be carrying quite so much buried grief as adults had we been parented with greater kindness and thoughtfulness when we were children. We cannot say with any certainty. It is different for each one of us. Each of us has our unique constellation of painful past experiences and our reactions to them, some buried, some unearthed.

It takes years of inner and outer work on oneself to heal from losses of one kind or another, and from a lack of recognition and honoring and being cared for appropriately in childhood. Often it takes years even to become aware of our deepest feelings about our experiences and how we were treated. It is not always that one's parents were abusive, or alcoholic, or grossly neglectful. Much of the hurt for many of us came about while our parents were trying to do the best they could with what they had and within the framework of their world and world view. They were formed by their own experiences, both positive and negative, and by what *their* parents passed down to them, just as we are. Each family has its own unique combinations of love, shame, guilt, blame, withholding, and neediness. They are most harmful when coupled with unconsciousness.

A woman told me that when her mother died, when she was still a young girl with a number of young siblings, her father refused to have any further mention of the mother in the household. It was as if, buried, she never existed. All the children were forced into this emotional closet. The father thought it would be better, less traumatic, to just move on and not dwell on the past. It did irreparable harm to the family.

So we see that it is ignorance (in the Buddhist sense of ignoring how things actually are) which so often lies at the root of our grief. This kind of ignorance can lead to parents not knowing their own children. Such ignorance can co-exist within a family in which there are many positive accomplishments and a surface appearance of harmony and love. The one does not preclude the other.

Unconscious grief casts a shadow that extends out and down in our psyche. It moves in the dark inner recesses of memory. It has a life of its own underground, even when the surface seems bright. Indeed, sometimes the brighter the surface, the longer and darker the emotional shadows.

Robert Bly, in *The Little Book on the Human Shadow*, describes the dynamics of our buried emotions using the image of an invisible bag we acquire early in life into which, as we grow, we progressively stuff all the parts of ourselves that we are made to feel aren't lovable in our attempts to be seen and accepted in the circle of those we value and hold in esteem. This can go on for one's entire lifetime, living something of a lie to keep up appearances or to fit in.

It may have started out at home with our parents when we were infants and young children, and were given messages about what pleased them and what didn't, what was "acceptable" in terms of thoughts, feelings, and behaviors, and what wasn't. But it continues in school among one's peers and teachers, and out in the world. Over time our bag gets longer and longer, and heavier and heavier as we stuff more and more of ourselves into it: our anger, our impulsiveness, our spontaneity, our softness, our strength, even our intelligence, in our sometimes desperate efforts to be likeable or accepted or well thought of, or to fit a certain framework we believe we are called upon to reflect—the stoic, the martyr, the wise one. It is truly dark in the bag because we are unwilling to let in any light and see what's going on in a large part of our own psyche.

If we pretend we don't have this bag over our shoulder, and we therefore refuse to open it from time to time for thirty or forty years, except to stuff more things in, those shadows we have stuffed inside, which are actually valid and important if unaccepted parts of ourselves, fester and grow toxic from lack of acknowledgment and expression. They linger there, and they can influence our life trajectory in momentous ways we may not know but only see on occasion in dreams, or when the fabric of our life seems to fray or suddenly disintegrate. What we don't want to look at in the inner world is often visible in our face in the outer world. The inner reflects the outer, and the outer the inner. To come to harmony requires marrying inner and outer, bringing them together again, in the embrace of awareness and acceptance.

Perhaps it is time to educate ourselves to this burden we carry once and for all and to consciously make ongoing, moment-to-moment efforts to accept all aspects of our being, to listen to and speak with our shadow and our subterranean river of buried grief, and hold ourselves in esteem and unconditional acceptance, with compassion. This is tantamount to parenting ourselves, or completing the job on the way to what we might call true adulthood.

If we can "parent" ourselves in this way, maybe—just maybe—we will have a clearer view of our children, and will be able to see and accept them in ways that will occasion less lopping off of parts of themselves in their heartbreaking attempts to be accepted for who they actually are, rather than for what we—in our own ignorance of how things are, and out of our own fears—might want them to be.

✳

Ring the bells that can still ring.
Forget your perfect offering.
There is a crack in everything.
That's how the light gets in.

LEONARD COHEN

Hanging
by a Thread

When our children are hurting, we hurt. When our children aren't hurting, parenting can be difficult enough. Sometimes it feels like we are hanging by a thread.

*

Kids fighting with each other, temper tantrums, "I'm bored!", teething, fussing, illness, sleepless nights, long winter days, dark rainy days, days when we are feeling low, tired, trying to meet different needs, balancing, juggling work and family and a hundred other things, negotiating, coming up with yet another creative idea, or uncreative idea, or even dinner . . . by the end of the day I (mkz) am feeling exhausted, exasperated, tremendously limited, and confined. My world has become too small. I feel an overpowering urge to run outside, to get some air, some distance, some space.

When the weather doesn't allow for outdoor activity and we are cooped up inside for long stretches of time, that's when I become acutely aware of my own limits as a person and all the skills I never acquired and thus can't teach my children. I'm also very aware of the limits of our culture. It seems like all there is to do is to consume in some fashion.

Whether it's shopping or eating or going to the movies, so often it all feels empty and lifeless. Where are the centers in our towns for dancing and music, storytelling, and conversation for all ages?

They say it takes a whole village to raise a child. But where are the villages in our society? We still see important vestiges of the village of old in extended family, community centers, support groups, cross-generational friendships, and communities of faith. Nevertheless, all too often parents find themselves isolated and alone. This may be especially true for single parents, who aren't able to share their day-to-day struggles, get a different perspective, or just have someone to commiserate with—although from another perspective, it might be said that sometimes partners can be unsupportive and create more work. Even with friends or supportive partners, the hardest times usually happen when we are on our own. Parenting can be lonely work.

We need community to round out our individual resources and necessarily limited skills, to provide a critical mass of ideas, enthusiasm, and life experience in the form of people with a variety of backgrounds and talents to back us up when our own repertoire feels exhausted. As parents, we have to provide the bedrock in the family, but we can't provide everything ourselves.

Our darkest times as parents of young children take many different forms. There is a huge gamut of circumstances and experiences that color what each family and each parent has to face and work with.

*

As our children get older and enter adolescence and the teen years, with all their complexity and problems, having babies and younger children may seem simple by comparison, and we may find ourselves confused, discouraged, even despairing at times. As we have already seen, it can feel as if we are losing our teenage children as they pull away from us, influenced more and more by their peers, and are sometimes drawn into self-destructive behaviors. We also understand that in some way, we *are* losing them as they move out into the world. We feel anguished at their vulnerability and our inability to protect them, and sometimes angry at the ways they express themselves—or don't.

The intuitive, elemental, and very physical parenting we did with young children is no longer appropriate. We may find that our physical exhaustion gives way to mental and emotional exhaustion, in part because we are continually adjusting our roles as parents, as our adolescents struggle with their needs for autonomy, connection, love, and meaning.

They grow and undergo metamorphoses in various astonishing, unexpected, and sometimes trying ways, and we are called upon to grow and change as well. As they become independent and need us less, we can find ourselves slipping into a business-as-usual routine where they are concerned, which can feel superficial, unsatisfying, and disconnected, to us and to them. They need more time alone, more space from us, and a *different* kind of sensitivity from us. In some ways we are irrelevant to them, but we are also *not* irrelevant to them.

It can be hard to see that they still need us, when they are angry and critical and closed off from us, and through the veil of our own anger and worry. Refusing to disappear and completely disconnect from them, even when we feel marginalized, confused, frustrated, and despairing, takes tremendous will and commitment.

Inevitably, there are times when adolescents find life unsatisfying, when their soul needs are not being met, when they are unhappy and questioning: "What's life about? Where is the meaning? Isn't there more to life than this? Where do I fit in?" They may become moody, withdrawn, and feel more distant from us than we could ever have imagined when they were little. They may actively push us away, with hostile, angry behavior. We see them hurting, but it's hard to reach them.

When they are feeling alienated and alone, they need to feel that we are still with them, in whatever way they will allow us to be. We may see them looking at us as if from across a large chasm. Reaching them can be difficult. The gulf can feel scary, to them and to us. We may feel powerless in a way that we never felt when they were little. They inadvertently give us a glimpse of our own fragility, our own doubts and fears, our own feelings of vulnerability, which are usually buried deep inside of us and shielded from daily examining.

When our children are questioning the authenticity of feelings, of people, and even of themselves, we would do well to locate a place within ourselves that is authentic, grounded, simple, and real. At such times, we might take a few moments to focus inwardly, bringing our attention to our breathing, to our body, and to our feelings. We may not feel very connected or close to our child in such moments, but we *can* be a sympathetic presence and reach for any threads they might hold out to us, however thin.

We might also extend some threads of our own, however tentative and delicate, if appropriate. This might involve just listening and acknowledging the reality of the difficulties they are experiencing, or their pain and uncertainty. Or it might call for something more dramatic, such as taking them off by themselves for a day, or a weekend, or a week. This may not be possible or feel possible, but truly hard times call for truly creative solutions. Choosing something they might like to do, and making the time to be together, in whatever way we can, can remind them of the deeper meaning that resides below their busy and sometimes monotonous everyday routines. And stepping outside of our everyday lives, even if precipitated by a crisis, can serve the same function for us as well, and can help us renew our connection with them.

There are times—when our older children are feeling stuck, limited, unhappy with their lives—in which decisive action is appropriate and necessary. This is particularly true when we sense that they are leaning toward doing things that are dangerous or self-destructive. They need to know that we are concerned about them, and what our concerns are. They may need us to problem-solve with them, advocate for them, help them find ways to make their lives more satisfying, more meaningful.

Teenagers often have their own clear insights into the heart of the matter. But there are also times when they know something is not right but don't know what it is, and at those times they may need us to bring whatever wisdom we have gleaned from our own life experience to the problem at hand. It takes a long time for children, for any of us, to understand how the world works (do we ever fully "understand?") and how to make things work for them.

Helping them in any way may be especially hard to do if we are seen as part of the problem. Although we can be open to making changes in our own behavior, we may or may not be able to help them make changes in their lives. We may or may not even agree on what is needed to make things better, or even what the problem is. But sometimes, just acknowledging the hard time they are having can make the difference between their feeling isolated and feeling connected, between feeling judged and feeling cared for. When they feel concern and loving acceptance from a parent, it can give them a more meaningful context within which to view their difficulties of the moment.

At other times, we can overwhelm them with our concerns, our worry, and our well-meaning overtures. Hard as this is for us, we may have to step back and give them more room.

*

There are times when our children, no matter how old they are, seem to "regress" to a younger age. This can be exasperating for parents and drive us to distraction. It can happen when we are feeling most vulnerable and depleted ourselves. It's almost as if they are resonating with our mental state, as well as their own.

*

A friend's sixteen-year-old boy had been emotionally withdrawn from his family and got very sick from an infection about the same time. His parents could have chosen to see his sudden illness as purely physical, having nothing to do with his emotional state or the difficulties he and the family had been experiencing. Instead, they were able to view his illness within a larger context, and began to examine the stresses, both physical and emotional, in their son's life and within the family. They then made use of this time in which he was sick and convalescing to promote a broader healing. They accepted his need to "regress" by being at home—slowing down, turning inward for a time, eating special healing foods, and reconnecting with his family—and recognized the restoring and transformative benefits of this to him and to their relationship with him.

"Regression" is a word with strong negative connotations. It usually connotes maladjustment, failure to act one's age, going backwards to a more "infantile" stage. But there are times when children, not just young children, need a period of being cared for, read to, sung to, a time in which to go inward in order to be able to move outward again. Responding with kindness and acceptance, and without judgment, when our children are regressing feeds that part of them that is struggling with growth. It ultimately helps them to move on, to shed an old skin. It is a true gift to them.

This is not always easy, or even possible. Work and other demands may not leave us with the time we need to attend fully to our child. It may only be possible for us to treat the symptom that our child is showing us, rather than attending to the problems that created the symptom. But if, over the long term, it is only the symptoms that get our attention, the root cause can grow and continue to create problems.

When a child is unhappy and out of balance and perhaps regressing, he or she can be very hard to live with. But when we take the difficult behavior personally and wall ourselves off, put on our armor, get stuck in our own hurt feelings, the walls between us just get thicker and higher. These are the times when it helps to see with eyes of wholeness. This means viewing what's happening in the largest possible context, with an intention to examine, to be fully present, and view it within the paradoxical framework of distance *and* compassion. When the crisis has passed, if we can let go of any hurt, resentment, or anger we may be feeling, we can move into a truly new moment with our children.

At the end of a day that felt like it was filled with unending criticism and negativity directed at me, one of my daughters, at the age of ten, snuggled up to me and told me very sincerely that she loved me. This wonderful capacity to be fluid, to let go of anger, changes as children get older. They need us to remind them by our own behavior that it is possible to be aware of ongoing issues at the same time that we meet each moment with a willingness to start afresh.

Ultimately, it is not our ideas that will count the most; rather, it will be the authenticity of our being and our embodiment of caring that we bring to the gut-wrenching moments we all find ourselves in as parents and that make us question everything. This is hard training, in the language of Zen practice.

You do not have to be good.

You do not have to walk on your knees

for a hundred miles through the desert, repenting.

You only have to let the soft animal of your body love what it
  loves.

Tell me about despair, yours, and I will tell you mine.

Meanwhile the world goes on

Meanwhile the sun and the clear pebbles of the rain

are moving across the landscapes,

over the prairies and the deep trees,

the mountains and the rivers.

Meanwhile the wild geese, high in the clean blue air,

are heading home again.

Whoever you are, no matter how lonely,

the world offers itself to your imagination,

calls to you like the wild geese, harsh and exciting—

over and over announcing your place

in the family of things.

MARY OLIVER, "WILD GEESE," *Dream Work*

Losing It

All parents lose it sometimes. We lose our temper, we lose our minds. We can lose our balance, our way, our dignity, our self-respect. When it happens, it is very painful, no matter what provoked it.

It usually happens when we are exhausted and have been pushed beyond our limits. Intense feelings of frustration arise and we may not recognize them in time, or we just don't know how to shift gears, or even care. Sometimes losing it takes the form of screaming and yelling, or mean-spirited speech. Sometimes, we lash out with a smack or slap. As soon as it happens, we feel terrible—angry with ourselves, sad for our children. All of a sudden, we're in the middle of a nightmare. I'll (mkz) give you an example:

I'm putting one of my daughters to bed. She has always had a hard time going to sleep, and at eight years old, she is still a night owl and can stay up forever. I'm at my worst after 10:00 P.M. I don't function well. I'm not patient. She often becomes especially sensitive at bedtime—to all sorts of things. It's often then that she'll want something to eat, she won't want to be left alone, she wants the light on, the nightlight is not enough.

When it's time for her to go to bed, I sit with her for a while. When I see, as I do on this particular night, that it's going to be one of those long hauls and I'm too tired to stay up, I say to her, "Sleep in my bed tonight." So off she goes. But I say, "You have to wear a shirt in my bed, that's the rule, because I don't want to spend the night keeping you covered so you won't get cold!" She knows this, objects anyway, but does put on a shirt. Then she immediately starts fussing about it and kicking and punching the bed. I get her another shirt, a softer, more comfortable one. By this time, she is even angrier and swearing at me. *She* wants the light on, *I* want the light off. It is turning into a battle of wills. I am afraid she'll wake her sister. I feel trapped. I feel controlled. I feel helpless. Things are moving in a certain direction and I can't seem to change it.

Then I hear her sister yelling at us to be quiet. She's been woken up. I am even angrier now. I yell at her to be quiet. She continues to make noise and pound the bed and fuss, and I finally feel so frustrated and angry and helpless that I slap her on the cheek. She starts crying and then screaming even more loudly. Her sister yells again for her to be quiet. I feel sick that I've smacked her. She's shouting that I'm a child abuser and that she's going to call the police. I'm paralyzed with shame and remorse. I'm in the middle of a gigantic nightmare. After about twenty minutes of screaming and crying that I'm sure the whole neighborhood can hear, she calls for her dad. Her dad's not home. Finally she starts sobbing, "Mommy!"

I bring her ice and a washcloth and sit there with her, crying with her, telling her what I did was very bad, and telling her I'm really sad I hurt her. Finally, an hour later, she's asleep in my bed, snuggled up to me. I lie there wide awake feeling terrible. What a bedtime!

As horrible as it is, there is usually *something* I can learn from this kind of wrenching experience that will make it easier to work with the next time something similar comes up. I begin by asking myself questions. Is there something that could have made the transition to sleep less difficult for her? How can I work with my own anger and frustration so that I don't make things worse?

Each child is so different. For some, the transition into sleep is resisted every night and the transition to wakefulness in the morning is just as hard. With others, it may be as easy as a bedtime story or a quiet song. But sometimes, no matter what we do, it seems like we're headed for disaster. That night, putting my daughter to bed started with reading stories by the fire, followed by sketching pictures sitting in her bed—a lovely beginning, ending in collective misery.

I ask myself, what could I have done differently? At times the answer is very clear. In this situation, it wasn't at all clear. Sometimes these night storms feel inevitable, as if they just have to play themselves out. But did this really have to happen the way it did? When do I bend? When do I bend too much? Could I have done something to change the direction we were moving in?

Showing remorse for my actions and concern for her feelings, rather than leaving what happened unacknowledged and unexamined, is extremely important for her and for me if healing is to occur, and some kind of learning. For me, this means acknowledging the awfulness of what happened and not trying to minimize it nor blame her for it. The next day, when we both have some distance from it, we can talk more about what happened and how we both felt.

It sometimes helps to go over our agreements and focus in on the things we can agree on in advance. After this episode, we agreed on a signal that would grab our attention and let each other know that something serious was happening so that we might have a chance to change course. Hopefully, each time an incident like this happens, we learn something that makes it less likely to happen again.

In the midst of the storm, it helps if we can stop for a moment, bring awareness to our breathing, and give ourselves permission to not necessarily have to solve anything in that moment. In doing so, we can avoid reacting with our own out-of-control anger, which only fuels the intensity and chaos.

Losing our temper can be horrible. Yet, we can use even this to learn and grow if we are not afraid to acknowledge that it happened rather than deny or minimize it, or spend our energy blaming ourselves or our children, or just wishing things could be different without taking responsibility for our actions. At the same time, depending on their age, we may have to help our children see their own part in what happened, and to strategize with them to find more effective ways to express their feelings, and to see the different choices they may have in difficult situations.

No Guarantees

Parents know all too painfully that there are many things we don't control, and that no matter what we do, there are no guarantees. Part of mindful parenting is facing our own expectations and our own limitations and working with each situation as best we can, without trying to force a certain outcome.

From the moment we become pregnant, to the birth of our child, and in the years that follow, there are a myriad of factors affecting each child's life trajectory and development. Some we know about, others we may not. Some are straightforward, others deeply mysterious. We can do all the "right things," only to find out later that they were not so "right," and that there were factors we were not aware of, perhaps that no one was aware of at the time. When it comes down to it, we can only rely on a combination of intuition, common sense, awareness, information, and most importantly, our love. Even with our best efforts to meet the needs of our children, it is important to recognize that there will be many things that can have an impact on them that we cannot necessarily control or prevent.

The most obvious examples are tragic mishaps that can leave a child forever changed and the family struggling to adjust their lives to meet their child's needs; or the death of a child, leaving a gigantic hole in the lives of the survivors.

A child's health can also be seriously hurt by long-term exposure to various environmental hazards. There is new information about such hazards coming out all the time, sometimes contradictory, and often confusing. Many factors in the environment are known to cause cancer and birth defects; others are suspected of being harmful, and some environmental hazards are yet to be identified.

Alcohol, smoking, drugs, asbestos, lead, radon, pesticides, and many other chemicals are known to have a detrimental effect on human health, and exert their strongest effects on children. The health effects of other ubiquitous factors, such as microwave radiation, are currently being researched. As parents, we have to strike some kind of balance between recognizing and accepting the limits of our knowledge and of what we can do to protect our children on the one hand, and on the other, being reasonably informed and doing the best we can to try to protect them.

Being mindful of the environment that a child is exposed to, whether during pregnancy, in the home, or out in the world, requires energy and attention. This whole area is anxiety-producing and intimidating because we often feel powerless and the stakes are high. It is also hard sometimes to find out what is known and then weigh the risks to our own individual family members. It is easier to ignore the whole domain of environmental risk.

Sometimes environmental hazards are right in front of our eyes in our own homes, such as asbestos disintegrating on heating pipes, or peeling lead paint. Sometimes our noses alert us to hazards such as formaldehyde or other volatile organic compounds, such as those venting from newly installed carpeting. Some are undetectable by our senses, like lead and other chemicals in our water. Environmental hazards such as chemical pollution of wells, pesticides in foods, indoor air quality in schools, may require us to organize in groups, to lobby and speak out to preserve or restore environmental safety for our children.

While it is of paramount importance for our children to feel emotionally safe, it is also our responsibility as parents to work to make our children's physical environment safe as well.

*

Other factors we can't control as parents but do have to work with are the unique physical and emotional qualities our children are born with. For instance, all parents know that each one of our children is born with unique qualities that unfold and change over time. One of these is what we might call their temperament. Rudolf Steiner, the German philosopher and educator, identified four major categories of temperament: the *choleric* (fiery, energetic, often athletic, intense, willful); the *melancholic* (inward, solitary, pessimistic, sensitive, loves rainy days and sad stories); the *sanguine* (easygoing, forgetful, changeable, sociable, dreamy); and the *phlegmatic* (loves to eat and be cozy, inwardly focused, cautious, observant, deliberate).

We all have a mix of different temperaments and at different times different aspects predominate. An infant who is very choleric, demanding, and intense may grow into a child who shows more sanguine qualities at times, and also may have a melancholic streak. A sanguine baby may grow into a teenager with a strong will and a fiery temper.

The temperamental features that make a child unique can sometimes be very trying for parents. They can be made even more difficult by our unconscious expectations or by our own temperaments. Different temperaments in families can create situations in which tremendous friction, unmet expectations, and anger come into play. An athletic, high-achieving parent may have trouble relating to a child who is more phlegmatic and prefers to curl up with a snack and a book. An articulate, verbally oriented parent may feel at a loss with a deeply feeling, non-verbal, artistic child. Being aware of such characteristics in our children and in ourselves can help us to be more understanding and accepting, and to work with situations with greater insight.

We may have had one baby that nursed easily and was very social, setting up expectations within us, and then have another baby who is a disinterested nurser, harder to reach and connect with, or one who has colic or allergies. An easygoing, flexible child may be followed by a child who finds every transition difficult and is always pushing the limits, whatever they are. A well-organized student and avid reader may be followed by a child who has trouble organizing himself and finds reading difficult.

Some children seem to have a harder time than others in all sorts of ways. They may be born with problems or develop problems or be drawn to paths that are worrisome, perhaps even dangerous or self-destructive. Being a good parent doesn't mean that our children will have completely problem-free lives. But imagine what their lives might have been like had they been born into a family in which they were not seen for who they were, in which the parents did not extend themselves and work with the actuality of situations mindfully, and in which they may have been ignored, rejected, or shamed because they had different and perhaps trying aspects to their being.

Parenting mindfully asks a lot of us. There is deep inner work and deep outer work to be done. Our awareness has to encompass the whole. We do this for our children, with the understanding that there are no guarantees.

Lost

Dante told the truth when he opened the *Divine Comedy* with the lines: "In the middle of this road we call our life/I found myself in a dark wood/With no clear path through"—in other words, lost. To really know where one is, his poem tells us, allegorically at least, one has first to descend, go underground, into the darkness of hell. Only then can one make the ascent to heaven.

When we feel that we have lost our way, perhaps during a time of darkness, or despair, or confusion, we might ask ourselves, "How did I get here?" "Where am I?" "What is this place I find myself in now?"

As soon as we start attending, we are no longer lost. We are simply where we are. Where we actually are is always a good place to begin, both physically, when we've lost our bearings, and metaphorically, when it feels as if we no longer know what we are doing as parents, or in our work, or in our lives in general. Perhaps, in some way, we are always lost, to the degree that we are not fully awake. Perhaps what is most important is our willingness to be where we actually are and dwell here fully, in darkness or in light, without having to go anywhere else. Only then may we know where to place our foot when it comes time to move.

A poem by David Wagoner, based on the Northwest Native American tradition, captures this spirit. It is what the elder might say in response to a young boy or girl who comes and asks, "What do I do when I am lost in the forest?"

> Stand still. The trees ahead and bushes beside you
> Are not lost. Wherever you are is called Here,
> And you must treat it as a powerful stranger,
> Must ask permission to know it and be known.
> The forest breathes. Listen. It answers,
> I have made this place around you,
> If you leave it you may come back again, saying Here.
>
> No two trees are the same to Raven.
> No two branches are the same to Wren.
> If what a tree or a bush does is lost on you,
> You are surely lost. Stand still. The forest knows
> Where you are. You must let it find you.

DAVID WAGONER, *Lost*

The poet reminds us that our lives depend on our sensitivity to the particulars, that if what the forest or a tree does, or the look of a child, is lost on us, then we are surely, in some deep way, lost. The call is to pay attention, to wake up to where we are, to what is before us and all around us, here, now. Can we learn to stand still? Can we hear the forest of life and of the world breathing, calling to us to be still for a moment, to wake up, to feel the interconnectedness of all things, to realize that no two moments are the same? Can we listen in this way to our children?

This is the challenge of bringing mindfulness into our parenting, especially at those moments that seem the darkest, and when we feel the most adrift, without bearings, lost. Can we stand still right there, right then, which may be right *here*, right *now*, and be in touch with and guided by what is most basic, through our own attention?

It's Never
Too Late

We are all to some degree a product of our times. The choices we make as young parents are influenced by the era in which we parent and its values, and by the people around us, our own parents, our friends, and, of course, the "experts." We tend to take authoritative pronouncements at face value and not see past their social contexts, whether it is the way our parents raised us, or well-meaning advice from a pediatrician. It's very hard to nurse a baby in a time when everyone is bottlefeeding, in an environment lacking support, guidance, and role models. Or we may have grown up in a family that didn't hug, where feelings were not acknowledged, or where love was always tied to conditions and expectations. We may have carried that way of being into our own parenting, relying on what was familiar and comfortable, without much thought, or unable to muster the will or courage to go against the prevailing tide.

At times, we may not have been comfortable with what we were doing as parents, and our intuition may have voiced discomfort or yearned for something else, but we may not have felt that we had options, that there was any other way. Our feelings, our instincts, our intuitions may have been buried; and now, later in life, we may be left with regret, sadness, loss, or pain.

A mother of grown children sent us the following reflections, which she had written several years before we met her:

"I am but a baby myself when I give birth to my first child. Twenty-three is wanting to be tripping off in Europe somewhere or going to grad school or dating more than one guy in the same week. Twenty-three is not wanting to change diapers, sterilize glass baby bottles and have cotton lap pads across my thighs. But it is the early 60s, and what's a nice Jewish girl to do at 20 but to marry a nice Jewish boy and produce a grand-child. . . .

"It is the early 60s and my husband simply drops me off at the hospital as I go into labor. The doctor says he will call him at home . . . not to worry and to grab some sleep. 'Good-bye, hon,' he says. The nurse wheels me off in the wheelchair and looks at my small frame. 'What are you here for?' 'To have a baby,' I say. 'Where is it?' she asks, looking at my belly. It is the early 60s and the less gain the better. I am 15 pounds over my normal weight. It is the early 60s and hiding a protrusion is in . . . showing, as in blossoming, is definitely out.

"I am wheeled into the labor room. It is the early 60s and consciousness is out . . . being unconscious is in, and I am given an injection to create twilight sleep. In the delivery room I feel nothing, I see nothing. My only recall is of someone shaking my arm, and I vaguely hear, 'You have a boy.' It is the early 60s, and I never get to see my son until many hours after the birth. It is the early 60s and rooming in (mother and child) is not permitted in hospitals. Fathers can only visit during hours. Breastfeeding is out . . . formula is in . . . having a nurse for four weeks is in . . . bonding with the baby is . . . well, no one really even talks about the bonding process.

"My husband and I may be parents, but we are still kids ourselves. Neither of us has worked out our deeper issues, and when the nurse leaves after four weeks, I begin to cry. The impact hits hard. At twenty-three, I am tied down. I am on a schedule of feeding, changing, bathing, sleeping. I am ripe for the advice that I hear . . . 'Don't spoil him . . . don't pick him up . . . let him cry. That's what we did with you. Listen to us . . . we are your parents and after raising two children, we know what is right. The worst thing is to give in when he cries . . . Oh, you can see if he needs to be changed or fed, but if he doesn't need that, then let him cry and eventually he'll go to sleep.'

"I buy their advice . . . I want to be a good mother and have an unspoiled child, and so I feed, I diaper, I bathe, and when I hear the crying, I let him cry.

"The word 'spoiled' hits hard . . . It brings back some unpleasant memories of when I was called spoiled by my parents:

" 'You should be grateful for what you have . . . for what we do for you . . . other children don't have it as good as you do . . . we've spoiled you . . . '

"I look at my infant son . . . No, I won't give in to his crying.

"It's the early 60s and live-in housekeepers are in; joining a country club is in; playing indoor tennis as part of a league is in. I don't do any of the forementioned, but I also don't meet my son's primary need for closeness and contact. I don't even learn about bonding until almost twenty-five years later.

"At some time during the early 80s, I begin to notice women breastfeeding their babies in public places and in the quiet confines of their homes. On the Oprah show I learn that having wants and needs are OK. I am hearing words like 'contact' and 'warmth' and the 'bonding process.' Something in me is painfully sad. Something in me is wanting to cry. I long to return to my infant son and pick him up and kiss his baby tears; I yearn to cuddle him and coo him to sleep, but having that second chance is out.

"It is the 90s . . . my son is a grown man and for me, feeling the pain and the feelings is in."

The grief of lost opportunities, for how we were or weren't in another time, lies deep within the human psyche. It can cause us to yearn for some way to heal our children's pain and our own, and bring us closer. We are forced to acknowledge that what is past cannot be undone, only known and known deeply, felt and felt deeply, and thereby, in a glimmer of new possibility and hope, perhaps transformed by our very recognition and our acceptance. It is only in the present that new possibilities exist. Acknowledging our anguish and grief and the pain we may have caused, is part of the shaping of those possibilities, of giving birth to something new in ourselves, which may require the shedding of something old, however tenaciously it clings to us and we to it.

In our view, it is never too late to try to heal relationships with grown children who may have been hurt by us through our past ignorance, however innocent or understandable, or through lack of attention, or busyness, or neglect, withholding, judgment, or abusiveness. It is never too late to work toward creating healthy new connections, even if our children are distrustful of us, or angry about past attitudes or actions, omissions, or commissions on our part, that they feel were harmful to them.

One way we might begin to heal these wounds is by sharing our regrets and our awareness of the things we did that were harmful or neglectful, either by letter or in person with our adult children. Doing this in a letter may be a more sensitive way to communicate at first, particularly if a child feels we have been intrusive or thoughtless about boundaries. To be of any real value, reaching out in this way must be a genuine overture, with the well-being of our child foremost in our mind, and, as hard as it might be for us, accepting the possibility that irreparable damage may have been done and no reconciliation possible. We need to stand in a place beyond looking for sympathy, understanding, reassurance, or affection, beyond any desire to be absolved of guilt. We can recognize these feelings when they arise, and yet bring our attention back to the question, "What is in the best interest of my child?" even when he or she is an adult.

*

In bringing mindfulness to our relationships with our adult children, we need to include an awareness of the ways in which our assumptions and expectations might be limiting or disrespectful of them. In addition, we need to be cognizant of the demands and stresses that they may be dealing with in their own lives.

This does not mean that, in our interactions with our adult children, we cannot voice our feelings or express our own needs. When something happens that bothers us, we need to pay attention and try, with some sensitivity, to talk about it soon after, rather than letting things build up. When we ask something of them, we need to recognize that they are adults and are free to say no, even to reject us altogether.

It helps to look at our grown children as if we were seeing them for the first time, seeing each not as a newborn but as a new being. Any moment together, even on the telephone, is a new chance to be present, to build trust, to attune to them, to be sensitive, to be empathic, to accept them as they are, and to honor their sovereignty.

If, on occasion, we lapse into an old familiar pattern, if we find ourselves critical, or unkind, or judging, or demanding, or withholding, or any of the myriad ways negativity can manifest, we need to take a moment and look at what has happened. We need to acknowledge what we did, learn from it, and apologize for our behavior. And then . . . we begin again.

*

Western medicine is founded on the cardinal principle, dating to Hippocates, to first do no harm. Perhaps we need to collectively affirm a Hippocratic Oath for parenting: that we will, above all, first do no harm. This would be a practice in itself.

Mindfulness is all about living the lives that are ours to live. This can only happen if we make room for our true nature to emerge—what is deepest and best in ourselves. While we may all be born miraculous beings, without proper nurturing our genius may be smothered and snuffed out for lack of oxygen. The oxygen that feeds our true nature is found in stillness, attention, love, sovereignty, and community. The challenge of mindful parenting is to find ways to nourish our children and ourselves, to remain true to the quest, the hero's journey that is a human life lived in awareness, across our entire life span, and so to grow into who we all are and can become for each other, for ourselves, and for the world.

Seven Intentions and
Twelve Exercises
for Mindful Parenting

Intentionality—
Parenting As
a Spiritual Discipline

Intentions remind us of what is important. When we form the intention to do something, and that intention in turn informs our choices and our actions, the chances that we will be sensitive to what is important in our lives increase greatly, and we are more likely to see the big picture. Our intentions serve as blueprints, allowing us to give shape and direction to our efforts, and to assess how we are doing as we work at developing something worthy of ourselves and our lives. So at some point, whenever that is, we have to decide what is really important for us, and then work at constantly keeping that framework in mind as things unfold.

In mindful parenting, certain principles are important to affirm from the very beginning. This does not mean that if we already have children, it is too late to become more mindful in our parenting. It means that we begin, when we are ready, wherever we are in our lives, and work with the here and now, formulating the intentions that are important for us to affirm and to implement, and that are realistic. Not only is it never too late to introduce mindfulness into our lives; the very moment that we make the conscious commitment to do so becomes the perfect moment to begin.

Here are some intentions that you may find helpful. Of course, you can also create your own.

INTENTION ONE: I will bring my entire creative genius to the work of mindful parenting.

INTENTION TWO: I will see parenting as a spiritual discipline, meaning that it provides me with every necessary opportunity to cultivate wisdom and openheartedness in myself, so that I may come to know and express my true nature and share what is best in me with my children and with the world.

INTENTION THREE: I will cultivate mindfulness and discernment in my daily life, especially with my children, using an awareness of my breathing to ground me in the present moment.

INTENTION FOUR: I will make every effort to see who my children actually are, and to remember to accept them for who they are at every age, rather than be blinded by my own expectations and fears. By making a commitment to live my own life fully and to work at seeing and accepting myself as I am, I will be better able to accord a similar acceptance to my children. In this way I can help them to grow and to realize their full potential as unique beings.

INTENTION FIVE: I will make every effort to see things from each child's point of view and understand what my children's needs are, and to meet them as best I can.

INTENTION SIX: I will use whatever comes up in my own life and in the lives of my children, including the darkest and most difficult times, as "grist for the mill," to grow as a human being so that I am better able to understand my children, their soul needs, and what is required of me as a parent.

INTENTION SEVEN: I will fold these intentions into my heart, and commit myself to putting them into practice as best I can, every day, and in appropriate ways that feel right to me and that honor my children's sovereignty, and my own.

Twelve Exercises
for Mindful Parenting

1. Try to imagine the world from your child's point of view, purposefully letting go of your own. Do this every day for at least a few moments to remind you of who this child is and what he or she faces in the world.

2. Imagine how you appear and sound from your child's point of view, i.e., having *you* as a parent today, in this moment. How might this modify how you carry yourself in your body and in space, how you speak, what you say? How do you want to relate to your child in *this* moment?

3. Practice seeing your children as perfect just the way they are. See if you can stay mindful of their sovereignty from moment to moment, and work at accepting them as they are when it is hardest for you to do so.

4. Be mindful of your expectations of your children and consider whether they are truly in your child's best interest. Also, be aware of how you communicate those expectations and how they affect your children.

5 Practice altruism, putting the needs of your children above your own whenever possible. Then see if there isn't some common ground, where your true needs can also be met. You may be surprised at how much overlap is possible, especially if you are patient, and strive for balance.

6 When you feel lost, or at a loss, remember to stand still, as in David Wagoner's poem: "The forest breathes . . ." Listen to what it is saying; "The forest knows/Where you are. You must let it find you. . . ." Meditate on the whole, by bringing your full attention to the situation, to your child, to yourself, to the family. In doing so, you may go beyond thinking, even good thinking, and perceive intuitively, with the whole of your being (your feelings, intuition, body, mind, and soul) what really needs to be done. If that is not clear in any moment, maybe the best thing is to not do anything until it becomes clearer. Sometimes it is good to remain silent.

7 Try embodying silent presence. This will grow out of both formal and informal mindfulness practice over time, if you attend to how you carry yourself and what you project in body, mind, and speech. Listen carefully.

8 Learn to live with tension without losing your own balance. In *Zen and the Art of Archery*, Herrigel describes how he was taught to stand at the point of highest tension effortlessly without shooting the arrow. At the right moment, the arrow mysteriously shoots itself. Do this by practicing moving into

any moment, however difficult, without trying to change anything and without having to have a particular outcome occur. Simply bring your full awareness and presence to this moment. Practice seeing that whatever comes up is "workable," if you are willing to stand in this way in the present, trusting your intuition and best instincts. Your child, especially when young, needs you to be a center of balance and trustworthiness, a reliable landmark by which he or she can take a bearing within his or her own landscape. Arrow and target need each other. Forcing doesn't help. They will find each other better through wise attention and patience.

9 Apologize to your child when you have betrayed a trust in even a little way. Apologies are healing. An apology demonstrates that you have thought about a situation and have come to see it more clearly, or perhaps more from your child's point of view. But we have to be mindful of being "sorry" too often. It loses its meaning if we are always saying it, or make regret into a habit. Then it can become a way for us not to take responsibility for our actions. Be aware of this. Cooking in remorse on occasion is a good meditation. Don't shut off the stove until the meal is ready.

10 Every child is special, and every child has special needs. Each sees in an entirely unique way. Hold an image of each child in your heart. Drink in their being, wishing them well.

11 There are very important times when we need to practice being clear and strong and unequivocal with our children. Let this come as much as possible out of awareness and generos-

ity and discernment, rather than out of fear, self-righteousness, or the desire to control. Mindful parenting does not mean being overindulgent, neglectful, or weak; nor does it mean being rigid, domineering, and controlling.

12. The greatest gift you can give your child is your self. This means that part of your work as a parent is to keep growing in self-knowledge and in awareness. We have to be grounded in the present moment to share what is deepest and best in ourselves. This is ongoing work, but it can be furthered by making a time for quiet contemplation in whatever ways feel comfortable to us. We only have right now. Let us use it to its best advantage, for our children's sake, and for our own.

Mindfulness Meditation Practice Tapes
with Jon Kabat-Zinn

*(Please note: These are **NOT** parenting tapes.*
They are for cultivating mindfulness through periods of formal practice.)

SERIES 1

The Series I tapes are those used by people who enroll in the
Stress Reduction Clinic at the University of Massachusetts
Medical Center. Their use is described in *Full Catastrophe Living*.
These tapes are sold only as a set.

Tape 1 / Side 1   45-minute guided body scan meditation
          Side 2   45-minute guided mindful hatha yoga 1

Tape 2 / Side 1   45-minute guided sitting meditation
          Side 2   45-minute guided mindful hatha yoga 2

Mindfulness Meditation Practice Tapes
with Jon Kabat-Zinn

(Please note: These are NOT parenting tapes.
They are for cultivating mindfulness through periods of formal practice.)

SERIES 2

This series of tapes is for people who want a range of shorter guided meditations to help them develop and/or expand a personal meditation practice based on mindfulness. The series includes the mountain and lake meditations, as well as a range of other methods on the different tapes. These tapes are sold only as a complete set.

Tape 1 / Side 1 10-minute guided sitting meditation with the focus on awareness of breathing

Side 2 10-minute guided meditation lying down with the focus on the breath

Tape 2 / Side 1 20-minute guided sitting meditation

Side 2 20-minute guided lying-down meditation

Tape 3 / Side 1 30-minute guided sitting meditation

Side 2 30-minute guided lying-down meditation

Tape 4 / Side 1 Mountain Meditation (sitting) 20 minutes

Side 2 Lake Meditation (lying down) 20 minutes

Tape 5 / Side 1 Silence, with bells at 5, 10, 15, 20, and 30 minutes

Side 2 Silence, with bells at random times up to 30 minutes

Mindfulness Meditation Practice Tapes
with Jon Kabat-Zinn

(Please note: These are NOT parenting tapes.
They are for cultivating mindfulness through periods of formal practice.)

ORDER FORM

Name _____

Address _____

_____

City / State / Zip _____

Country* _____

Telephone (_____) _____

Send orders to:

STRESS REDUCTION TAPES

P.O. BOX 547

LEXINGTON, MA 02173-0005

Please note: Telephone orders cannot be accepted.

SERIES 1	# of sets		Total $
Set of 2 tapes	_____	$20.00 per set	_____
	add $2.00 *per set* for postage & handling		_____
Massachusetts residents add 5% ($1.00) sales tax *per set*			_____
	TOTAL SERIES 1 ORDER		_____

SERIES 2	# of sets		Total $
Set of 5 tapes	_____	$35.00 per set	_____
	add $4.00 *per set* for postage & handling		_____
Massachusetts residents add 5% ($1.75) sales tax *per set*			_____
	TOTAL SERIES 2 ORDER		_____
	TOTAL ENCLOSED (SERIES 1 & SERIES 2)		_____

Note: SERIES 1 and SERIES 2 are shipped separately
All orders shipped First Class (SERIES 1) or Priority (SERIES 2)
*For orders outside North America, please add an *additional* postage charge
of $3.00 per set for SERIES 1 and $4.00 per set for SERIES 2.
SEE NEXT PAGE FOR METHOD OF PAYMENT

Check ❏   Amount Enclosed $_____

Visa ❏   MasterCard ❏   DiscoverCard ❏   American Express ❏

ACCOUNT NUMBER

MO/YR

_____ / _____

Expiration Date

_____

Signature of Authorized Buyer

Make checks payable to: STRESS REDUCTION TAPES

For tape orders from outside the U.S. please use credit card,
or check drawn on a U.S. bank in U.S. dollars, or an International
Postal Money Order in U.S. dollars.

The authors gratefully acknowledge permission from these sources to reprint the following:

Excerpt from *Letters to a Young Poet* by Rainer Maria Rilke, translated by Stephen Mitchell, copyright © 1984 by Stephen Mitchell. Reprinted by permission of Random House, Inc.

"Angry Fathers" by Mel Lazarus, copyright © 1995 by The New York Times Company. Reprinted by permission.

Excerpts from *Emotional Intelligence* by Daniel Goleman, copyright © 1995 by Daniel Goleman. Used by permission of Bantam Books.

Excerpts from *When Singing Just Sing—Life as Meditation* by Narayan Liebenson Grady. Reprinted by permission of the author.

Excerpts from *The Baby Book* by William and Martha Sears, copyright © 1992 by William Sears and Martha Sears. Reprinted by permission of Little, Brown and Company.

Excerpts from *The Blue Jay's Dance* by Louise Erdrich, copyright © 1995 by Louise Erdrich. Reprinted by permission of HarperCollins Publishers, Inc.

Excerpts from *Four Quartets* by T. S. Elliot, copyright © 1943 by T. S. Eliot and renewed 1971 by Esme Valerie Eliot. Reprinted by permission of Harcourt Brace & Company.

"Loaves and Fishes" and an excerpt from "Looking Back the Night" by David Whyte. Reprinted by permission of David Whyte and Many Rivers Press.

"Wu-Men's Verse" from "CASE 45: 'Who Is That Other?' " from *The Gateless Barrier: The Wu-Men Kuan* (Mumonkan), translated by Robert Aiken, copyright © 1991 by Diamond Sangha. Reprinted by permission of North Point Press, a division of Farrar, Straus, & Giroux, Inc.

Excerpt from Rumi's "You are the notes . . ." reprinted from *When Grapes Turn to Wine*, Yellow Moon Press, Cambridge, MA, 1986, copyright © 1986 by Robert Bly. Reprinted with his permission.

Excerpts from "A Dialogue of Self and Soul" by W. B. Yeats, reprinted with the permission of Simon & Schuster from *The Collected Works of W. B. Yeats, Volume 1: The Poems*, revised and edited by Richard J. Finneran, copyright © 1933 by Macmillan Publishing Company; copyright © renewed 1961 by Bertha Georgie Yeats.

Excerpts from *The Long Road Turns to Joy: A Guide to Walking Meditation* by Thich Nhat Hanh (1996). Reprinted with permission of Parallax Press, Berkeley, California.

Reprinted, by permission, from Ethel Johnston Phelps, "Tatterhood," in *Tatterhood and Other Tales*, edited by Ethel Johnston Phelps, illustrated by Pamela Baldwin Ford (New York: The Feminist Press at The City University of New York, 1978), pp. 1–6, copyright © 1978 by Ethel Johnston Phelps.

"Anthem" written by Leonard Cohen, copyright © 1993 by Leonard Cohen Stranger Music, Inc. Used by permission. All rights reserved.

"Wild Geese" from *Dream Work* by Mary Oliver, copyright © 1986 by Mary Oliver. Used by permission of Grove/Atlantic, Inc.

"Lost" by David Wagoner, copyright © 1976 by David Wagoner. Reprinted by permission of the author.

Citation from *Women Who Run With the Wolves* by Clarissa Pinkola Estes, Ph.D., copyright © 1992, 1995. Used by kind permission of the author, Dr. Estes, and Ballantine Books, a division of Random House, Inc.